ISSUES PAST and PRESENT

An American History Sourcebook

VOLUME I

Issues Past and PRESENT

An American History Sourcebook

VOLUME I

EDITED BY

Phillip S. Paludan
University of Kansas

Robert M. Calhoon
*University of North Carolina
at Greensboro*

Michael A. Moore
Bowling Green State University

Jonathan G. Utley
University of Tennessee, Knoxville

BIOGRAPHIES BY

Donald C. Lord
Unity College

D. C. HEATH AND COMPANY
Lexington, Massachusetts   Toronto

Acknowledgment is made to the following sources for permission to reproduce material from their collections:

Cover: Beinecke Rare Book and Manuscript Library, Yale University
           Elliott Erwitt/Magnum

p. 9:   Reproduced through courtesy of the Virginia Historical Society.
p. 61:   Courtesy Oberlin College.
p. 111;   Courtesy Missouri Historical Society.
p. 189:   Courtesy Illinois State Historical Library.

Copyright © 1978 by D. C. Heath and Company

Published simultaneously in Canada.

Printed in the United States of America.

International Standard Book Number: 0-669-00784-6

Library of Congress Catalog Card Number: 77-78614

Preface

Our concerns in presenting this book are contemporary—we believe that modern problems can be clarified by studying the past. Our major assumption is that at certain periods in American history, men and women faced problems that still exist today and that their efforts must be considered if *our* confrontation is to be understood. We gather around us, then, people like Jonathan Edwards, Benjamin Franklin, Sam Adams, Daniel Webster, Henry David Thoreau, Abraham Lincoln, Andrew Carnegie, Woodrow Wilson, Jane Addams, Oliver Wendell Holmes, Jr., Franklin Roosevelt, and ask their advice. We also call to us people less well known to history—a former slave, an early immigrant, an assembly of unknown women organizing to fight slavery, a black historian, a labor organizer, a veteran trying to survive the Depression, a couple of Peace Corps workers — and ask their counsel. Finally, we bring men and women who have confronted these problems in our own times, and we solicit their understandings and proposals. We ask of the historical figures, "When you faced issues like those confronting us, how did *you* try to resolve them?" We require a dialogue about the enduring issues in American life with both our contemporaries and our ancestors.

There are limitations in the answers provided by the past. Earlier Americans confronted the issues at times when the structure of society, beliefs about man's place in the universe, and other fundamental concepts and experiences were quite different from today. We must perceive therefore how these differences may limit potential answers to today's problems.

But the fact of limitations does not invalidate the method. The best demonstration of its validity is provided by reading the documents themselves. When the Puritans dealt with the question of creating a sense of community, they were as aware as we are of the vital role played in the process by the family, the individual's moral sense, the school, and the state. When the people of the Civil War era agonized over whether or not war could be justified, they posed a question yet to be answered: Will the result of victory be worth the numbers of the dead? When Americans at the turn of the century calculated the cost of achievement, they wrestled as we do with the question "What will getting ahead cost my family, my society, my own humanity?" When we discover that our parents' generation also wondered how their government could be responsive to the needs of "little people," the "generation gap" narrows a bit.

Finding answers in the past will not uncover a blueprint for today — will not ensure resolution of modern dilemmas. In order to deal with today's problems, we need to understand clearly today's world. Knowledge of the past, however, will make us recognize the dimensions of the issues which have troubled men and women for centuries. We shall become aware of alternative responses extending beyond our time. Studying the past frees us from the present, providing us greater opportunity to shape our future, because we are able to expand our options and increase our choices. As T. S. Eliot put it, "This is the use of memory, for liberation — not less of love, but expanding of love beyond desire, and so liberation from the future as well as the past." Here, then, is the ideological foundation for this text.

There is a pedagogical foundation also. We believe that, for students, "doing history" is as important as reading it and that reading the sources and coming to conclusions based on them is an imperative preliminary step to evaluating what historians or anyone else — past and present — write and say.

Our format for "doing history" pivots on the issues, juxtaposing the past and the present in several ways: first, by an introductory essay which provides the background needed to understand a topic in its time as well as its meaning for us today; second, by a biography of a prominent person whose efforts in dealing with an issue altered existing beliefs; third, by introductory comments preceding the documents which suggest questions thoughtful persons might ask themselves were they living at the time; and finally, by a modern essay which illustrates today's discussion of an issue.

The *introductory essays* to each section of the book are designed to show how these issues remain vital and suggest the range of argument that they have provoked. Though the Puritans are gone, the central problems of their life continue to demand answers of us. Though John Brown's body "lies a molderin' in the grave," the issues tormenting his soul go marching on. Though Jane Addams is dead, the conflicts which threaded through her life exist today also. Though Franklin Roosevelt is no more, many of the problems he wrestled with remain.

The *biographies* following the introductory essays help make the issues more vivid by relating them to the lives of thoughtful, interesting men and women. They offer readers a chance to examine why people like William Byrd, Thomas Hart Benton, William Jennings Bryan, Paul Robeson responded as they did to these persistent problems. We hope that the biographies will also provoke you to question how your life relates to the issues today: What is *my* community based on? Can it, should it, endure? What would *I* fight, kill, or die for? What price am I willing to pay for success? How much of my comfort would I give up so that others might live?

The *documents* bring to life the conflicts of the past. They recreate the sense of being alive in another age, of listening, as it were, to an ancient radio and hearing history being made in the accents and dialects of the time. By reflecting a wide range of opinions on issues, they suggest the past be viewed not in black and white but rather in infinitely subtle shades of gray. The editors' comments and questions which precede each document are designed to stimulate thought, discussions, and argument. They encourage the reader to ponder the complex evolution and subsequent mutations of the issues through time. Indeed, encountering the issues again in the *modern essays,* the reader realizes how bound we are to today's imperatives and how important it is to call forth yesterday's forgotten insights, in order to understand the dimensions of problems which have persisted throughout the American experience.

We believe that *Issues Past and Present* will stimulate an encounter with and respect for this nation's roots by showing that the tree which has emerged from these roots flourishes in our own time. Students in introductory American history courses will benefit from confronting a past shown to be relevant to modern dilemmas. But this book is not just a text for students in school. It is offered for all people who are concerned about the world they live in and who recognize that the issues our ancestors wrestled with in the past continue to shape the present. We cannot afford to ignore their experiences as we try to shape our future.

P. S. P.
R. M. C.
M. A. M.
J. G. U.
D. C. L.

Acknowledgments

Although this work is the product of much mutual discussion and criticism, each of the authors has made specific contributions. Robert Calhoon prepared "Colonial and Revolutionary America" and "The Young Republic." Phillip Paludan is responsible for "Manifest Destiny and Reform" and "Civil War and Reconstruction." He collaborated with Calhoon on the section on colonial community. Michael Moore wrote and edited "The Gilded Age" and "The Progressive Era." Jonathan Utley wrote and edited "Prosperity and Depression" and "An Insecure World." Donald Lord prepared the biographies. Paludan coordinated the efforts and acted as general editor.

We have accumulated debts to others who have contributed to this effort, and they must be recognized. We would like to thank Clifford Griffin, Donald McCoy, Mark Rose, and John Lomax of the University of Kansas; William Bruce Wheeler, Charles W. Johnson, Stephen V. Ash, James A. Burran, Nancy-Ann E. Min, Bonnie B. Gilley of the University of Tennessee, Knoxville; and Kathleen Swiger and David C. Roller.

Our families sustained the effort with their love, their diversions, and their encouragement, and to them we also owe our thanks.

Contents

PART II

The Young Republic

PART III

Manifest Destiny and Reform

PART IV

The Civil War and Reconstruction

PART I

Colonial and Revolutionary America

Introduction

The Quest for Community and Identity in Early America

Early one morning in March of 1964, a young woman named Kitty Genovese was returning home from a night job when a man approached her with a knife and began stabbing her. She eluded the man for a moment and began screaming for help, but no one responded. She continued to cry out after the attacker caught her and stabbed her repeatedly. Eventually she died. When questioned the next day, thirty-eight of her neighbors admitted that they had heard her cries for help, knew that something terrible was happening, but had done nothing: they had not even called the police until she had died.

The incident aroused an enormous outcry — senators spoke of it in Congress, papers editorialized about Kitty Genovese, a major law school held a "Conference on the Good Samaritan and the Bad — The Law and Morality of Volunteering in Situations of Peril, or of Failing to Do So." The focus of public indignation and outrage was not just on the death of a young woman, but the failure of the community to protect her. The circumstances of her death were roughly paralleled throughout urban life: muggings on subways while bystanders watched and did nothing; victims of heart attacks gasping as they lay on the sidewalk while pedestrians passed by.

Incidents such as these have generated social criticism directed at the excessive emphasis on individualism and the resulting destruction of a sense of community. As a result, our sense of social responsibility is meager at best, the critics note, and is subordinated constantly to the ideals of private wealth and comfort. Incidents similar to the Kitty Genovese slaying make this clear.

The problem is not just the lack of reaction to violence, but a general unresponsiveness: major corporations demand profits while they pollute the nation's air and water; individuals protest increasing taxes although U.S. citizens pay fewer taxes than in any other modern industrial state; we create images of welfare as a hand-out for the immoral and indigent; with the money we hoard we buy televisions, telephones, and cars for each family member. All these attitudes and devices serve further to isolate us — to make us increasingly self-centered. In a world that increases recklessly in population and that increasingly demands cooperation, we diminish our responsibility to and for each other daily. The problem is compounded by the communication media's ability to reveal our differences and divisions without providing real-life contact or resolutions of difficulties, giving us a sense of involvement even though we have not been at all involved. In consequence, we feel accountable to no one, and no one is accountable to us.

In reaction to these conditions, large numbers of Americans (most of them under thirty) are seeking an alternative life style. They are establishing communes, forming cooperatives, and developing a counterculture. Although many of these communitarian efforts fail, the fact that they are begun warrants thought about the weaknesses of the existing system and about the viability of the alternatives that are being suggested. It demands careful consideration, because these efforts are signs of a more profound problem: perhaps the major demand of our time is to discover how to create a sense of community, with shared values and goals, and mutual responsibility in a world of high mobility, large populations, and specialized occupations.

Trends to counter excessive individualism are hardly new. From the first, Americans have cooperated with each other, and developed associations on all levels for both temporary and permanent purposes: claim clubs of squatters to protect land rights, wagon trains to convoy pioneers, vigilantes to secure order, and business fraternal clubs to satisfy social and economic needs are a few of the testimonies to our search for community. Most notable of all the past alternatives to individualism have been the hundreds of attempts to establish utopian communities. Throughout the nineteenth century there were numerous efforts to establish a community in harmony with itself, rejecting all selfish goals. Resting on a desire to develop ideals of mutual love, concern, and responsibility, communities such as Brook Farm, New Harmony, Hopedale, and Oneida sprang up all over the nation. A few flourished briefly, but most of them died leaving little more than a trace of their existence. There was one utopian community, however, that had profound impact on American life, providing thought and experiences which shape even elements of the modern world: the community of the Puritans.

The modern popular image of the Puritans is neither complimentary nor accurate. Puritans were *not* all narrow-minded witch-hunters. They were *not* motivated by the awful fear that someone, somewhere, was having a good time, and were determined to put an end to it. As Edmund Morgan says, "We have to caricature the Puritans in order to feel comfortable in their presence. They found answers to some human problems we would rather forget." Perhaps the most important of these problems was that of developing and maintaining a sense of community. It is a problem we cannot afford to forget.

Fleeing from the religious persecutions of England in the 1620s and 1630s, the Puritans sought to establish in the colonies a state devoted to the worship of God in the Puritan manner. They wanted to create what they called "A City Upon a Hill," which the world might admire and perhaps one day copy. To achieve that goal, they established stable, harmonious communities where citizens respected and felt personally responsible for the order of society and for the welfare of their neighbors. They established a community in the sense described by the modern sociologist Robert Nisbet:

> By community, I mean something that goes far beyond mere local community. The word as we find it in much nineteenth- and twentieth-century thought encompasses all forms of relationships which are characterized by a high degree of personal intimacy, emotional depth, moral commitment, social cohesion, and continuity in time. Community is founded on man conceived in his wholeness rather than in one or another of the roles, taken separately, that he may hold in the social order. It draws its psychological strength from levels of motivation deeper than those of mere volition or interest, and it achieves its fulfillment in a submergence of individual will that is not possible in unions of mere convenience or rational assent. Community is a fusion of feeling and thought, of tradition and commitment, of membership and volition. It may be found in, or given symbolic expression by, locality, religion, nation, race, occupation, or crusade.

It was not an easy achievement, the building of such a community. Within Puritan thought were attitudes that contradicted its establishment: the emphasis on each individual's responsibility to be his or her own confessor in seeking salvation promoted self-centeredness; the assertion that God's reaction to earthly activities would bring earthly as well as eternal rewards encouraged the acquisition of private fortunes; the importance of a calling (an occupation to which God called an individual) suggested God's sanction for purely selfish labors. The Puritans recognized these dangers. Their ministers constantly reminded them that the endurance of the community and their own salvation were inextricably linked, that no one could gain salvation if duties to the community were forgotten. For almost a century, the selfish consequences of individualism were restrained, and the Puritan community endured.

Behind its idyllic appearance, the colonial New England town was a social institution designed to inhibit individualism and channel all energies. Though the towns were dominated by a wealthy elite, nearly all male citizens voted in town meetings. Elected officials lacked the coercive power to impose the will of the majority on recalcitrant individuals. They feared that open conflicts would divide the town into hostile segments and jeopardize the very existence of the community. They therefore strained to avoid controversies, and the elite maintained their dominance only by strenuous efforts to secure public support. Puritanism was a vital ingredient in this kind of communal life. It taught that both government officials and citizens were sinful — the magistrate was liable to become corrupt or tyrannical, and the subject prone to disobedience or civic indifference — and Puritan clergy developed an elaborate series of warnings and inducements to keep both the ruler and the ruled aware of their social responsibilities. This attitude was not confined to New England. In Pennsylvania and West Jersey, during the last quarter of the seventeenth century, Quaker settlers created religious communities which were also designed to contain human aggression and direct the members' energies into socially useful and humanitarian pursuits. The Quakers practiced pacifism toward the Indian tribes, they extended care to the poor, and they disciplined members who became greedy or extravagant.

Puritans and Quakers were not the only groups of colonial Americans who tried to create closely knit communities. Throughout the tidewater regions of the southern colonies, for example, county courts became the focal point of a closely integrated and self-regulated society. The courts regulated a wide variety of economic activities such as civil debt collection, road maintenance, estate inheritance, and tobacco inspection. Elections and court days were festive public occurrences on which planters, farmers and tradespeople came together and recognized their mutual dependence upon each other.

Every settlement in colonial America resembled in some respects these experiments in community. All of them were based on a theoretical contract between ruler and ruled; all sought to impose order and civility on a relatively crude colonial environment; in all of them the absence of venerable institutions, the availability of land, and the shortage of labor critically weakened the power of constituted authority to impose order on the society; and finally, all colonial communities were to some extent built upon exploitation and violence. Slave labor in the southern colonies accounted for the immense profitability of plantation agriculture, and ultimately slavery contributed to the prosperity of all of colonial America. Moreover, fear of black insurrection drew the white community more closely together, so that in a perverse way, slavery hastened the political maturity of American society. Likewise, mob violence in colonial America often helped to solve problems which law and government seemed unwilling or unable to solve. The first vigilantes appeared on the South Carolina frontier in the early 1760s when regular law enforcement there collapsed. Common seamen resorted to mob violence to resist illegal impressment into the British Navy. Tenant farmers in New York and New Jersey periodically rioted against their landlords. Mob violence against British officials during the Stamp Act and Townshend duties crises seemed to many respectable leaders like encouraging proof of American readiness and ability to resist oppression. The American Revolution was the culmination of this search for community in American life.

British policies restricting colonial autonomy and impinging on traditional liberties forced the colonists to examine the nature of the compact between themselves and the Crown and the proper role of parliamentary power in their political life. They concluded that the ultimate power to review the legitimacy of governmental policy rested in the people and could be exercised only by the representatives of the people. British actions which transferred more and more decision-making from the colonies to the Crown jeopardized this vital theoretical arrangement. In order to preserve social coherence and harmony, white leaders sought to enlist the whole community in resistance against British authority and in the creation of a revolutionary government.

Paralleling and reinforcing this search for community was the search for identity in early colonial life. It was the effort of colonial Americans to understand who they were as a people, to make the best use of their virtues and abilities, to learn from their weaknesses, and to devise meaningful standards for conduct and goals for their society. In this respect, Americans today are probably closer to the spirit of the eighteenth century than they have been at any intervening time in our history. We are uncertain of our ability to confront problems of ecology, population, racism, and relations between rich nations and poor nations because we are unsure of our capabilities and no longer confident of our character as a people. Colonial Americans wrestled with this same dilemma. Their answer to the question of their own worth was to repress people unlike themselves. By dispossessing Indians and enslaving blacks, colonial Americans became confident of their superiority and prowess. Whatever they tried became a successful learning experience: economic prosperity, religious revivalism, self-government, cultural diversity and urbanity all served to help Americans realize who they were as a people. The Revolution was the culmination of the Americans' search to discover their collective character — democratic, virtuous, and enlightened — and to enact those qualities in their newly created country.

In a society dominated by a conscientious and intellectually curious elite, this search for self-discovery was the central experience of many aristocrats. Such a man was William Byrd II. His education, his reading in European classics, his pious devotional life, his careful management of vast estates, and above all, his natural sense of superiority over his family, slaves, and underlings all defined who he was. This hierarchical network of relationships and influences connected the various communities in which he lived.

Personalizing the Issues

William Byrd of Westover: The Great Gentleman

William Byrd II was an important man in American history, yet his most important contributions were not made as a politician, writer, diplomat, or soldier. Historians are interested in him because his diaries destroyed many myths about colonial Virginia and helped scholars rewrite the history of the plantation South.

Unlike most famous diarists, Byrd did not intend that his words would be made public. For this reason, he wrote his diaries in an obscure shorthand and kept them hidden away, hoping that no one, either in his lifetime or after, would read them. Unfortu-

nately his strategy was too successful: most of his diaries were lost. The three that have been found were not discovered until the 1930s: the first at the Huntington Library in California, the second at the University of North Carolina, and the third in the Virginia Historical Society. Fortunately there were three scholars working in colonial history — Louis B. Wright, Marion Tinling and Maude Woodfin — who could transcribe the shorthand. Ever since the publication of *The Secret Diary of William Byrd* (1941), *Another Secret Diary of William Byrd* (1942) and the *London Diary* (1958), historians have been reevaluating the history of colonial America and making significant changes in the established concept of eighteenth-century Virginia.

Historians have accepted the Byrd diaries as much more valid than other colonial diaries because they are consistent with other available sources. Because he never intended to make them public, many entries are dull and repetitious, while others are full of interesting and spicy detail which Byrd obviously meant to be kept secret. His sex life, for example, including both his successes and failures, is chronicled in detail.

Byrd's secrecy raises the basic question of why he kept his diaries. It seems that he started the first one as an exercise in shorthand and soon discovered that this was a good, quick way to keep daily records. There were many instances when he used them later for references. Possibly he kept them also for self-analysis, but it is difficult to tell at this late date what other purpose he had. Most colonial diarists wrote basically of their spiritual growth and thus their works have limited value as historical sources. This was not the case with Byrd. He was a very religious man, yet his accounts gave a sensual record of life in America and showed details of daily living found in few other sources.

But Byrd's fame does not rest solely on his diaries; as the master of Westover Plantation, he has long been considered the embodiment of the Virginia gentleman. Like most of the gentry, he patterned his life after the fashion established in Castiglione's *Book of the Courtier,* and behaved as a gentleman should. This behavior pattern gave Byrd much latitude to enjoy the good life.

Although he was born in Virginia in 1674, Byrd spent thirty of his first fifty-two years in England. Thus, even more than most of his contemporaries, he suffered from the divided identity which characterized the gentry of his era. In 1681, at the age of seven, his father sent him to London to receive a classical education. At sixteen, he journeyed to Holland to study business techniques under the best businessmen of the era. Later, he returned to London, studied at the Middle Temple, England's famous law school, and became a lawyer in 1695.

The next year, after a brief visit to Virginia, he returned to England to represent the Virginia Assembly before Parliament, the Crown, and the Board of Trade. This experience (and another in 1715–1726) made the young courtier aware of his dual identity. He loved England and the English, and he always behaved like, and was accepted as, an English gentleman. Indeed, one of his greatest honors was his election to the Royal Society, an exclusive intellectual society devoted to scientific knowledge. Yet as the representative for the colonial assembly, he was a bold, but respectful, arbiter for Virginia. Often he was angry with governors who cared more for "English interests than Virginian liberties." His career illustrates that colonial assemblies waged a relentless struggle against the will of their governors long before the American Revolution.

Byrd was a successful representative and often persuaded Parliament to repeal laws that were harmful to Virginia's interests. In 1717, for example, he secured the repeal of two laws instituted by Lieutenant Governor Alexander Spotswood, one establishing a monopoly of the Indian trade and another allowing for the payment of debts with tobacco. These and other successes created political animosity between the two men. But the conflict was political, not personal, and later when Spotswood was no longer the Crown's representative, the two Virginians had a cordial relationship. Earlier their rivalry was so intense that Spotswood vetoed the bill that would have established a salary for Byrd as Virginia's official representative. This action soon proved ineffective because the burgesses decided to pay Byrd directly out of their pockets.

In 1705, during Byrd's second stay in England, his father died. Byrd returned to Virginia to manage his plantations, and as was usually the custom, to inherit also his father's status and positions. William Byrd I had been the Auditor and Receiver General in Virginia, but rather than continue to allow one man to wield power through two positions, the Board of Trade split them, and William Byrd II inherited only his father's role as the Receiver General. As such, he collected the quitrents (land tax) due the Crown on plantations in Virginia. Byrd kept first 3 percent, then later 5 percent, of the taxes he collected.

Annoyed as he was by the decision to separate the two positions, Byrd complained loudly that no governor, in this case Spotswood, should have sole authority to spend 20,000 pounds. Actually, he was more annoyed with his own failure to receive his father's seat on the Council. He had to wait five years before another vacancy occurred, at which time his application was accepted. In the meantime, he busied himself with his social and political life.

Thirty-one years old when he returned to Virginia in 1705, he was one of the colony's most eligible bachelors. He soon courted and married Lucy Parke, the youngest daughter of the wild and violent Colonel Daniel Parke. Parke had spoiled his daughters and permitted them to indulge in a family characteristic — a violent temper — at will. Thus Byrd's first marriage was marked by constant squabbling. Fortunately, the diarist recorded as many reconciliations as arguments. It should be noted, furthermore, that both Byrd and his wife lived passionately. Once, for example, Byrd recorded that he "roguered [seduced his] wife on the pool table."

As it was, Byrd was quite lucky — he might have married the older daughter, Frances, who married his close friend, John Custis. Custis later wrote his own epitaph, noting that the only peace he had ever known was in bachelorhood. Neither of the daughters, however, could match their father's temper. Once, when angered by one of the numerous sermons preached by the Reverend James Blair on Parke's notorious adulterous behavior, the colonel dragged Mrs. Blair from a church pew that he claimed belonged to him, and publicly implied that Blair preached more often on adultery than on drinking because Mrs. Blair was the most infamous drunk in Virginia.

When Byrd married Lucy Parke, he had expected a dowry, but he never received any because Parke was always in trouble, debt, or both. Parke's future, and that of a forthcoming dowry, looked brightest when he became the governor of the Leeward Islands. Unfortunately, he was killed in a riot in Antigua caused by his authoritarian policies. Characteristically, Parke left most of his estate to an illegitimate daughter, and only 1,000 pounds to Lucy Byrd. Parke's many land holdings were to be sold for the payment of debts until Byrd arranged to inherit the lands in return for assuming the debts. This decision was a disastrous mistake, as the debts proved to be staggering. Byrd had probably been deceived about the exact amount Parke owed the English merchant. Thus he spent the rest of his life in debt for his father-in-law's lands.

That the shrewd Byrd willingly blundered into such a bad situation illustrates one of the outstanding characteristics of the Virginia gentry: their hunger for land. Land, of course, was not only a strategic form of money in a barter economy, but it also gave one power and status. Throughout the colonial era, a small number of gentlemen landowners controlled the social, economic, and political destiny of the colony. For this reason, when Byrd died in 1744, he had accumulated 179,000 acres.

Byrd's struggle to pay off his debts was aided by the frugal housekeeping of his second wife. Lucy Parke Byrd died in London in 1716 from smallpox. As was the custom in early Virginia, Byrd spent little time mourning, and looked for an English heiress to return home with him. This is not as callous as it seems. Courting in the colonies often began at funerals. He was unsuccessful, however, as few heiresses wanted to live in a "wilderness." It was, as one of them said, "like having a plantation on the moon." In between his unsuccessful courting, the planter visited the bawdy houses frequented by gentlemen, often paying the price for his folly since social diseases were then quite common.

Byrd finally became a successful suitor in 1724, when he met and married Maria Taylor. He was then 50 and his wife, 25. She returned with him to Westover in 1726 and ran the plantation as well as Lucy Parke had run it poorly. She was a faithful and dutiful wife who bore him four children (just as Lucy Parke Byrd had done). Byrd spoke of her lovingly in his diary, but this did not stop him from "committing folly" with the servants. Due to his position and status, it was expected that he act like a gentleman, and gentlemen often seduced their maidservants.

Status, of course, was all-important to the transplanted Virginia English gentleman. While the many long rivers flowing into the Chesapeake Bay and

Virginia's fertile soil made the plantation system possible, they also hindered the development of urban life. Thus, status had to be achieved on the plantation. This situation increased the Virginian's land hunger as land meant status, power, wealth, and often a seat on the Council. To achieve these goals colonial planters worked long hours. While Byrd often noted in his diary that "we were as merry as we could be . . . ," this gaiety took place only after a day of exhausting labor. Like most other planters of the era, Byrd was a busy man who kept his own accounts, doctored his slaves, and supervised the work on the Westover Plantation. His many other plantations were run by overseers, but he visited them periodically to keep these undependable men under control.

Thus one myth destroyed by the Byrd diaries was that of the Virginia cavalier who lived in ease while servants and overseers directed a smoothly organized plantation life. Nothing could be farther from the truth. Not only were the planters industrious, but their plantation life was often chaotic. As an example, he noted that the only way Governor Spotswood kept his servants from drinking at the annual Governor's Ball was to promise them a two-day drunk if they remained sober during the ball. When Byrd visited other plantations he often slept in beds that smelled foul, and had to eat poorly cooked foods.

His own plantation was not much better. He once "whipped the cook" for serving "half-raw bacon," and he noted numerous incidents when slaves were punished for their clumsiness. Even then runaways were a problem and a frequent source of annoyance. Runaway slaves were whipped, of course, and constant offenders were forced to wear a bit in their mouths. Byrd never resorted, however, to the branding iron, as his first wife had.

Despite their constant labor and their chaotic home life, the Byrds had an exciting social life. Indeed, the chaos often added to the excitement. In Williamsburg, for example, the drunken burgesses often tossed their sober peers out of bed or tossed water on the maids. Dancing, card-playing, horse races, parties, and dinners were very common. So too was flirting — or even more. Byrd once annoyed his wife by kissing a Mrs. Chiswell, and noted many times that "we did little dancing but much kissing."

Byrd's writings destroyed other myths about colonial life. It has too often been assumed that Virginians were neither as religious nor as intellectual as New Englanders. Possibly this situation was true in the nineteenth century, but it was not true in the eighteenth. Byrd's day usually started between 3–6 A.M. when he read the classics or the Bible in either Greek, Latin, or Hebrew. He also read books on history and religion, particularly the sermons of the famous English clergyman Dr. John Tillotson. Not all the planters had as many books as Byrd, or read as much as he, but when they visited each other they discussed what they had read, and much of it was theology. Often, during times of stress, Byrd turned to the Bible or his books of sermons for strength, as did other planters. Somehow, like his Puritan contemporaries, he found a way to reconcile his "sinful sexual excesses" with his religion.

Puritan "bundling" helped contribute to so many illegitimate births that colonial laws on bastardy had to be altered. English law provided that any child born before the ninth month of the marriage was illegitimate; New Englanders changed this law rather than be faced with the prospect of a whole village of illegitimate townsfolk.

A myth — created by Hollywood — that has misrepresented Byrd and his peers is the image of their exaggerated snobbishness. Most movies on colonial life portray the gentry as unrealistic snobs, while the common folk are the great heroes. There is some evidence to support this thesis, since the gentry seldom mixed socially with commoners. Even the earthy Byrd would not partake of the charms offered by Indian maidens while on a surveying expedition because many of the men accompanying him were commoners. He also was shocked when one planter allowed his daughter to marry an overseer.

But the yeoman farmer accepted most of these proscriptions willingly since he shared the planters' sense of structural community. Byrd had inherited his father's position as the Receiver General only because the common folk in Virginia willingly accepted the leadership of the gentry. This acquiescence was due to a variety of factors, including the planters' role in the economy of the colony: transportation was the key to colonial economy and only the gentlemen planters had wharves from which to ship their goods. For a modest fee, these facilities were available to the yeomen. The planters could have destroyed their competition at will by monopolizing the wharves or charging excessive fees for their use, but they did not.

In an economic sense, then, the planters met the responsibility of power. Other obligations entrusted to them because of their position were equally well met. Like the ideal English gentlemen they mimicked, the gentry felt a strong duty to the community. They were elected repeatedly to public office because they represented the interests of the entire community fairly. It was expected that these political offices would benefit the gentry in every way — socially, politically, and economically — but this was considered a small price for the good service Virginians received from the gentry. They were trusted to the extent that they were given leadership in every area; they were the burgesses, the church elders, and the militia officers, and their sons could expect that such honors would eventually be bestowed upon them. Common folk realized that while royal governors would come and go, the gentry would always be in Virginia. For this reason, leadership was given to them rather than to the royal representative. As idealistic as it sounds, this leadership was deserved and seldom abused. Eventually the yeomen farmers followed the gentry into two civil wars. And why not? Was it not the gentry who had challenged the authority of both the Crown and the federal government?

The sense of community which gave the gentry its staying power in the eighteenth century, as well as the Virginians' dual identity, were both evident in Byrd's epitaph when he died in 1744 at the age of 70. Laudatory as all epitaphs are, it was nonetheless accepted by the vast majority of Virginians as valid. It stated, among other things, that Byrd was:

> The well-bred gentleman and polite companion
> The splendid economist and prudent father of a family,
> ... the constant enemy of all exorbitant power
> And (the) hearty friend to the liberties of his country.

Issue

The Quest for Community

Technological change, mobility, and the individualistic ethos combine to rupture the bonds that tie each individual to a family, a community, a kinship network, a geographical location — bonds that give him a comfortable sense of himself.

Philip Slater, 1970

That common saying, "Every man for himself, and God for us all," is wicked, and is directly against the end of every calling or honest kinde of life.

William Perkins, 1616

During much of American history, towns and small cities have given their inhabitants a way of life — that is, a code of behavior, a web of protective relationships, a set of common experiences and associations. Even the narrow provincialism of these communities has provided people with an impetus to succeed in the larger and more impersonal world which exists beyond the town.

What is the process by which a community stamps its imprint so indelibly on the lives of individuals? Does the community require conformity only as a way of preserving the *status quo,* or do the restrictions of community life also serve to curb just enough individualism to enable people to function as a group?

What is the role of religion in this communal experience? Churches claim a special means of discovering moral truth and possess in their theology an elaborate understanding of human weaknesses and capabilities. The language of religious experience is therefore a candid and direct account of how people should perceive their moral duty.

Similarly, Americans have relied heavily on law as a means of holding the community together. Statutes not only prohibit a wide range of antisocial conduct; they also regulate many social, family, and economic relationships.

As creators and inhabitants of new communities, colonial Americans expended a great deal of effort in making communal life vibrant and dynamic.

◆ DOCUMENTS ◆

Religion and Community

THOMAS HOOKER

Thomas Hooker describes the prerequisites for the realization of the Puritan community's goals. What does Hooker see as the danger to community? Why is that threat destructive? What would be the cost to personal freedom of following Hooker's ideas? Why must this cost be paid to bring about the successful community?

For if each man may do what is good in his owne eyes, proceed according to his owne pleasure, so that none may crosse him or controll him by any power; there must of necessity follow the distraction and desolation of the whole, when each man hath liberty to follow his owne imagination and humorous devices, and seek his particular, but oppose one another, and all prejudice the publicke good.

In the building, if the parts be neither mortised nor braced, as there will be little beauty, so there can be no strength. Its so in setting up the frames of societies among men, when their mindes and hearts are not mortised by mutuall consent of subjection one to another, there is no expectation of any successfull proceeding with the advantage to the publicke. To this appertains that of the Apostle, Every one submit unto another.

Mutuall subjection is as it were the sinewes of society, by which it is sustained and supported.

Hence every man is above another, while he walkes according to rule; and when he departs from it, he must be subject to another.

Hence every part is subject to the whole, and must be serviceable to the good thereof, and must be ordered by the power thereof. . . .

From Thomas Hooker, *A Survey of the Summe of Church-Discipline* (London, 1648), p. 188.

It is the highest law in all Policy Civill or Spirituall to preserve the good of the whole; at this all must aime, and unto this all must be subordinate. . . .

Hence each man and member of society, in a just way, may be directed, censured, reformed, removed, by the power of the whole: this belongs to all the Members, and therefore to any that shall be in office, if they be Members. They are superior as Officers, when they keep the rule: but inferior as Members, and in subjection to any when they break the rule. So it is in any corporation; so in the Parliament. The whole can censure any part.

Work and Community
WILLIAM PERKINS

English Puritan scholar William Perkins describes the duty of individuals to follow the calling to which God directs them. What are the advantages of each person being assigned by God to a calling in society? How important is work in maintaining the order of a community? How is a person to recognize God's calling? Why is a calling which helps only the individual "against the end of every calling or honest kind of life"?

> *Let everie man abide in that calling,*
> *wherein hee was called. . . .*
>
> 1 Cor. 7: verse 20

A vocation or calling, is a certaine kinde of life ordained and imposed on man by God, for the common good. First of all I say, it is a certaine condition or kinde of life: that is, a certaine manner of leading our lives in this world. For example, the life of a King is to spend his time in the governing of his Subjects, and that is his calling: and the life of a Subject is to live in obedience to the Magistrate, and that is his calling. The state and condition of a Minister is, to lead his life in preaching of the Gospell and word of God, and that is his calling. A master of his family, is to lead his life in the government of his family, and that is his calling. In a word, that particular and honest manner of conversation, whereunto everie man is called and set apart, that is (I say) his calling.

Now in everie calling we must consider two causes. . . . The author of everie calling, is God himself: and therefore Paul saith; As God hath called everie man, let him walke vers. 17. And for this cause, the order and manner

From William Perkins, *Works* (Cambridge, 1616), I, 750–751.

of living in this world, is called a Vocation; because everie man is to live as he is called of God. For looke as in the camp, the Generall appointeth to everie man his place and standing; one place for the horse-man, & another for the foot-man, and to everie particular Souldier likewise, his office and standing; in which hee is to abide against the enemie, and therein to live and die: even so it is in humane societies: God is the Generall appointing to everie man his particular calling, and as it were his standing: and in that calling hee assignes unto him his particular office; in performance whereof he is to live and die. And as in a camp, no Souldier can depart his standing, without the leave of the Generall; no more may any man leave his calling, except hee receive libertie from God. . . .

The finall cause or end of every calling, I note in the last words of the description; For the common good: that is, for the benefit and good estate of mankinde. In mans body there be sundry parts and members, and every one hath his severall use and office, which it performeth not for itself, but for the good of the whole bodie; as the office of the eye, is to see, of the eare to heare, and the foote to goe. Now all societies of men, are bodies, a family is a bodie, and so is every particular Church a bodie, and the Common-wealth also: and in these bodies there be severall members, which are men walking in severall callings and offices, the execution whereof, must tend to the happie and good state of the rest; yea of all men every where, as much as possible is. The common good of men stands in this, not onely that they live, but that they live well, in righteousnesse & holinesse, and consequently in true happinesse. And for the attainement hereunto, God hath ordained and disposed all callings, and in his providence designed the persons to beare them. Here then wee must in generall know, that he abuseth his calling, whosoever he be that against the end thereof, imployes it for himself, seeking wholly his own, and not the common good. And that common saying, Every man for himself, and God for us all, is wicked, and is directly against the end of every calling or honest kinde of life.

Sustaining Community Cohesion

COTTON MATHER

Cotton Mather suggests practical ways for the community to inculcate virtuous conduct and for individuals to gain the moral guidance they need. How will this behavior help develop a sense of community — a sense of shared ideals

From Cotton Mather, *Bonifacius: An Essay . . . to Do Good* (Boston, 1710), pp. 19, 82–83, 87.

and behavior? Will such behavior interfere with the privacy of individuals? Why does Mather hope to keep political discussion out of the groups he proposes? What sacrifices are necessary to create and nurture a sense of community?

Such *glorious things are spoken* in the oracles of our good God, concerning them who *devise good,* that A BOOK OF GOOD DEVICES may very reasonably demand attention and acceptance from them that have any impressions of the most *reasonable religion* upon them. I am *devising* such a BOOK. . . .

[For example]

The *rules* observed by some, ASSOCIATED FAMILIES, may be offered on this occasion with some advantage. They will tell us what *good* may be done by such *societies* in a neighborhood.

I. It is to be proposed, that about a dozen *families,* more or less, of a vicinity, agree to meet (the men and their wives) at each other's houses, once in a fortnight, or a month, at such a time as may be agreed upon, and spend a convenient quantity of time together, in the *exercises of religion.*

II. The *exercises of religion* proper for a *meeting,* are: for the brethren to begin and conclude with PRAYERS in their turns; for PSALMS to be sung; and for SERMONS to be repeated.

III. It were desirable, for the MINISTERS now and then, to afford their presence at the meeting, and *pray* with them, and *instruct* them, and *exhort* them, as they may see occasion.

IV. The *candidates* of the ministry may do well, to perform some of their *first services* here, and here shape and mold themselves for *further services.*

V. One special *design* of the *meeting,* should be, with *united prayers,* to ask the blessings of Heaven on the family where they are assembled, as well as on the rest: that with the wondrous force of *united prayers, two or three may agree on earth, to ask such things,* as are to be done for the families, by *our Father which is in Heaven.*

VI. Such a *meeting* should look upon themselves, as bound up in one *bundle of love;* and count themselves obliged, in very close and strong bonds, to be serviceable unto one another. If anyone in the society should fall into *affliction,* all the rest should presently study to relieve and support the afflicted person, in all the ways imaginable. If anyone should fall into *temptation,* the rest should watch over him, and with the *spirit of meekness,* with the *meekness of wisdom,* endeavor to recover him. . . .

VIII. Let the whole *Society,* be exceedingly careful, that their discourse while they are together, after the other services of religion are over, have nothing in it, that shall have any taint of *backbiting* or *vanity,* or the least relation to the affairs of *government,* or to things which do not concern them, and do not serve the interests of holiness in their own conversation. But let their discourse be wholly on the matters of religion; and those also, not the disputable and controversial matters, but the points of *practical piety.* . . .

IX. Let every person in the *Society,* look upon it, as a special task incumbent on him, to look out, for some other hopeful *young man,* and use all proper pains, to engage him in the resolutions of godliness, until he also shall be joined unto the *Society.* And when a *society* shall in this way be increased unto a fit number, let it *swarm* into *more;* who may hold an useful correspondence with one another.

Confronting Community Ideals

JONATHAN EDWARDS

Writing in 1736, Jonathan Edwards describes the religious experiences of a community during the Great Awakening. What do these experiences suggest about the nature and condition of the sense of community in Northampton? Does the intensity of the experience suggest a pre-existing weakness or strength in the community?

The town of Northampton is of about eighty-two years standing, and has now about two hundred families; which mostly dwell more compactly together than any town of such a bigness in these parts of the country; which probably has been an occasion that both our corruptions and reformations have been from time to time, the more swiftly propagated, from one to another, through the town. Take the town in general, and so far as I can judge, they are as rational and understanding a people as most I have been acquainted with: many of them have been noted for religion, and particularly, have been remarkable for their distinct knowledge in things that relate to heart religion, and Christian experience, and their great regards thereto. . . .

But though the people did not ordinarily neglect their worldly business, yet there then was the reverse of what commonly is: religion was with all sorts the great concern, and the world was a thing only by the by. The only thing in their view was to get the kingdom of heaven, and every one appeared

From Jonathan Edwards, *Works* (New York, 1879), III, 231–249 passim.

pressing into it: the engagedness of their hearts in this great concern could not be hid; it appeared in their very countenances. It then was a dreadful thing amongst us to lie out of Christ, in danger every day of dropping into hell; and what persons' minds were intent upon was to escape for their lives, and to *fly from the wrath to come.* All would eagerly lay hold of opportunities for their souls; and were wont very often to meet together in private houses for religious purposes: and such meetings, when appointed, were wont greatly to be thronged.

There was scarcely a single person in the town, either old or young, that was left unconcerned about the great things of the eternal world. Those that were wont to be the vainest, and loosest, and those that had been most dis-posed to think and speak slightly of vital and experimental religion, were now generally subject to great awakenings. And the work of conversion was carried on in a most astonishing manner, and increased more and more; souls did, as it were, come by flocks to Jesus Christ. From day to day, for many months together, might be seen evident instances of sinners brought *out of darkness into marvellous light,* and delivered *out of a horrible pit, and from the miry clay, and set upon a rock,* with a *new song of praise to God in their mouths.*

This work of God, as it was carried on, and the number of true saints multiplied, soon made a glorious alteration in the town; so that in the spring and summer following, anno 1735, the town seemed to be full of the presence of God: it never was so full of love, nor so full of joy; and yet so full of distress as it was then. There were remarkable tokens of God's presence in almost every house. It was a time of joy in families on the account of salva-tion's being brought unto them; parents rejoicing over their children as new born, and husbands over their wives, and wives over their husbands. *The goings of God were then seen in his sanctuary, God's day was a delight, and his tabernacles were amiable.* Our public assemblies were then beautiful; the congregation was alive in God's service, every one earnestly intent on the public worship, every hearer eager to drink in the words of the minister as they came from his mouth; the assembly in general were, from time to time, in tears while the word was preached; some weeping with sorrow and distress, others with joy and love, others with pity and concern for the souls of their neighbors. . . .

God's work has also appeared very extraordinary, in the degrees of the influences of his Spirit, both in the degree of awakening and conviction, and also in a degree of saving light, and love, and joy, that many have experienced. It has also been very extraordinary in the extent of it, and its being so swiftly propagated from town to town. In former times of the pouring out of the Spirit of God on this town, though in some of them it was very remarkable, yet it reached no further than this town, the neighboring towns all around continued unmoved.

The work of God's Spirit seemed to be at its greatest height in this town, in the former part of the spring, in March and April; at which time God's work in the conversion of souls was carried on amongst us in so wonderful a manner, that so far as I, by looking back, can judge from the particular acquaintance I have had with souls in this work, it appears to me probable, to have been at the rate, at least of four persons in a day, or near thirty in a week, take one with another, for five or six weeks together: when God in so remarkable a manner took the work into his own hands, there was as much done in a day or two, as at ordinary times, with all endeavors that men can use, and with such a blessing as we commonly have, is done in a year.

I am very sensible how apt many would be, if they should see the account I have here given, presently to think with themselves that I am very fond of making a great many converts, and of magnifying and aggrandizing the matter; and to think that, for want of judgment, I take every religious pang, and enthusiastic conceit, for saving conversion; and I do not much wonder if they should be apt to think so: and for this reason, I have forborne to publish an account of this great work of God, though I have often been put upon it; but having now as I thought a special call to give an account of it, upon mature consideration I thought it might not be beside my duty to declare this amazing work, as it appeared to me, to be indeed divine, and to conceal no part of the glory of it, leaving it with God to take care of the credit of his own work, and running the venture of any censorious thoughts, which might be entertained of me to my disadvantage. But that distant persons may be under as great advantage as may be, to judge for themselves of this matter, I would be a little more large, and particular. . . .

These awakenings when they have first seized on persons, have had two effects: one was, that they have brought them immediately to quit their sinful practices, and the looser sort have been brought to forsake and dread their former vices and extravagancies. When once the Spirit of God began to be so wonderfully poured out in a general way through the town, people had soon done with their old quarrels, backbitings, and intermeddling with other men's matters; the tavern was soon left empty, and persons kept very much at home; none went abroad unless on necessary business, or on some religious account, and every day seemed in many respects like a Sabbath day. And the other effect was, that it put them on earnest application to the means of salvation, reading, prayer, meditation, the ordinances of God's house, and private conference; their cry was, *What shall we do to be saved?* The place of resort was now altered, it was no longer the tavern, but the minister's house; that was thronged far more than ever the tavern had been wont to be.

There is a very great variety, as to the degree of fear and trouble that persons are exercised with, before they obtain any comfortable evidences of pardon and acceptance with God: some are from the beginning carried on with abundantly more encouragement and hope, than others: some have had ten times less trouble of mind than others, in whom yet the issue seems to be the same. Some have had such a sense of the displeasure of God, and the great danger they were in of damnation, that they could not sleep at nights; and many have said that when they have laid down, the thoughts of sleeping in such a condition have been frightful to them, and they have scarcely been free from terror while they have been asleep, and they have awaked with fear, heaviness, and distress still abiding on their spirits. It has been very common, that the deep and fixed concern that has been on persons' minds, has had a painful influence on their bodies, and given disturbance to animal nature.

The awful apprehensions persons have had of their misery, have for the most part been increasing, the nearer they have approached to deliverance; though they often pass through many changes, and alterations in the frame and circumstances of their minds: sometimes they think themselves wholly senseless, and fear that the Spirit of God has left them, and that they are given up to judicial hardness; yet they appear very deeply exercised about that fear, and are in great earnest to obtain convictions again. . . .

There is wrought in them a holy repose of soul in God through Christ, and a secret disposition to fear and love him, and to hope for blessings from him in this way: and yet they have no imagination that they are now converted, it does not so much as come into their minds; and very often the reason is, that they do not see that they do accept of this sufficiency of salvation, that they behold in Christ, having entertained a wrong notion of acceptance; not being sensible that the obedient and joyful entertainment which their hearts give to this discovery of grace, is a real acceptance of it: they know not that the sweet complacence they feel in the mercy and complete salvation of God, as it includes pardon and sanctification, and is held forth to them only through Christ, is a true receiving of this mercy, or a plain evidence of their receiving it. They expected I know not what kind of act of soul, and perhaps they had no distinct idea of it themselves.

And indeed it appears very plainly in some of them, that before their own conversion they had very imperfect ideas what conversion was: it is all new and strange, and what there was no clear conception of before. It is most evident, as they themselves acknowledge, that the expressions that were used to describe conversion, and the graces of God's Spirit, such as a spiritual sight of Christ, faith in Christ, poverty of spirit, trust in God, resignedness to God, &c., were expressions that did not convey those special and distinct ideas to their minds which they were intended to signify: perhaps to some of them it was but little more than the names of colors are to convey the ideas to one that is blind from his birth.

This town is a place where there has always been a great deal of talk of conversion, and spiritual experiences; and therefore people in general had before formed a notion in their own minds what these things were; but when they come to be the subjects of them themselves, they find themselves much confounded in their notions, and overthrown in many of their former conceits. And it has been very observable, that persons of the greatest understanding, and that had studied most about things of this nature, have been more confounded than others. Some such persons that have lately been converted, declare that all their former wisdom is brought to nought, and that they appear to have been mere babes, who knew nothing. It has appeared that none have stood more in need of enlightening and instruction, even of their fellow Christians, concerning their own circumstances and difficulties, than they, and it has seemed to have been with delight, that they have seen themselves thus brought down and become nothing, that free grace and divine power may be exalted in them.

Personal Ethics and Community

JOHN WOOLMAN

Quaker John Woolman describes the growing dissolution of community during the 1740s as economic prosperity drives a deep wedge between the well-to-do and the poor. What are the consequences of these gaps between rich and poor? What should the rich do to heal the division? What values exist in having all people share the same sort of labor? Is there any role for the poor in helping to secure a strong sense of community?

Wealth desired for its own sake obstructs the increase of virtue, and large possessions in the hands of selfish men have a bad tendency, for by their means too small a number of people are employed in things useful; and therefore they, or some of them, are necessitated to labour too hard, while others would want business to earn their bread were not employments invented which, having no real use, serve only to please the vain mind.

Rents set on lands are often so high that persons who have but small substance are straitened in hiring a plantation; and while tenants are healthy and prosperous in business, they often find occasion to labour harder than was intended by our gracious Creator.

Oxen and horses are often seen at work when, through heat and too much labour, their eyes and the emotion of their bodies manifest that they are oppressed. Their loads in wagons are frequently so heavy that when weary with hauling it far, their drivers find occasion in going up hills or through mire to raise their spirits by whipping to get forward. Many poor people are so thronged in their business that it is difficult for them to provide shelter suitable for their animals in great storms.

These things are common when in health, but through sickness and inability to labour, through loss of creatures and miscarriage in business, many are straitened; and so much of their increase goes annually to pay rent or interest that they have not wherewith to hire so much as their case requires.

From "A Word of Remembrance and Caution to the Rich," *The Works of John Woolman* (Philadelphia: Benjamin Johnson, 1806), pp. 391–397.

Hence one poor woman, in attending on her children, providing for her family, and helping the sick, does as much business as would for the time be suitable employment for two or three; and honest persons are often straitened to give their children suitable learning. The money which the wealthy receive from the poor, who do more than a proper share of business in raising it, is frequently paid to other poor people for doing business which is foreign to the true use of things. . . .

Our gracious Creator cares and provides for all his creatures. His tender mercies are over all his works; and so far as his love influences our minds, so far we become interested in his workmanship and feel a desire to take hold of every opportunity to lessen the distresses of the afflicted and increase the happiness of the creation. Here we have a prospect of one common interest from which our own is inseparable — that to turn all the treasures we possess into the channel of universal love becomes the business of our lives. Men of large estates whose hearts are thus enlarged are like fathers to the poor, and in looking over their brethren in distressed circumstances and considering their own more easy condition, find a field for humble meditation and feel the strength of those obligations they are under to be kind and tender-hearted toward them.

Poor men eased of their burdens and released from too close an application to business are at liberty to hire others to their assistance, to provide well for their animals, and find time to perform those visits amongst their acquaintance which belongs to a well-guided social life.

When these reflect on the opportunity those had to oppress them, and consider the goodness of their conduct, they behold it lovely and consistent with brotherhood; and as the man whose mind is conformed to universal love hath his trust settled in God and finds a firm foundation to stand on in any changes or revolutions that happen amongst men, so also the goodness of his conduct tends to spread a kind, benevolent disposition in the world.

Our blessed Redeemer, in directing us how to conduct one towards another, appeals to our own feeling: "Whatsoever ye would that other men should do to you, do ye even so to them." Now where such live in fullness on the labour of others, who have never had experience of hard labour themselves, there is often a danger of their not having a right feeling of the labourer's condition, and therefore of being disqualified to judge candidly in their case, not knowing what they themselves would desire were they to labour hard from one year to another to raise the necessities of life and to pay large rents beside — that it's good for those who live in fullness to labour for tenderness of heart, to improve every opportunity of being acquainted with the hardships and fatigues of those who labour for their living, and think seriously with themselves: Am I influenced with true charity in fixing all my demands? Have I no desire to support myself in expensive customs because my acquaintance live in those customs? Were I to labour as they do toward supporting them and their children in a station like mine, in such sort as they and their children labour for us, could I not on such a change, before I entered into agreements of rents or interest, name some costly articles now used by me or in my family which have no real use in them, the expense whereof might be lessened? And should I not in such case strongly desire the disuse of those needless expenses, that less answering their way of life the terms might be the easier to me?

If a wealthy man, on serious reflection, finds a witness in his own conscience that there are some expenses which he indulgeth himself in that are in conformity to custom, which might be omitted consistent with the true design of living, and which was he to change places with those who occupy his estate he would desire to be discontinued by them — whoever are thus awakened to their feeling will necessarily find the injunction binding on them: "Do thou even so to them."

Divine love imposeth no rigorous or unreasonable commands, but graciously points out the spirit of brotherhood and way to happiness, in the attaining to which it is necessary that we go forth out of all that is selfish.

Controlling Community Disruption
NORTH CAROLINA ASSEMBLY

The North Carolina Assembly acts to control the classes that lack reasons for helping to sustain the community. Those classes are servants and slaves. Is there a difference between the attitude toward "servants" and "slaves"? Do these laws suggest a breakdown of community, or are they an attempt to produce a community containing superior and subservient classes? How does this solution to the problem of economic class compare with Woolman's? Can a community be sustained by force as well as by admonition?

An Act Concerning Servants and Slaves
Be it Enacted, by his Excellency Gabriel Johnston, Esq., Governor, by and with the Advice and Consent of his Majesty's Council, and General Assembly of this Province, and it is hereby Enacted, by the Authority of the same, That no Person whatsoever, being a Christian, or of Christian Parentage, who, from and after the Ratification of this Act, shall be imported or brought into this Province, shall be deemed a Servant for any Term of Years, unless the Person importing him or her shall produce an Indenture, or some Specialty or Agreement, signifying that the Person so imported did contract to serve such Importer, or his Assigns, any Number of Years, in Consideration of his or her Passage; . . .

From *The State Records of North Carolina* (Goldsboro, 1904), XXIII, 191–202 passim.

... That if any Christian Servant, whether he or she be a Servant by Importation or otherwise, shall at any Time or Times absent him or herself from the service of his or her Master or Mistress, without Licence first had, he or she shall satisfy and make good such Loss of Time by serving after their Time of Service by Indenture or otherwise is expired, double the Time of Service lost or neglected by such Absence; ...

... That if any Christian Servant shall lay violent Hands on his or her Master or Mistress, or Overseer, or shall obstinately refuse to obey the lawful Commands of any of them, upon Proof thereof by one or more Evidences before any Justice of the Peace, he or she shall, for every such Offence, suffer such Corporal Punishment as the said Judge shall think fit to adjudge, not exceeding Twenty One Lashes. ...

... And as an Encouragement for Christian Servants to perform their Service with Fidelity and Cheerfulness; Be it further Enacted, by the Authority aforesaid, That all Masters and Owners of any Servant or Servants shall find and provide for their Servant or Servants wholesome and competent Diet, Clothing and Lodging, at the Discretion of the County Court, and shall not, at any Time, give immoderate Correction, neither shall at any Time whip a Christian Servant naked, without an Order from the Justice of the Peace; ...

... That if any Servant or Servants shall unjustly vex and trouble his, her or their Master or Owner with Groundless Complaints against them to the County Court, or any Justice or Justices of the Peace, such Servant or Servants shall, by the County Court, be ordered to serve his, her or their Master or Owner so injured by such unjust and groundless Vexation, after the Expiration of the Time he, she or they have then to serve, the double Term and Space of that Time he, she or they neglected and lost in Prosecution of such Complaints. ...

... That every Servant, by Indenture or otherwise, who shall imbezzel, purloin, wilfully waste or shall trade, sell or barter, or otherwise make away any of his or her Master or Mistress' Corn, Cattle, Sheep, Hogs, Stock, or other Goods or Provisions, or Commodities whatsoever, shall, upon Conviction of every such Offence, by one or more Testimonies, upon Oath, or Confession of the Party, before any County Court within this Government, be adjudged by the said Court, to serve his or her said Master or Mistress such Time as the said Court shall think reasonable, for the said Offence, after the said Time by Indenture or otherwise, as aforesaid, is expired. ...

... And whereas many Women Servants are begotten with Child by free Men, or Servants, to the great Prejudice of their Master or Mistress, whom they serve, Be it therefore further Enacted, by the Authority aforesaid, That if any Woman Servant shall hereafter be with Child, and bring forth the same during the Time of her Servitude, she shall for such Offence be adjudged by the County Court to serve her Master or Mistress one Year after her Term of Service by Indenture or otherwise is expired. ...

... That no Slave shall go armed with Gun, Sword, Club or other Weapon, or shall keep any such Weapon, or shall Hunt or Range in the Woods, upon any pretence whatsoever (except such Slave or Slaves who shall have a Certificate, as is hereinafter provided), and if any Slave shall be found offending herein, it shall and may be lawful for any Person or Persons to seize and take, to his own Use, such Gun, Sword or other Weapon, and to apprehend and to deliver such Slave to the next Constable, who is enjoined and required, without further Order or Warrant, to give such Slave Twenty Lashes on his or her bare Back, and to send him or her home, and the Master or Owner of such Slave shall pay the taker-up of such armed Slave the same Reward as by this Act is allowed for taking up of Runaways. . . .

. . . And whereas many Times Slaves run away and lie out hid and lurking in the Swamps, Woods and other Obscure Places, killing Cattle and Hogs, and committing other Injuries to the Inhabitants in this Government: Be it therefore Enacted, by the Authority aforesaid, That in all such Cases, upon Intelligence of any Slave or Slaves lying out as aforesaid, any Two Justices of the Peace for the County wherein such Slave or Slaves is or are supposed to lurk to do Mischief, shall, and they are hereby impowered and required, to issue Proclamation against such Slave or Slaves (reciting his or their Name or Names, and the Name or Names of the Owner or Owners, if known), thereby requiring him or them, and every of them, forthwith to surrender him or themselves; and also, to impower and require the Sheriff of the said County to take such Power with him as he shall think fit and necessary for going in search and pursuit of and effectual apprehending such outlying Slave or Slaves; which Proclamation shall be published on a Sabbath Day, at the Door of every Church or Chappel, or for want of such, at the Place where Divine Service shall be performed in the said County, by the Parish Clerk or Reader, immediately after Divine Service: And if any Slave or Slaves against whom Proclamation hath been thus issued, stay out and do not immediately return home, it shall be lawful for any Person or Persons whatsoever to kill and destroy such Slave or Slaves by such Ways and Means as he or she shall think fit, without Accusation or Impeachment of any Crime for the same. . . .

. . . That if any Number of Negroes or other Slaves, that is to say, Three or more, shall at any Time hereafter, consult, advise or conspire to rebell, or make insurrection, or shall plot or conspire the Murther of any Person or Persons whatsoever, every such consulting, plotting, or conspiring, shall be adjudged and deemed Felony; And the Slave or Slaves convicted thereof, in Manner hereafter directed, shall suffer Death.

◆ MODERN ESSAY ◆

The Death of Community

PHILIP SLATER

In The Pursuit of Loneliness, *Philip Slater questions the value of individual autonomy and freedom as ultimate societal goals. The social and psychological results of individualism, he argues, have been loneliness, fear, and alienation. Is traditional liberty compatible with close human relationships? Can durable human institutions also be humane? Are people today ready for the hard task of building a more sensitive and cohesive society?*

We are so accustomed to living in a society that stresses individualism that we need to be reminded that "collectivism" in a broad sense has always been the more usual lot of mankind, as well as of most other species. Most people in most societies have been born into and died in stable communities in which the subordination of the individual to the welfare of the group was taken for granted, while the aggrandizement of the individual at the expense of his fellows was simply a crime.

   This is not to say that competition is an American invention — all societies involve some sort of admixture of cooperative and competitive institutions. But our society lies near or on the competitive extreme, and although it contains cooperative institutions I think it is fair to say that Americans suffer from their relative weakness and peripherality. Studies of business executives have revealed, for example, a deep hunger for an atmosphere of trust and fraternity with their colleagues (with whom they must, in the short run, engage in what Riesman calls "antagonistic cooperation"). The competitive life is a lonely one, and its satisfactions are very short-lived indeed, for each race leads only to a new one.

   In the past, as so many have pointed out, there were in our society many oases in which one could take refuge from the frenzied invidiousness of our economic system — institutions such as the extended family and the stable local neighborhood in which one could take pleasure from something other than winning a symbolic victory over one of his fellows. But these have disappeared one by one, leaving the individual more and more in a situation in which he must try to satisfy his affiliative and invidious needs in the same place. This has made the balance a more brittle one — the appeal of cooperative living more seductive, and the need to suppress our longing for it more acute.

In recent decades the principal vehicle for the tolerated expression of this longing has been the mass media. Popular songs and film comedies have continually engaged in a sentimental rejection of the dominant mores, maintaining that the best things in life are free, that love is more important than success, that keeping up with the Joneses is absurd, that personal integrity should take precedence over winning, and so on. But these protestations must be understood for what they are: a safety valve for the dissatisfactions that the modal American experiences when he behaves as he thinks he should. The same man who chuckles and sentimentalizes over a happy-go-lucky hero in a film would view his real-life counterpart as frivolous and irresponsible, and suburbanites who philosophize over their back fence with complete sincerity about their "dog-eat-dog-world," and what-is-it-all-for, and you-can't-take-it-with-you, and success-doesn't-make-you-happy-it-just-gives-you-ulcers-and-a-heart-condition — would be enraged should their children pay serious attention to such a viewpoint. Indeed, the degree of rage is, up to a point, a function of the degree of sincerity: if the individual did not feel these things he would not have to fight them so vigorously. The peculiarly exaggerated hostility that hippies tend to arouse suggests that the life they strive for is highly seductive to middle-aged Americans.

The intensity of this reaction can in part be attributed to a kind of circularity that characterizes American individualism. When a value is as strongly held as is individualism in America the illnesses it produces tend to be treated by increasing the dosage, in the same way an alcoholic treats a hangover or a drug addict his withdrawal symptoms. Technological change, mobility, and the individualistic ethos combine to rupture the bonds that tie each individual to a family, a community, a kinship network, a geographical location — bonds that give him a comfortable sense of himself. As this sense of himself erodes, he seeks ways of affirming it. But his efforts at self-enhancement automatically accelerate the very erosion he seeks to halt.

It is easy to produce examples of the many ways in which Americans attempt to minimize, circumvent, or deny the interdependence upon which all human societies are based. We seek a private house, a private means of transportation, a private garden, a private laundry, self-service stores, and do-it-yourself skills of every kind. An enormous technology seems to have set itself the task of making it unnecessary for one human being ever to ask anything of another in the course of going about his daily business. Even within the family Americans are unique in their feeling that each member should have a separate room, and even a separate telephone, television, and car, when economically possible. We seek more and more privacy, and feel more and more alienated and lonely when we get it. What accidental contacts we do have, furthermore, seem more intrusive, not only because they are unsought but because they are unconnected with any familiar pattern of interdependence.

Most important, our encounters with others tend increasingly to be competitive as a result of the search for privacy. We less and less often meet our fellow man to share and exchange, and more and more often encounter him as an impediment or a nuisance: making the highway crowded when we are rushing somewhere, cluttering and littering the beach or park or wood, pushing in front of us at the supermarket, taking the last parking place, polluting our air and water, building a highway through our house, blocking our view, and so on. Because we have cut off so much communication with each other we keep bumping into each other, and thus a higher and higher percentage of our interpersonal contacts are abrasive.

We seem unable to foresee that the gratification of a wish might turn out to be something of a monkey's paw if the wish were shared by many others. We cheer the new road that initially shaves ten minutes off the drive to our country retreat but ultimately transforms it into a crowded resort and increases both the traffic and the time. We are continually surprised to find, when we want something, that thousands or millions of others want it, too — that other human beings get hot in summer and cold in winter. The worst traffic jams occur when a mass of vacationing tourists departs for home early to "beat the traffic." We are too enamored of the individualistic fantasy that everyone is, or should be, different — that each person could somehow build his entire life around some single, unique eccentricity without boring himself and everyone else to death. Each of us of course has his quirks, which provide a surface variety that is briefly entertaining, but aside from this human beings have little basis for their persistent claim that they are not all members of the same species.

Since our contacts with others are increasingly competitive, unanticipated, and abrasive, we seek still more apartness and accelerate the trend. The desire to be somehow special inaugurates an even more competitive quest for progressively more rare and expensive symbols — a quest that is ultimately futile since it is individualism itself that produces uniformity.

This is poorly understood by Americans, who tend to confuse uniformity with "conformity," in the sense of compliance with or submission to group demands. Many societies exert far more pressure on the individual to mold himself to fit a particularized segment of a total group pattern, but there is variation among these circumscribed roles. Our society gives far more leeway to the individual to pursue his own ends, but since *it* defines what is worthy and desirable, everyone tends, independently but monotonously, to pursue the same things in the same way. The first pattern combines cooperation, conformity, and variety; the second, competition, individualism and uniformity.

These relationships are exemplified by two familiar processes in contemporary America: the flight to the suburb and the do-it-yourself movement. Both attempt to deny human interdependence and pursue unrealistic fantasies of self-sufficiency. The first tries to overlook our dependence upon the city for the maintenance of the level of culture we demand. "Civilized" means, literally, "citified," and the state of the city is an accurate index of the condition of the culture as a whole. We behave toward our cities like an irascible farmer who never feeds his cow and then kicks her when she fails to give enough milk. But the flight to the suburb is in any case self-defeating, its goals subverted by the mass quality of the exodus. The suburban dweller seeks peace, privacy, nature, community, and a child-rearing environment which is healthy and culturally optimal. Instead he finds neither the beauty and serenity of the countryside, the stimulation of the city, nor the stability and sense of community of the small town, and his children are exposed to a cultural deprivation equaling that of any slum child with a television set. Living in a narrow age-graded and class-segregated society, it is little wonder that suburban families have contributed so little to the national talent pool in proportion to their numbers, wealth, and other social advantages. And this transplantation, which has caused the transplants to atrophy, has blighted the countryside and impoverished the city. A final irony of the suburban dream is that, for many Americans, reaching the pinnacle of one's social ambitions (owning a house in the suburbs) requires one to perform all kinds of menial tasks (carrying garbage cans, mowing lawns, shoveling snow, and so on) that were performed for him when he occupied a less exalted status.

Some of this manual labor, however, is voluntary — an attempt to deny the elaborate division of labor required in a complex society. Many Americans seem quite willing to pay this price for their reluctance to engage in inter-personal encounters with servants and artisans — a price which is rather high unless the householder particularly relishes the work (some find in it a tangible relief from the intangibles they manipulate in their own jobs) or is especially good at it, or cannot command a higher rate of pay in the job market than the servant or artisan.

The do-it-yourself movement has accompanied, paradoxically, increasing specialization in the occupational sphere. As one's job narrows, perhaps, one seeks the challenge of new skill-acquisition in the home. But specialization also means that one's interpersonal encounters with artisans in the home proliferate and become more impersonal. It is not a matter of a familiar encounter with the local smith or grocer — a few well-known individuals performing a relatively large number of functions, and with whom one's casual interpersonal contacts may be a source of satisfaction, and are in any case a testimony to the stability and meaningful interrelatedness of human affairs. One finds instead a multiplicity of narrow specialists — each perhaps a stranger (the same type of repair may be performed by a different person each time). Every relationship, such as it is, must start from scratch, and it is small wonder that the householder turns away from such an unrewarding prospect in apathy and despair.

Americans thus find themselves in a vicious circle, in which their extra-familial relationships are increasingly arduous, competitive, trivial, and irksome, in part as a result of efforts to avoid or minimize potentially irksome or competitive relationships. As the few vestiges of stable and familiar community life erode, the desire for a simple, cooperative life style grows in intensity. The most seductive appeal of radical ideologies for Americans consists in the fact that all in one way or another attack the competitive foundations of our society. Each touches a responsive doubt, and the stimuli arousing this doubt must be carefully unearthed and rooted out, just as the Puritan must unearth and root out the sexual stimuli that excite him.

Now it may be objected that American society is far less competitive than it once was, and the appeal of radical ideologies should hence be diminished. A generation of critics has argued that the entrepreneurial individualist of the past has been replaced by a bureaucratic, security-minded, Organization Man. Much of this historical drama was written through the simple device of comparing yesterday's owner-president with today's assistant sales manager; certainly these nostalgia-merchants never visited a nineteenth-century company town. Another distortion is introduced by the fact that it was only the most ruthlessly competitive robber barons who survived to tell us how it was. Little is written about the neighborhood store that extended credit to the poor, or the small town industry that refused to lay off local workers in hard times — they all went under together. And as for the organization men — they left us no sagas.

Despite these biases real changes have undoubtedly occurred, but even if we grant that the business world as such was more competitive, the total environment contained more cooperative, stable, and personal elements. The individual worked in a smaller firm with lower turnover in which his relationships were more enduring and less impersonal, and in which the ideology of Adam Smith was tempered by the fact that the participants were neighbors and might have been childhood playmates. Even if the business world was as "dog-eat-dog" as we imagine it (which seems highly unlikely), one encountered it as a deviant episode in what was otherwise a more comfortable and familiar environment than the organization man can find today in or out of his office. The organization man complex is simply an attempt to restore the personal, particularistic, paternalistic environment of the family business and the company town; and the other-directed "group-think" of the suburban community is a desperate attempt to bring some old-fashioned small-town collectivism into the transient and impersonal life-style of the suburb. The social critics of the 1950's were so preoccupied with assailing these rather synthetic substitutes for traditional forms of human interdependence that they lost sight of the underlying pathogenic forces that produced them. Medical symptoms usually result from attempts made by the body to counteract disease, and attacking such symptoms often aggravates and prolongs the illness. This appears to be the case with the feeble and self-defeating efforts of twentieth-century Americans to find themselves a viable social context.

Issue

The Quest for Identity

A society that fears it has no future is not likely to give much attention to the needs of the next generation, and the ever-present sense of historical discontinuity, the blight of our society, falls with particularly devastating effect on the family.

Christopher Lasch, 1976

If he is a good man, [the American] forms schemes of future prosperity, he proposes to educate his children better than he has been educated himself; he thinks of future modes of conduct, feels an ardor to labour he never felt before.

J. Hector St. John de Crèvecoeur, ca. 1770

Colonial Americans were acutely aware that they were provincials separated by distance and relative sophistication from the dazzling culture of the London metropolis and the mature stability of the English countryside. As the intense piety of the seventeenth century waned and as people moved away from the little communities founded by the early settlers, colonial society became fluid and middle-class; its booming economy and burgeoning population presented individuals with more and more opportunities for advancement. This tendency, in turn, reduced the hold of the community on individuals.

Experiencing a loss of community, the people sought a self-image and a strategy for conducting themselves in new, impersonal social situations. The crafty and self-centered outlook expressed in Benjamin Franklin's *Poor Richard's Almanack* provided just such guidance: "To lengthen thy life, lessen thy meals"; "Distrust and caution are the parents of security"; "Take counsel in wine but resolve afterwards in water." These maxims were a way of helping people come to terms with an increasingly complex environment, with a more intricate, less sustaining world than that of small stable communities. Was this style of living satisfying? Was it liberating? Was it humane?

By inculcating this sense of identity — a self-consciousness of one's own interests and rights — colonial culture was itself a major cause of the American Revolution. These attitudes also collided directly with British attempts to tighten control of the Empire after 1760 and to curb colonial resistance.

◆ DOCUMENTS ◆

Prudence, Reputation, and Identity

SIR WALTER RALEIGH and HENRY PEACHAM

Behavior manuals, widely read by aspiring young men in the colonies, advocated self-discipline and acute self-scrutiny as a way of achieving the standards of the community and securing identity. Two of the most popular of these books were written by Sir Walter Raleigh and Henry Peacham, respectively. What assumptions do these writers make about human drives, passions, and potentialities? Were the community standards described in these manuals capricious and restrictive, or disciplinary and civilizing?

[From *Raleigh's Advice*]

There is nothing more becoming a wise man than to make choice of friends, for by them thou shalt be judged what thou are. Let them, therefore, be wise and virtuous and none of those that follow thee for gain. But make election rather of thy betters than thy inferiors, shunning always such as are poor and needy, for if thou givest twenty gifts and refuse to do the like but once, all that thou hast done will be lost and such men will become thy mortal enemies. . . .

The next and greatest care ought to be in choice of a wife, and the only danger therein is beauty, by which all men in all ages, wise and foolish, have been betrayed. And although I know it vain to use reasons or arguments to dissuade thee from being captivated therewith, there being few or none that ever resisted that witchery, yet I cannot omit to warn thee as of other things which may be thy ruin and destruction. . . .

Take care thou be not made a fool by flatterers, for even the wisest men are abused by these. Know, therefore, that flatterers are the worst kind of traitors, for they will strengthen thy imperfections, encourage thee in all evils, correct thee in nothing, but so shadow and paint all thy vices and follies as thou shalt never by their will discern evil from good or vice from virtue. . . .

Be careful to avoid public disputations at feasts or at tables amongst choleric or quarrelsome persons, and eschew evermore to be acquainted or familiar with ruffians, for thou shalt be in as much danger in contending with a brawler in a private quarrel as in a battle wherein thou mayest get honor

---

From *Sir Walter Raleigh's Advice to His Son and to Posterity* (London, 1632), and from Henry Peacham, *The Compleat Gentleman . . .* (London, 1627).

to thyself and safety to thy prince and country; but if thou be once engaged, carry thyself bravely that they may fear thee after. To shun, therefore, private fight be well advised in thy words and behavior, for honor and shame is in the talk and the tongue of a man causeth him to fall. . . .

Amongst all other things of the world take care of thy estate, which thou shalt ever preserve if thou observe three things. First, that thou know what thou hast, what everything is worth that thou hast, and to see that thou art not wasted by thy servants and officers. The second is that thou never spend anything before thou have it, for borrowing is the canker and death of every man's estate. The third is that thou suffer not thyself to be wounded for other men's faults and scourged for other men's offenses, which is to be surety for another. . . .

On the other side, take heed that thou seek not riches basely nor attain them by evil means; destroy no man for his wealth nor take anything from the poor, for the cry and complaint thereof will pierce the heavens. . . .

Take especial care that thou delight not in wine, for there never was any man that came to honor or preferment that loved it; for it transformeth a man into a beast, decayeth health, poisoneth the breath, destroyeth natural heat, brings a man's stomach to an artificial heat, deformeth the face, rotteth the teeth, and, to conclude, maketh a man contemptible, soon old and despised of all wise and worthy men, hated in thy servants, in thyself, and companions, for it is a bewitching and infectious vice. . . .

. . . Serve God; let Him be the author of all thy actions; commend all thy endeavors to Him that must either wither or prosper them; please Him with prayer lest if He frown He confound all thy fortunes and labors. . . .

[Peacham, from *The Compleat Gentleman*]

There is no one thing that setteth a fairer stamp upon nobility than evenness of carriage and care of our reputation, without which our most graceful gifts are dead and dull, as the diamond without his foil. For hereupon as on the frontispiece of a magnificent palace are fixed the eyes of all passengers and hereby the height of our judgments (even ourselves) is taken. . . .

. . . The principal means to preserve it is temperance and that moderation of the mind wherewith as a bridle we curb and break our rank and unruly passions, keeping, as the Caspian Sea, ourselves ever at one height without ebb or reflux. And albeit true it is that Galen saith, we are commonly beholden for the disposition of our minds to the temperature of our bodies, yet much lieth in our power to keep that fount from empoisoning by taking heed to ourselves. . . .

The first use, then, hereof (I mean your learning) as an antidote against the common plague of our times: let it confirm and persuade you that as your understanding is by it ennobled with the richest dowry in the world, so hereby learn to know your own worth and value and in the choice of your companions to entertain those who are religious and learned. . . .

Whom, then, you shall entertain into the closet of your breast, first sound their religion; then look into their lives and carriage, how they have been reckoned of others; lastly, to their quality, how or wherein they may be useful unto you, whether by advice and counsel, direction, help in your studies, or serviceable in your exercise and recreations. . . .

Wherefore I must next commend unto you frugality, the mother of virtues, a virtue which holdeth her own, layeth out profitably, avoideth idle expenses, superfluity, lavish bestowing or giving, borrowing, building, and the like, yet, when reason requireth, can be royally bountiful, a virtue as requisite in a noble or gentleman as the care of his whole estate and preservation of his name and posterity. . . .

Be thrifty also in your apparel and clothing lest you incur the censure of the most grave and wisest censor. . . .

I now come to your diet, wherein be not only frugal for the saving of your purse, but moderate in regard of your health, which is impaired by nothing more than excess in eating and drinking (let me also add tobacco-taking). Many dishes breed many diseases, dulleth the mind and understanding, and not only shorten but take away life. . . .

Above all, learn betimes to avoid excessive drinking, than which there is no one vice more common and reigning and ill-beseeming a gentleman, which, if grown to a habit, is hardly left; remembering that hereby you become not fit for anything, having your reason degraded, your body distempered, your soul hazarded, your esteem and reputation abased, while you sit taking your unwholesome healths. . . .

But above all in your talk and discourse have a care ever to speak the truth, remembering there is nothing that can more prejudice your esteem than to be lavish-tongued in speaking that which is false, and disgracefully of others in their absence.

Creating Social Identity

BENJAMIN FRANKLIN

Prudence, realism, and caution were only the first attributes required by colonial society. Benjamin Franklin spelled out the rules for being an agreeable companion and for living in peace with one's own shortcomings and moral compromises. Does morality depend on fixed rules, or does it arise from the demands of each social situation and from the dynamics of each human relationship? Is the good opinion of one's fellows the only test of virtue?

From the *Pennsylvania Gazette,* November 15, 1770, and February 18, 1734.

[November 15, 1770]

Rules, by the Observation of which, a Man of Wit and Learning may nevertheless make himself a *disagreeable* Companion.

Your Business is to *shine;* therefore you must by all means prevent the shining of others, for their Brightness may make yours the less distinguish'd. To this End,

1. If possible engross the whole Discourse; and when other Matter fails, talk much of your-self, your Education, your Knowledge, your Circumstances, your Successes in Business, your Victories in Disputes, your own wise Sayings and Observations on particular Occasions, &c. &c. &c.

2. If when you are out of Breath, one of the Company should seize the Opportunity of saying something; watch his Words, and, if possible, find somewhat either in his Sentiment or Expression, immediately to contradict and raise a Dispute upon. Rather than fail, criticise even his Grammar.

3. If another should be saying an indisputably good Thing; either give no Attention to it; or interrupt him; or draw away the Attention of others; or, if you can guess what he would be at, be quick and say it before him; or, if he gets it said, and you perceive the Company pleas'd with it, own it to be a good Thing, and withal remark that it had been said by Bacon, Locke, Bayle, or some other eminent Writer: thus you deprive him of the Reputation he might have gain'd by it, and gain some yourself, as you hereby show your great Reading and Memory.

4. When modest Men have been thus treated by you a few times, they will chuse ever after to be silent in your Company; then you may shine on without Fear of a Rival; rallying them at the same time for their Dullness, which will be to you a new Fund of Wit.

Thus you will be sure to please *yourself*. The polite Man aims at pleasing *others,* but you shall go beyond him even in that. A Man can be present only in one Company, but may at the same time be absent in twenty. He can please only where he *is,* you whereever you are *not*.

[February 18, 1734]

That SELF-DENIAL *is not the* ESSENCE OF VIRTUE.

It is commonly asserted, that without *Self-Denial* there is no Virtue, and that the greater the *Self-Denial* the greater the Virtue.

If it were said, that he who cannot deny himself in any Thing he inclines to, tho' he knows it will be to his Hurt, has not the Virtue of *Resolution* or *Fortitude,* it would be intelligible enough; but as it stands it seems obscure or erroneous.

Let us consider some of the Virtues singly.

If a Man has no inclination to *wrong* People in his Dealings, if he feels no Temptation to it, and therefore never does it; can it be said that he is not a just Man? If he is a just Man, has he not the Virtue of Justice?

If to a certain Man, idle Diversions have nothing in them that is tempting, and therefore he never relaxes his Application to Business for their Sake; is he not an Industrious Man? Or has he not the Virtue of Industry?

I might in like manner instance in all the rest of the Virtues: But to make the Thing short, As it is certain, that the more we strive against the Temptation to any Vice, and practise the contrary Virtue, the weaker will that Temptation be, and the stronger will be that Habit; 'till at length the Temptation has no Force, or entirely vanishes: Does it follow from thence, that in our Endeavours to overcome Vice, we grow continually less and less Virtuous; till at length we have no Virtue at all?

If Self-Denial be the Essence of Virtue, then it follows, that the Man who is naturally temperate, just, &c. is not virtuous; but that in order to be virtuous, he must, in spight of his natural Inclinations, wrong his Neighbours, and eat and drink, &c. to excess.

But perhaps it may be said, that by the Word *Virtue* in the above Assertion, is meant, *Merit;* and so it should stand thus; Without Self-Denial there is no Merit; and the greater the Self-Denial the greater the Merit.

The Self-Denial here meant, must be when our Inclinations are towards Vice, or else it would still be Nonsense.

By Merit is understood, Desert; and when we say a Man merits, we mean that he deserves Praise or Reward.

We do not pretend to merit any thing of God, for he is above our Services; and the Benefits he confers on us, are the Effects of his Goodness and Bounty.

All our Merit then is with regard to one another, and from one to another.

The Sources of Personal Identity

WILLIAM BYRD II

While Franklin addressed himself to people still in search of success, Virginia planter William Byrd knew exactly who he was. He used his diary to record his efforts at intellectual, spiritual, and social achievement. He took pride in

From Louis B. Wright and Marion Tinling, eds., *The Secret Diary of William Byrd ...,* *1709–1712* (Richmond: Dietz Press, 1941), pp. 105, 174, 400, 420. Reprinted by permission.

his daily reading of works in several languages, his morning calisthenics ("I danced my dance"), and his busy, purposeful day of social and business affairs. What did this life of striving and achievement cost Byrd? Why was he, for all his self-confidence, a driven man? What fears and insecurities underlay his pride and composure?

[November 11, 1709]

I rose at 7 o'clock and read some Greek in Anacreon. I said a short prayer and about 11 o'clock we went to breakfast and I ate goose. In the afternoon we went to visit Colonel Waters, a very honest man, who lives about six miles off. He gave us some good wine called [Saint George's] wine. We took a walk by the side of the Bay and then went to supper and I ate some roast beef. Then we returned in the dark to Arlington where we found some of the women sick and some out of humor and particularly my wife quarreled with Mr. Dunn and me for talking Latin and called it bad manners. This put me out of humor with her which set her to crying. I wholly made the reconciliation. The parson was more affronted than I, and went to bed. I neglected to say my prayers but had good health, good thoughts, and indifferent good humor, thanks be to God Almighty.

[May 5, 1710]

I rose at 7 o'clock and read a chapter in Hebrew and some Greek in Anacreon. I said my prayers and ate milk for breakfast. I danced my dance. My sick boys were a little better. The wind blew cold at northwest. I settled several accounts. About 11 o'clock there came abundance of people to visit us and among them Mr. Goodwin and his wife. We played at billiards till dinner. I ate boiled beef for dinner. In the afternoon we played again at billiards. The company stayed till about 6 o'clock and then took leave and went away. Then my wife and I took a walk to Mrs. Harrison's, who was indisposed with a cold. We stayed there about half an hour and then walked back again. I read some French. I said my prayers and had good health, good thoughts, and good humor, thank God Almighty.

[September 4, 1711]

I rose about 6 o'clock and read a chapter in Hebrew and 200 verses in Homer. I said my prayers and ate water gruel for breakfast. I danced my dance. I was not well, nor I was not sick, but out of order a little, I believe for want of sleep. I settled several matters in the library. The weather was grown warmer, the wind at southwest. About 12 o'clock came Colonel Frank Eppes and his son Frank and Tom Randolph to discourse about the militia of Henrico. I ordered that every week two troops should range at the head of the river and if they found any Indians on patented land to take away their guns. They stayed to dinner and I ate some salt crab for dinner. In the afternoon the company went away about 4 o'clock and then I read a little Latin and afterwards took a walk about the plantation and finished my walk in the garden. I was a little displeased with my wife for talking impertinently. I said my prayers and had good health, good humor, and good thoughts, thank God Almighty. When I went to bed my ague returned but not with great violence; however I slept very indifferently.

[October 13, 1711]

I rose about 7 o'clock and read a chapter in Hebrew and some Greek in Lucian. I said my prayers and ate boiled milk for breakfast. I danced my dance. I had a looseness which gave me above 12 stools but I shit but a little at a time. It did not rain much in the night and was cold this morning. I took a walk to see my people at work and then settled several accounts till dinner. I ate boiled mutton with a good stomach and after dinner cleaned my gilt knives and forks [and] spoons and then I settled more accounts. Mrs. Hamlin came to account with me and would borrow money of me but I had the discretion not to do it. My looseness continued with great violence. In the evening I took a walk about the plantation and at night came one of my people from the Falls and told me Tom Osborne began to recover and walk about, thank God. I read some Latin in Terence and then said my prayers and had good health, good thoughts, and good humor, thank God Almighty. My looseness continued with griping.

America's English Identity

ISAAC WILKINS

For the loyalists, the Empire itself was a special form of community, one resembling a family in which the wisdom and resources of the parent state lent stability and direction to the lives of its colonial children. In a debate in the New York Assembly in 1775, Isaac Wilkins advocated obedience and submission as the course the colonists should follow in their conflict with Great Britain. What room would such colonial subordination leave the colonists for self-fulfillment? How would the Puritans have reacted to Wilkins's views on liberty and authority? Is Wilkins's argument simply an extension of the dictates of the behavior manuals, such as Sir Walter Raleigh's and Henry Peacham's?

From Rivington's *New-York Gazetteer*, April 6, 1775.

Mr. Speaker,

The subject now under consideration is the most important, I believe, that has ever come before this House. Nothing less than the welfare, I had almost said the existence, of this colony, and perhaps of all America, depends upon the result of our present deliberations.

. . . For my own part, I feel more real concern than I can well express, at the gloomy prospect of our affairs, and I would sacrifice more, much more, than most men would be willing to believe, if I could . . . rescue my country from the ruin and destruction, that is now ready to overwhelm her.

The necessity of a speedy reconciliation between us and our mother country, must be obvious to every one, who is not totally destitute of sense and feeling: so that there can be no dispute now, I presume, but about the means of accomplishing it.

. . . We have too much understanding, not to know, that the interest of these colonies and of Great-Britain are the same, — that we are all one people, of the same laws, language, and religion, each of us, equally bound to each other by the ties of reciprocal affection; and we have too much loyalty to the best of Sovereigns, too great a regard to order and good government, to affect that insurrections and tumults in one colony, can, or ought to justify them in another.

. . . The Americans love liberty; 'tis their grand, their darling object; and may they ever have virtue and spirit enough to affect and defend it, as well as wisdom and prudence to enjoy it. But that love of liberty which beats so strongly at our hearts, and which seems to animate and inspirit almost every individual, if not carefully watched and attended to, will on some future day (should we be so fortunate as to escape our present danger) prove a dreadful source of misfortune to us, if not of ruin.

Liberty and licentiousness are nearly allied to each other; like wit and madness, there is but a thin partition between them; and licentiousness invariably leads to slavery. Almost every page of history will furnish abundant proofs of the truth of these observations; and God grant that the annals of this country may not add to the number, but I fear from our present licentious conduct, we are much nearer to a state of slavery and oppression, than we seem to be aware of.

. . . We have this day before us the choice either of peace or war, of happiness or misery, of freedom or slavery; and surely we can hesitate a moment which to choose. . . .

I have therefore, Mr. Speaker, nothing more to add, than that, if contrary to my hopes, and my most ardent wishes; if contrary to the honour and dignity of this house; if contrary to the dictates of humanity; and to the duty which we owe to our constituents, and to our country, you adopt the unjust and destructive measures of the Congress, and by that means, involve our country in a civil war; the most dreadful calamity that can befall a people, I hereby declare my honest indignation to that measure, and now call heaven and this house to witness, that I am guiltless of the blood of my fellow-subjects that will be shed upon the occasion. I am guiltless of the ruin of my country.

Demanding a National Identity

SAMUEL ADAMS

In rebuttal to loyalist strictures about obedience to imperial authority, patriots like Samuel Adams found a sense of community in collective radical action in defying what they regarded as illegitimate authority. On the basis of what principles should the leaders of such action be selected? What kinds of evil compel the community to act in self-defense against external tyranny? How do Adams and Wilkins differ in their interpretations of human nature and the sources of virtue in human society? How do they differ on the nature of American identity?

Dependence of one man or state upon another is either absolute or limited by some certain terms of agreement. The dependence of these Colonies, which Great Britain calls constitutional, as declared by acts of Parliament, is absolute. If the contrary of this be the bugbear so many have been disclaiming against, I could wish my countrymen would consider the consequence of so stupid a profession. If a limited dependence is intended, I would be much obliged to any one who will show me the Britannico-American Magna Charta, wherein the terms of our limited dependence are precisely stated. If no such thing can be found, and absolute dependence be accounted inadmissible, the sound we are squabbling about has certainly no determinate meaning. If we say we mean that kind of dependence we acknowledged at and before the year 1763, I answer, vague and uncertain laws, and more especially constitutions, are the very instruments of slavery. The Magna Charta of England was very explicit, considering the time it was formed, and yet much blood was spilled in disputes concerning its meaning.

Besides the danger of an indefinite dependence upon an undetermined power, it might be worth while to consider what the characters are on whom we are so ready to acknowledge ourselves dependent. The votaries of this idol tell us, upon the good people of our mother country, whom they represent as the most just, humane, and affectionate friends we can have in the world. Were this true, it were some encouragement; but who can pretend ignorance, that these just and humane friends are as much under the tyranny of men of a

From H. A. Cushing, ed., *The Writings of Samuel Adams* (New York, 1907), III, 262–266.

reverse character as we should be, could these miscreants gain their ends? I disclaim any more than a mutual dependence on any man or number of men on earth; but an indefinite dependence upon a combination of men who have, in the face of the sun, broken through the most solemn covenants, debauched the hereditary, and corrupted the elective guardians of the people's rights; who have, in fact, established an absolute tyranny in Great Britain and Ireland, and openly declared themselves competent to bind the Colonies in all cases whatsoever, — I say, indefinite dependence on such a combination of usurping innovators is evidently as dangerous to liberty, as fatal to civil and social happiness, as any one step that could be proposed even by the destroyer of men. The utmost that the honest party in Great Britain can do is to warn us to avoid this dependence at all hazards. Does not even a Duke of Grafton declare the ministerial measures illegal and dangerous? And shall America, no way connected with this Administration, press our submission to such measures and reconciliation to the authors of them? Would not such pigeon-hearted wretches equally forward the recall of the Stuart family and establishment of Popery throughout Christendom, did they consider the party in favor of those loyal measures the strongest? Shame on the men who can court exemption from present trouble and expense at the price of their own posterity's liberty! The honest party in England cannot wish for the reconciliation proposed. It is as unsafe to them as to us, and they thoroughly apprehend it. What check have they now upon the Crown, and what shadow of control can they pretend, when the Crown can command fifteen or twenty millions a year which they have nothing to say to? A proper proportion of our commerce is all that can benefit any good man in Britain or Ireland; and God forbid we should be so cruel as to furnish bad men with the power to enslave both Britain and America. Administration has now fairly dissevered the dangerous tie. Execrated will he be by the latest posterity who again joins the fatal cord!

"But," say the puling, pusillanimous cowards, "we shall be subject to a long and bloody war, if we declare independence." On the contrary, I affirm it the only step that can bring the contest to a speedy and happy issue. By declaring independence we put ourselves on a footing for an equal negotiation. Now we are called a pack of villainous rebels, who, like the St. Vincent's Indians, can expect nothing more than a pardon for our lives, and the sovereign favor respecting freedom, and property to be at the King's will. Grant, Almighty God, that I may be numbered with the dead before that sable day dawns on North America.

All Europe knows the illegal and inhuman treatment we have received from Britons. All Europe wishes the haughty Empress of the Main reduced to a more humble deportment. After herself has thrust her Colonies from her, the maritime powers cannot be such idiots as to suffer her to reduce them to a more absolute obedience of her dictates than they were heretofore obliged to yield. Does not the most superficial politician know, that while we profess ourselves the subjects of Great Britain, and yet hold arms against her, they have a right to treat us as rebels, and that, according to the laws of nature and nations, no other state has a right to interfere in the dispute? But, on the other hand, on our declaration of independence, the maritime states, at least, will find it their interest (which always secures the question of inclination) to protect a people who can be so advantageous to them. So that those short-sighted politicians, who conclude that this step will involve us in slaughter and devastation, may plainly perceive that no measure in our power will so naturally and effectually work our deliverance. The motion of a finger of the Grand Monarch would produce as gentle a temper in the omnipotent British minister as appeared in the Manilla ransom and Falkland Island affairs. From without, certainly, we have everything to hope, nothing to fear. From within, some tell us that the Presbyterians, if freed from the restraining power of Great Britain, would overrun the peaceable Quakers in this government. For my own part, I despise and detest the bickerings of sectaries, and am apprehensive of no trouble from that quarter, especially while no peculiar honors or emoluments are annexed to either. I heartily wish too many of the Quakers did not give cause of complaint, by endeavoring to counteract the measures of their fellow-citizens for the common safety. If they profess themselves only pilgrims here, let them walk through the men of this world without interfering with their actions on either side. If they would not pull down kings, let them not support tyrants; for, whether they understand it or not, there is, and ever has been, an essential difference in the characters.

Finally . . . I account a state a moral person, having an interest and will of its own; and I think that state a monster whose prime mover has an interest and will in direct opposition to its prosperity and security. This position has been so clearly demonstrated in the pamphlet first mentioned in this essay, that I shall only add, if there are any arguments in favor of returning to a state of dependence on Great Britain, that is, on the present Administration of Great Britain, I could wish they were timely offered, that they may be soberly considered before the cunning proposals of the Cabinet set all the timid, lazy, and irresolute members of the community into a clamor for peace at any rate.

The Uniqueness of American Identity

J. HECTOR ST. JOHN de CREVECOEUR

A French emigrant to the colonies, Michel Guillaume St. Jean de Crèvecoeur, under the above pseudonym, examines the impact of the American environment on the consciousness of the newly settled colonists. How do the absence of powerful social institutions, the ready availability of land, and the opportunity to rise through one's own industry each affect the emigrant? How does

From J. Hector St. John de Crèvecoeur, *Letter from an American Farmer* (New York, 1782), pp. 76–80.

the new identity of being an American serve to release and channel each person's energies? Is there any limit to this new sense of boundlessness? How did this strong sense of belonging contribute to the ideology of the American Revolution?

An European, when he first arrives, seems limited in his intentions, as well as in his views; but he very suddenly alters his scale; two hundred miles formerly appeared a very great distance, it is now but a trifle; he no sooner breathes our air than he forms schemes, and embarks in designs he never would have thought of in his own country. There the plentitude of society confines many useful ideas, and often extinguishes the most laudable schemes which here ripen into maturity. Thus Europeans become Americans.

But how is this accomplished in that croud of low, indigent people, who flock here every year from all parts of Europe? I will tell you; they no sooner arrive than they immediately feel the good effects of that plenty of provisions we possess: they fare on our best food, and are kindly entertained; their talents, character, and peculiar industry are immediately inquired into; they find countrymen every where disseminated, let them come from whatever part of Europe. Let me select one as an epitome of the rest; he is hired, he goes to work, and works moderately; instead of being employed by a haughty person, he finds himself with his equal, placed at the substantial table of the farmer, or else at an inferior one as good; his wages are high, his bed is not like that bed of sorrow on which he used to lie: if he behaves with propriety, and is faithful, he is caressed, and becomes as it were a member of the family. He begins to feel the effects of a sort of resurrection; hitherto he had not lived, but simply vegetated; he now feels himself a man, because he is treated as such; the laws of his own country had overlooked him in his insignificancy; the laws of this cover him with their mantle. Judge what an alteration there must arise in the mind and thoughts of this man; he begins to forget his former servitude and dependence, his heart involuntarily swells and glows; this first swell inspires him with those new thoughts which constitute an American. What love can he entertain for a country where his existence was a burthen to him; if he is a generous good man, the love of this new adoptive parent will sink deep into his heart. He looks around, and sees many a prosperous person, who but a few years before was as poor as himself. This encourages him much, he begins to form some little scheme, the first, alas, he ever formed in his life. If he is wise he thus spends two or three years, in which time he acquires knowledge, the use of tools, the modes of working the lands, felling trees, &c. This prepares the foundation of a good name, the most useful acquisition he can make. He is encouraged, he has gained friends; he is advised and directed, he feels bold, he purchases some land; he gives all the money he has brought over, as well as what he has earned, and trusts to the God of harvests for the discharge of the rest. His good name procures him credit. He is now possessed of the deed, conveying to him and his posterity the fee simple and absolute property of two hundred acres of land, situated on such a river. What an epocha in this man's life! He is become a freeholder, from perhaps a German boor — he is now an American, a Pennsylvanian, an English subject. He is naturalized, his name is enrolled with those of the other citizens of the province. Instead of being a vagrant, he has a place of residence; he is called the inhabitant of such a county, or of such a district, and for the first time in his life counts for something; for hitherto he has been a cypher. I only repeat what I have heard many say, and no wonder their hearts should glow, and be agitated with a multitude of feelings, not easy to describe. From nothing to start into being; from a servant to the rank of a master; from being the slave of some despotic prince, to become a free man, invested with lands, to which every municipal blessing is annexed! What a change indeed! It is in consequence of that change that he becomes an American. This great metamorphosis has a double effect, it extinguishes all his European prejudices, he forgets that mechanism of subordination, that servility of disposition which poverty had taught him; and sometimes he is apt to forget too much, often passing from one extreme to the other. If he is a good man, he forms schemes of future prosperity, he proposes to educate his children better than he has been educated himself; he thinks of future modes of conduct, feels an ardor to labour he never felt before. Pride steps in and leads him to every thing that the laws do not forbid: he respects them; with a heart-felt gratitude he looks toward the east, toward that insular government from whose wisdom all his new felicity is derived, and under whose wings and protection he now lives. These reflections constitute him the good man and the good subject.

♦ MODERN ESSAY ♦

Identity vs. Narcissism
CHRISTOPHER LASCH

This review of recent books on the problem of identity in modern America reports that we are retreating into ourselves in a way that is unhealthy and bodes ill for the future of our society. Have Americans ceased to expect and attain healthy and vital relationships with people in their own community, and with political and social institutions which affect their lives? Are they so traumatized by modern life that their capacity for such relationships has been impaired? What qualities of human nature and what elements in the social order provide grounds for believing that individuals can and will rediscover a

---

Excerpts from Christopher Lasch, "The Narcissist Society," *The New York Review of Books,* September 30, 1976. Reprinted by permission of the author.

*meaningful place and role in their society? What is happening to the qualities
of joy, serenity, and faith in the experience of Americans?*

*How would Lasch evaluate the efforts of eighteenth-century writers to
define and embrace a view of their own identity? Did their perplexity and
anxiety necessarily interfere with having constructive lives, and handling social
and political problems?*

I

It is no secret that Americans have lost faith in politics. The retreat to purely
personal satisfactions — such as they are — is one of the main themes of
the Seventies. A growing despair of changing society — even of understanding it — has generated on the one hand a revival of old-time religion, on the
other a cult of expanded consciousness, health, and personal "growth."

Having no hope of improving their lives in any of the ways that matter,
people have convinced themselves that what matters is psychic self-improve-
ment: getting in touch with their feelings, eating health food, taking lessons
in ballet or belly dancing, immersing themselves in the wisdom of the East,
jogging, learning how to "relate," overcoming the "fear of pleasure." Harm-
less in themselves, these pursuits, elevated to a program and wrapped in the
rhetoric of "authenticity" and "awareness," signify a retreat from the political
turmoil of the recent past. Indeed Americans seem to wish to forget not only
the Sixties, the riots, the New Left, the disruptions on college campuses, Vietnam, Watergate, and the Nixon presidency, but their entire collective past,
even in the antiseptic form of the Bicentennial.

To live for the moment is the prevailing passion — to live for yourself,
not for your predecessors or posterity. We are fast losing the sense of historical
continuity, the sense of belonging to a succession of generations originating in
the past and stretching into the future.

Bertrand Russell long ago predicted that the assumption of parental responsibilities by the state would encourage "a certain triviality in all personal
relations" and "make it far more difficult to take an interest in anything after
one's own death." It is this erosion of the concern for posterity that distinguishes the spiritual crisis of the Seventies from earlier outbreaks of millenarian
religion, to which it bears a superficial resemblance. Many commentators have
seized on this resemblance as a means of characterizing the contemporary
"cultural revolution," ignoring the features that distinguish it from the religions of the past. A few years ago Leslie Fiedler proclaimed a "New Age of
Faith." In a recent issue of *New York*, Tom Wolfe interprets the new "narcissism" as a "third great awakening," an outbreak of orgiastic, ecstatic re-
ligiosity. Jim Hougan compares it to the millennialism of the waning Middle
Ages. "The anxieties of the Middle Ages are not much different from those of
the present," he writes in *Decadence,* a book that seems to present itself
simultaneously as a critique and a celebration of decadence. Then as now,
according to Hougan, social upheaval gave rise to "millenarian sects." [See

James Hougan, *Decadence, Radical Nostalgia, and Decline in the Seventies.*] . . .

The contemporary climate is therapeutic, not religious. People today hunger not for personal salvation, let alone for the restoration of an earlier golden age, but for the feeling — even if it is only a momentary illusion — of personal well-being, health, and psychic security. Therapy is the modern successor to religion; but this does not imply that the "triumph of the therapeutic" constitutes a new religion in its own right. Therapy constitutes instead an antireligion, not always to be sure because it adheres to rational explanation or scientific methods of healing, as its practitioners would have us believe, but because modern society "has no future" and therefore gives no thought to anything beyond its immediate needs.

Even when they speak of the need for "meaning" and "love," therapists define love and meaning simply as the fulfillment of the patient's emotional requirements. It hardly occurs to them — nor is there any reason why it should, given the nature of the therapeutic enterprise — to encourage the subject to subordinate his needs and interests to those of others, to someone or some cause or tradition outside himself. Love as self-sacrifice or self-abasement, "meaning" as submission to a higher loyalty — these sublimations strike the therapeutic sensibility as intolerably oppressive, offensive to common sense and injurious to personal health and well-being. To "liberate" humanity from such outmoded ideas of love and duty has become the mission of the post-Freudian therapies and particularly of their converts and popularizers, for whom mental health means the overthrow of "inhibitions" and the nonstop celebration of the self.

Jerry Rubin, never one to shrink from publicity, conducts such a celebration in his coyly titled memoir *Growing (Up) at Thirty-Seven.* Having a few years ago reached the dreaded age of thirty, the former Yippie leader found himself without a following. Forced, he says, to confront his private fears and anxieties, he moved from New York to San Francisco, where he shopped voraciously, on an apparently inexhaustible income, in the spiritual supermarkets of the West Coast. "In five years, from 1971 to 1975, I directly experienced est, gestalt therapy, bioenergetics, rolfing, massage, jogging, health foods, tai chi, Esalen, hypnotism, modern dance, meditation, Silva Mind Control, Arica, acupuncture, sex therapy, Reichian therapy, and More House — a smorgasbord course in New Consciousness." His book has the quality of a testimonial, of a series of endorsements for health products and therapeutic regimens of every kind. After years of neglecting his body, he gave himself "permission to be healthy" and quickly lost thirty pounds. Health foods, jogging, yoga, sauna baths, chiropractors, and acupuncturists have made him feel, at thirty-seven, "like twenty-five."

Spiritual progress proved equally gratifying and painless. He shed his protective armor, his sexism, his "addiction to love," and learned "to love myself enough so that I do not need another to make me happy." He came to understand that his revolutionary politics concealed a "puritan conditioning," which occasionally made him uneasy about his celebrity and its material rewards. No strenuous psychic exertions seem to have been required to convince Rubin that "it's O.K. to enjoy the rewards of life that money brings."

Paul Zweig's book [*Three Journeys: An Automythology*] records a similar quest, with the difference that Zweig, a poet instead of a propagandist, provides a glimpse into the pain that gives rise to the search for psychic peace. Zweig speaks persuasively of his growing "conviction, amounting to a faith, that my life was organized around a core of blandness which shed anonymity upon everything I touched"; of "the emotional hibernation which lasted until I was almost thirty"; of the "inner dryness" that drove him, in 1974, to test himself against the Sahara Desert; of the persisting "suspicion of personal emptiness which all my talking and my anxious attempts at charm surround and decorate, but don't penetrate or even come close to."

The central section of his "automythology" recounts, obliquely but with a desperate intensity, ten years spent as an exile in Paris in the Fifties and Sixties. During this period Zweig became a communist, took part in the agitation against the Algerian War, and eventually discovered communism's "antidote: the inner life." Although Zweig says that the war "gradually became an environment pervading every aspect" of his existence, external events play only a shadowy part in his narrative. They have the quality of hallucination, a vague background of "terror and vulnerability." At the height of the violent protest against the Algerian war, "he recalled a phrase he had once read in a book about the inner feeling of schizophrenia. The patient, with the pungency of an oracle, had said: '*La terre bouge, elle ne m'inspire aucune confiance.*' " The same feeling, Zweig says, overwhelmed him in the Sahara: "The earth moves about, I can have no confidence in it."

... The difference between Zweig and Rubin is that Zweig has not lost the capacity to move us, whatever else he may have lost, with the account of a spiritual ordeal whose very vagueness and indeterminacy explain its poignancy. He has written a painfully authentic description of the feeling of inauthenticity. Such writers as Rubin, by contrast, merely echo current therapeutic slogans, which have replaced the political slogans they used to mouth with equal disregard of their content.

It is essential to realize that the "inner revolution of the Seventies," as Rubin calls it, grew in part out of an awareness that the radicalism of the Sixties had failed to address itself to the quality of personal life or to cultural questions, in the mistaken belief that questions of "personal growth," in Rubin's words, could wait "until after the revolution." To speak of personal growth as something that can be achieved by eating health food, however, falsifies this perception. The problem for the Left — the problem for everyone — is to understand why personal growth and development have become so hard to accomplish; why the fear of growing up and aging — of "becoming a man" — haunts our society; why personal relations have become so brittle and precarious; and why the "inner life" no longer offers any refuge from the dangers around us. . . .

As a guide to the ideology of the "consciousness movement," Edwin Schur's book [*The Awareness Trap: Self-Absorption Instead of Social Change*] is invaluable. He recognizes that the movement appeals to an older tradition of self-help, which it restates in therapeutic terms. He explains why the newer forms of therapy, eager for unearned enlightenment, have rejected psychoanalysis, often on the spurious "radical" grounds that it merely adjusts people to a sick society. In place of the understanding that comes from confronting painful conflicts, the new therapies equate enlightenment with peace of mind. They invite the patient to satisfy his own needs before considering those of others and to reject the "roles" in which others would imprison him. They stress the need to live for the moment. According to Philip Slater, the former Parsonian sociologist who has become one of the spokesmen of the consciousness "revolution," postponement of gratification amounts to arrogance. "Setting oneself above one's own bodily responses is an act of snobbery, of satanic pride."

The Awareness Trap contains so many keen observations and so much good sense — including excellent discussions of the influence of awareness thinking on the women's movement and of the hollow claims of radical therapy — that one hesitates to find fault with it. Yet the grounds on which Schur condemns the "awareness craze" — that it addresses problems peculiar to the affluent, neglects those of the poor, and converts "social discontent to personal inadequacy" — seem to me highly misleading. Schur thinks it is "criminal" for "white middle-class citizens to become complacently self-preoccupied while their less fortunate fellow Americans struggle and starve." But the self-preoccupation on which the awareness movement capitalizes arises not from complacency but from desperation; nor is this desperation confined to the middle class. Schur seems to think that the transient, provisional character of personal relations is a problem only for affluent executives always on the move. Are we to believe that things are different among the poor? That working-class marriages are happy and free of conflict? That the ghetto produces stable, loving, and nonmanipulative friendships? Studies of lower-class life have repeatedly shown that poverty has damaging effects on marriage and friendship. The collapse of personal life originates not in the spiritual torments of affluence but in the war of all against all, which is now spreading from the lower class, where it has long raged without interruption, to the rest of society. . . .

Schur himself notes that "what seems ultimately to emerge out of this very mixed message is an ethic of self-preservation." But his condemnation of the survival ethic as a "retreat into privatism" misses the point. When personal relations are conducted with no other object than psychic survival, "privatism" no longer provides a haven from a heartless world. On the contrary, private life takes on the very qualities of the anarchic social order from which it is supposed to provide a refuge.

It is the devastation of personal life, not the retreat into privatism, that needs to be criticized and condemned. The trouble with the consciousness movement is not that it addresses trivial or unreal issues but that it provides self-defeating solutions. Arising out of a pervasive dissatisfaction with the quality of personal relations, it advises people not to make too large an investment in love and friendship, to avoid excessive dependence on others, and to live for the moment — the very conditions that created the crisis of personal relations in the first place.

The notion that our social and political problems originate in "privatism" is an illusion. One of the gravest indictments of our society is precisely that it has made deep and lasting friendships, love affairs, and marriages so difficult to achieve. As social life becomes more and more warlike and barbaric, personal relations, which ostensibly provide relief from these conditions, take on the character of combat. Some of the new therapies dignify this combat as "assertiveness" and "fighting fair in love and marriage." Others celebrate impermanent attachments under such formulas as "open marriage" and "open-ended commitments." Thus they intensify the disease they pretend to cure. They do this, however, not by diverting attention from social problems to personal ones, from real issues to false issues, but by obscuring the social origins of the suffering that is painfully but falsely experienced as purely personal and private. An account of awareness movements that mistakes this suffering for complacent self-absorption — middle-class self-indulgence — does little to clear up the confusion.

II

Narcissism holds the key to the consciousness movement and to the moral climate of contemporary society, as Hougan, Wolfe, and Schur in various ways suggest. Unless we are content merely to moralize under the cover of psychiatric jargon, however, we need to use this concept more rigorously than it is used in popular social criticism, and with an awareness of its clinical implications.

Narcissism is more than a metaphorical term for self-absorption. In modern psychiatric practice, it has come to be recognized as an important element in the so-called character disorders that have absorbed much of the clinical attention once given to hysteria and obsessional neuroses. Psychoanalysis, a therapy that grew out of experience with these classical neuroses, often finds itself today confronted with a "chaotic and impulse-ridden character," as Dr. Otto Kernberg observes in his new book [*Borderline Conditions and Pathological Narcissism*]. It must deal with patients who "act out" their conflicts instead of repressing or sublimating them. These patients, though often ingratiating and successful, tend to cultivate a protective shallowness in emotional relations. Promiscuous, they avoid close involvements, which might release intense feelings of rage. Their personalities consist largely of defenses against this rage and against feelings of moral deprivation that originate, as many psychoanalysts believe, in the pre-Oedipal stage of psychic development.

Often these patients suffer from hypochondria and complain of a sense of inner emptiness. At the same time they entertain fantasies of omnipotence and a strong belief in their right to exploit others and be gratified. "Archaic," punitive, and sadistic elements predominate in the superegos of these patients, and they conform to social rules more out of the fear of punishment than from a sense of guilt. What analysts call "primary process" thinking, which relies on magic and symbolism rather than linear causality and has little tolerance of ambiguity or doubt, plays a prominent part in their mental lives.

On the principle that pathology frequently represents a heightened version of normality, the "pathological narcissism" found in character disorders of this type should tell us something about narcissism as a social phenomenon. Kernberg's study of personality disorders that occupy the "borderline" between neurosis and psychosis, though written for clinicians and making no claims to shed light on social or cultural issues, depicts a type of personality that ought to be immediately recognizable, in a more subdued form, to observers of the contemporary cultural scene: facile at managing the impressions he gives to others, ravenous for admiration but contemptuous of those he manipulates into providing it; unappeasably hungry for emotional experiences with which to fill an inner void; terrified of aging and death. . . .

It is not merely that narcissism appears realistically to represent the best way of coping with a dangerous world, and that the prevailing social conditions therefore tend to bring out narcissistic traits that are present, in varying degrees, in everyone. These conditions have also transformed the family, which in turn shapes the underlying structure of personality. A society that fears it has no future is not likely to give much attention to the needs of the next generation, and the ever-present sense of historical discontinuity, the blight of our society, falls with particularly devastating effect on the family.

Whereas parents formerly sought to live vicariously through their offspring, now they tend to resent them as intrusions and to envy their youth. Formerly the young sought to escape the smothering embrace of the older generation, but for the last several decades they have been more likely to complain of emotional neglect. The modern parent's attempt to make children feel loved and wanted does not conceal an underlying coolness — the remoteness of those who have little to pass on to the next generation and who in any case give priority to their own right to self-fulfillment. The combination of emotional detachment with attempts to convince a child of his favored position in the family is a good prescription for a narcissistic personality structure.

Through the intermediary of the family, social patterns reproduce themselves in personality. Social arrangements live on in the individual, buried in the mind below the level of consciousness, even after they have become objectively undesirable and unnecessary — as many of our present arrangements are now widely acknowledged to have become. The perception of the world as a dangerous and forbidding place, though it originates in a realistic awareness of the insecurity of contemporary social life, receives reinforcement from the narcissistic projection of aggressive impulses outward. The belief that society has no future, while it rests on a certain realism about the dangers ahead, also incorporates a narcissistic inability to identify with posterity or to feel oneself part of a historical stream.

The weakening of social ties, which originates in the prevailing state of social warfare, at the same time reflects a narcissistic defense against dependence. A warlike society tends to produce men and women who are at heart antisocial. It should therefore not surprise us to find that the narcissist, although he conforms to social norms for fear of external retribution, often thinks of himself as an outlaw and sees others in the same way, "as basically dishonest and unreliable, or only reliable because of external pressures." "The value systems of narcissistic personalities are generally corruptible," writes Kernberg, "in contrast to the rigid morality of the obsessive personality."

The ethic of self-preservation and psychic survival is rooted, then, not merely in objective conditions of economic warfare, rising rates of crime, and social chaos, but in the subjective experience of emptiness and isolation. It reflects the conviction — as much a projection of inner anxieties as a perception of the way things are — that envy and exploitation dominate even the most intimate relations. The cult of personal relations, which becomes increasingly intense as the hope of political solutions recedes, conceals a thoroughgoing disenchantment with personal relations, just as the cult of sensuality implies a repudiation of sensuality in all but its most primitive forms. The ideology of personal growth, superficially optimistic about the power of positive thinking, radiates pessimism. It is the world view of the resigned.

PART II

The Young Republic

Introduction

Authority and Responsibility in the Young Republic

In August, 1974, as the House of Representatives prepared to impeach him for abuses of power, Richard M. Nixon resigned from the office of president of the United States. The new president, Gerald R. Ford, rightly called the Watergate scandal and the uncovering of criminal misconduct by the president "our long national nightmare." Nixon's struggle to hold on to the authority of the presidency and the effort by Congress to investigate and punish him made constitutional government a vital reality for the American people.

Watergate was what some would label a natural outcome of a much larger crisis of authority in American political life. The nation had poured 50,000 lives, $200 million, and an incalculable amount of physical and emotional anguish into the prosecution of a war in Vietnam, started in stealth and deception and continued in the cause of saving national "face." The Vietnam War placed such serious strains on the economy and public finance of the country that it caused rampant inflation and then a serious national economic recession. Coming on the heels of a period of expanding social services from the federal, state, and local governments, this inflation and recession brought many local governments, by the mid-1970s, to the brink of bankruptcy.

Most costly of all, the extravagant use of national power and wealth in the 1960s blighted the idealism of the people, and produced cynicism among large numbers of people who previously had implicit trust in their political institutions.

The estrangement of government from the people was symbolized by the ordeal of the Mullen family of Iowa. In early 1970, the Army informed the parents of Sergeant Michael Mullen that their son had been killed in Vietnam "when artillery fire from friendly forces landed in the area. . . ." Unable to receive any satisfactory explanation of how their son died, Mr. and Mrs. Mullen used the funeral gratuity paid them by the Army to buy an advertisement in the *Des Moines Register*. The ad contained 714 small crosses — the number of Iowans already killed in Vietnam — and asked the people of Iowa "how many more lives do you wish to sacrifice because of your silence." The Mullens never received an acknowledgment from the federal government that they were even *entitled* to know how Michael could have died from "friendly fire."

There are at least two causes of the general antigovernment sentiment. First, a resentment toward governmental unresponsiveness, which in the past has provoked people to demand the reform of political institutions, has reappeared. More fundamentally, recent events have called into question the very legitimacy of public policy. By the bicentennial year of 1976 the very survival of the American Republic had been called into question. Can our environment, social order, consumer economy, and life in the major cities survive the threats of pollution, racial integration, resource scarcity, and international turmoil? Can any political leadership, no matter how able, deal effectively with these overwhelming problems and dangers?

The young Republic was not as vulnerable to social and ecological catastrophe as American society today seems to be. The world's ozone layer and other natural resources seemed safe in 1800, but thoughtful people during the first generation after independence were nonetheless uncertain whether their experiment in republicanism could survive. They sensed that their own conduct would determine the fate of the new nation, and they were not certain that they, or their children, were equal to the task.

This sense of responsibility for their own destiny arose from their common participation in the American Revolution. The Revolution dominated the American people from 1776 through the era of Andrew Jackson. It not only established them as a free people under a democratic national government: it fulfilled the deep yearnings they had felt as colonists to protect their own interests and preserve their own liberty. The sudden transformation from a dependent to an independent people and the control of their country produced by the Revolution forced early Americans to think seriously about political authority — what it was, how it could be used or abused, what its impact on society might be, and whether the skillful distribution and regulation of power might actually tame human nature, and civilize and enrich the lives of the people who lived under it.

The Revolutionary generation had risked the prospect of the failure of the Revolution; the degeneration of the republican government into anarchy or despotism; and the manipulation of the fragile young nation by the European powers. Most important, the Revolution released an enormous amount of human energy which secured a large territorial expanse of land from the Appalachians to the Mississippi — and later, as a result of post-Revolutionary diplomacy, included the Louisiana Purchase. The Revolution launched a vast westward migration. As a result, by the 1820s Americans no longer thought of themselves and their culture in terms of European and classical origins. Rather, as Gordon S. Wood writes, Americans had become "a huge expansive nation whose cultural focus was no longer abroad but inward at its own boundlessness."

The Revolution excited the imagination and anticipation of the people. Old problems persisted, and new ones were created. Most strikingly, the Revolution and the constitutional government which followed it actually strengthened the institution of slavery. The enormous inconsistency of slavery in a free society troubled the consciences of many patriots and affected everything which transpired during the Revolution. The slave states bartered their support for a single national government in return for constitutional provisions protecting the institution of slavery itself. Many framers of the Constitution, slave-owners and non-slave-owners alike, hoped that they had limited the expansion of slavery enough to lead to gradual extinction.

The Virginia planters took the first steps toward gradual emancipation in 1782 by simplifying the state's manumission statute, but the fear of slave insurrection in the West Indies and an abortive uprising in Virginia itself in 1800 (known as "Gabriel's rebellion") caused the repeal of those voluntary emancipation provisions. Southerners soon realized that the Revolution had begun a movement toward racial equality which they could only attempt to resist. The determination to end slavery was fiercely articulated by one of Gabriel's fellow conspirators at his trial: "I have nothing more to offer [in my defense] than what General Washington would have had to offer had he been taken by the British officers and put to trial by them. I have ventured my life in endeavoring to obtain the liberty of my countrymen and am a willing sacrifice to their cause."

The need to protect the young Republic from economic stagnation prompted Alexander Hamilton and his allies in the 1790s to design fiscal and foreign policies to encourage investment, speculation, and the expansion of commerce, and to restore trade with Great Britain. Those policies became the foundation of the Federalist Party. Coupled with the Federalists' intolerance of criticism, those policies provoked the opposition under James Madison and Thomas Jefferson to organize a rival party, the Republicans. There was fierce rivalry and suspicion between the two parties. The Federalists feared that the Republicans would allow anarchy to infect American politics, and they believed that the anticommercial prejudice of the Republicans would stunt economic growth. The Federalists envisioned a decentralized, ungovernable, and stagnant republic. The opposing Republicans feared the Federalists would make the country into an economic and diplomatic vassal of Britain, serving the interests of a privileged minority of New England merchants and others who preferred a high-toned, genteel social order. The Republicans were convinced that the Federalists would forfeit America's hard-won independence and make government of the people into a mockery.

These hostilities finally ended with the War of 1812 and the subsequent demise of the Federalist Party. From 1815 to 1824 an "era of good feelings" followed the beginning of the two-party system.

This period also saw the resurgence of partisan political conflict between the supporters and enemies of Andrew Jackson. Nothing united the Jacksonian Democrats so much as the desire to restore a simple agrarian republic, which they believed had existed in the late eighteenth century. The greatest of the Jacksonian thinkers, historian George Bancroft, published a ten-volume *History of the United States* in 1834, depicting Jackson as the last of the long line of American freedom-fighters, which included the first colonists and the patriots who had fought for freedom. Jackson's opponents, the Whigs, were depicted as latter-day Hamiltonians who regarded the crudeness and raw quality of American life in the mid-nineteenth century as a blemish on the stable, elitist society created by the Revolution.

These conflicts reflected the presence of fundamental, unresolved issues concerning the nature of republican government in the new nation. If power belonged to the people and if the authority of government was a sacred trust placed in the hands of elected and appointed officials, what exactly was the nature of that authority? What was the extent of the power of the people and the authority of government? How could a government transcend the personal weaknesses and intellectual limitations of its officials? How could government draw from the wisdom of the whole society? And how could the whole body of the people be expected to become wise and moral citizens? In short, could a written constitution modify the behavior of the people who lived under it? Could a constitution actually increase general trust and agreement necessary for self-government?

In addition to these vexing problems of authority, consent, and obedience in American politics, the history of the young Republic raises questions of what government owes to the people it serves. If it passively submits to the whim of the populace, is it really fulfilling its function? If those in power allow their own judgment and expertise to be controlled by the less knowledgeable, will not destructive tensions and animosities arise within the political and social order?

The government must respond, anticipate, and guide the aspirations that will set social change into motion. The first half-century of the independent nation can be seen as an experiment in democratic politics and national leadership.

Charles G. Finney, the intellectual spokesman for evangelical Christianity in America from the 1820s until the Civil War, pondered the potential of the American people for wise and virtuous behavior. He believed that the nation had a moral destiny, and he identified the sins which delayed the coming of the millennium.

Personalizing the Issues

Charles Grandison Finney:
The Beginning of an American Theology

The congregation sat entranced, eyes fixed on the pulpit, where a tall, handsome man twisted and stretched as his warm mellow voice excited the audience. The speaker was Charles Grandison Finney, the greatest and possibly the most influential evangelist in American history. He was so effective that his impact upon the Age of Jackson was every bit as powerful as that of "Old Hickory" himself.

Finney's impact was due in part to the gradual changes which had taken place in American theology since the landing of the *Mayflower*. The Puritan fathers brought a reli-

gion based on Calvin's concept of predestination to the New World, but like many imported ideas, the doctrine of the chosen few was severely altered by the American environment. Nineteenth-century America was a society in motion; change was its only constant factor. Such societies tend to be individualistic in nature. In a static society institutions flourish, thus individuals merge into groups and appeal to these institutions. But in a dynamic, changing society, institutions are constantly in a state of flux and must appeal to the individual. This simple fact doomed rigid Calvinism from the start of the American adventure, a phenomenon noted by more than one Calvinistic cleric.

Calvin's ideas were simple, stern, and in terms of impact, effective. Finney's Puritan ancestors believed that God was an absolute sovereign who preordained man's destiny. Calvin accepted the idea that the first man and woman had once been pure in the Garden of Eden, but had fallen from grace by a voluntary act. Thus salvation could be gained only through the grace of God, mediated through Jesus Christ. According to Calvin, people were helpless to promote their own salvations. Those destined to be saved would be saved and they could not fall from grace; those destined to be damned were likewise powerless to control their fate. Thus people were divided into two classes: the elect and the damned — and salvation was granted only to the elect by the sovereign grace of God.

Being chosen, however, was no easy role. One could not fall from grace, but the elect were obligated to rule society, including those who had not been chosen. To accomplish this goal, Calvin turned to the state as the agency to make people behave. The established church and the state worked together to insure that only moral, chosen men would rule society. The elect of God were to regulate their neighbors' lives by moral example and political action.

But the Calvinists had a problem in America, where first tradition and later the constitution provided for separation of church and state. Thus the moral stewards had to devise organizations to undertake the job intended for Calvin's state. This gave rise to numerous organizations, such as the American Tract Society, the Bible Society, the Home Mission Society, the Sunday School Union, the American Missionary Association, and the American Board of Commissioners for Foreign Missions, which were very effective during Finney's lifetime. It was the duty of these organizations to insure the Calvinist intention that the elect should help others for the stability of society as well as for the glory of God.

John Calvin met and conquered many foes in Europe, but he never had an opponent comparable to the American frontier. Unbending principles were short-lived in a harsh wilderness which demanded the ultimate in flexibility for survival. In an environment where people often determined their social and economic salvation, they soon believed that they should also have some control over their spiritual salvation. To forestall a direct attack upon their theology, the Calvinists concluded that the elect were a constantly expanding group. This decision prevented a direct assault upon established theological ideas before Finney rose to prominence.

But the frontier was not alone in undermining Calvin's theology in the New World. His own concept of benevolence worked against it. Calvin commanded the elect to practice benevolence even though no one could be saved by the performance of this duty. Thus while the concept grew in America that selfishness was a sin and benevolence a virtue, so did the concept that it was illogical to do so much good for no reason other than to fulfill one's duty. How long would a practical people continue to be involved in a fruitless endeavor? Thus while benevolence grew in America, it also became modified. In simple form, benevolence was the golden rule. But nothing impractical could take deep root in America, and slowly, over the years, local religious thinking changed, setting the background for the First and Second Great Awakenings of 1725–1750 and 1795–1835, respectively.

Fortunately for the early American settlers, their pre-Finney Calvinist leaders, who wrote extensively about the doctrines of election and predestination, preached a more personalized religion to their flocks. Calvin was against free will; their American experience was not. Many great Calvinist preachers in America were inconsistent in their theology, and even before Finney they preached a religion in which there was hope for all people. Indeed, this inconsistency was one of the basic causes of the First Great Awakening. The conflict between the pure Calvinism of their ancestors and the American environment was resolved in favor of the environment. Great Puritan divines like Jonathan Edwards stressed a religion that appealed to common men and women, and provided a less ceremonial religion than was emphasized by the early clerics. Cutting across denominational lines, the divines who led the Awakening were both opportunistic and democratic. When the revival was over, it left a severely modified Calvinism as the intellectual core of America's Protestant religions.

But it was left to the divines of the early nineteenth century to replace this modified Calvinism with the concept of free will advocated by the famous Dutch theologian Arminius. One factor precipitating the Puritan exodus to the New World was the infiltration of Arminian views into the Church of England. But doctrines can be transported as well as people and Calvinism never had a monopoly on religious thought in America. The First Great Awakening was in part a clash between the beliefs in Calvinist predestination and Arminian free will in a new habitat.

During the Second Great Awakening, the conflict between the two ideologies was more pronounced. Arminian denial of the doctrine of the chosen few, and the view that any individual could be saved if the necessary grace through good works was acquired prevailed in America. By stressing personal religion in a society dominated by individualism, the Arminians assured their ultimate triumph. After the Civil War, when institutions became more important, native religion was again subjected to change, but in an egalitarian age, Calvinism was subdued. Calvin and his disciples brought about their own defeat by not being democratic, although their New England congregational church structure was very much so. The Arminians, on the other hand, used the autonomy and independence of the individual congregation to bring about a democratic church in a democratic age.

Westward migration also hastened the downfall of the elect. Beginning with the earliest of religions, history offers many examples of migrating peoples who alter their beliefs as they move to new environments. Indeed, one of the basic causes of both great religious revivals was the disruptive force of the American frontier upon established religion; and Finney's America was definitely a nation on the move. Its religion changed as people migrated westward, and each migration created a greater receptiveness to theological change.

The Arminians' success in the nineteenth century changed the basic character of American religion. They saw to it that the churches passed from clerical to lay control, that interdenominational cooperation was reestablished, and that Christian ethics superseded Christian dogma. Theologians now stressed the acquisition of grace through a program of good works. No longer was salvation limited to the chosen few. Eventually this doctrine spread to become the search for Christian perfection that culminated in the reform movements of pre-Civil War society. Christians could save themselves through good works, the most important of which was the salvation of others. But in the Second Great Awakening, salvation meant the elevation of the whole person, not just the soul, because like the later advocates of the Social Gospel, the Arminians preached the Kingdom of Christ on earth. The spread of Christian ethics and the individual's search for personal holiness were based on a new sense of responsibility. Unlike the Calvinist doctrine of duty, this new benevolence could bear important fruit, one's personal salvation as well as the salvation of others.

But Arminius, like Calvin, was a European theologian, and if he was to have great impact in America his views had to be expressed in the American idiom. This task was accomplished by Charles Grandison Finney. Born in 1792 in Warren, Connecticut, Finney was basically self-educated because his family considered him too bright to waste his time with a slower program of formal education at Yale. In 1821, he decided to give up his successful law practice and, in his twenty-ninth year, he began his second career, a vocation that would forever alter religious thinking in America.

Finney considered himself anti-Calvinist, unlike his counterpart in the First Great Awakening, Jonathan Edwards, who was a modified Calvinist. In many ways the differences between the two men symbolize the differences in the two periods. Edwards was a medieval man who saw God as the center of the universe, but Finney was a modern thinker who saw men and women in that position. Edwards would have been out of place in the Second Great Awakening because Finney's generation lived in a more settled, prosperous, confident society that had great faith in its own ability to progress. It was an optimistic world which rejected the pessimism of predestination.

Thus as influential as Finney was, the way had been prepared for him by the gradual changes which had taken place in America. Based on the common-sense theology of a kind God who had given men and women the free will to accept or reject the beauty of salvation through the precepts of Jesus Christ, Finney's ideas were as simple as Calvin's. The generation that found humor in the anti-Calvinist jingle, "You can and you can't, You will and you won't, You're damned if you do and you're damned if you don't," was receptive to the dynamic man who told them they had a great deal to say about their own salvation. As a result, his evangelism spread over the northern portion of the nation, particularly in the area known as the Burned-Over District of New York, a region which earned its name from the many emotional revivals which took place there in the first quarter of the nineteenth century.

Finney's simple theology that God is love was delivered in emotional sermons which combined his humanistic and rational beliefs to exhort his listeners to great efforts. Cold prayers, he said, "would not rise six feet above the earth." People should pray "until [their noses] bled" or their prayers would be to no avail. Finney could demand so much because he seemed to promise so much: do as he asked and one's soul would be saved. Actually, Finney's methods had almost as great an impact upon society as his theology. Believing in the priesthood of the believers, Finney wanted all lay people to be priests, and all ministers to be evangelists. He established the norm for these evangelist-ministers from the methods of the circuit riders, and used a plain and simple way of preaching to replace the literary sermons used in the wealthy churches and the more emotional approaches used in the poorer churches. He pointed out that Christ had taught by telling stories. It was, in Finney's words, the only way to teach.

Finney accompanied his story-telling with dramatic gestures and innovations: the "anxious seat" where sinners sat as entire congregations prayed for their souls; the "holy band" of helpers who preached at street-corner gatherings before and after the master's sermons; the use of music in the services; the pointed finger of accusation; the mellow, wide-ranging voice; the great dramatic talent and the body which writhed and gestured as he spoke. So effective was he that he often converted his enemies. Once, after one of his better sermons, a member of the congregation addressed the local minister with the remark that if Finney was correct, the minister had not been preaching the true Gospel. Without any explanation, the minister merely agreed with that observation.

Another example which illustrates Finney's effect was his first meeting with Theodore Dwight Weld. As a student at Hamilton College, in the heart of New York's Burned-Over District, Weld knew of Finney's teachings. He hated both the man and his ideas, since they were exactly the opposite of those of Weld's Calvinistic father. Weld hated Finney from what he knew of him, but refused to hear him preach. He was tricked into visiting a local church where the evangelist was speaking, and forced to stay for the entire sermon because he was seated in the inside seat of a pew. As Finney spoke, Weld's anger grew. After the sermon, the student went to a local store and shouted his disapproval of the evangelist. In the middle of Weld's harangue,

Finney entered the store but left when he heard the younger man's attack on his ideas. This gentlemanly behavior forced Weld to realize that he had acted badly, and he went to Finney's house to apologize. When the evangelist opened the door, he asked if Weld had "followed a minister of the Lord Jesus to his own door to abuse him?" This single statement shocked Weld. He realized that his anger and hatred were produced by the realization that if Finney was correct, Weld and his father were wrong. Immediately the young man dropped to his knees, as did Finney, and the two men prayed together for understanding. When Weld arose, he was no longer a Calvinist, and within a few years he became as famous as his mentor. Converted to Finney's idea that men and women could control their destinies and change the world, Weld became the most effective abolitionist in America.

What converted Weld was not Finney's method, as exciting as it was, but his theology. Called the "New Heart" theology, Finney denounced the concept that people were depraved and could do nothing about it. He combined reason with emotion, faith in the Bible with faith in people, belief in the benevolence of God with the perfectibility of people, and preached of a rational God who had great appeal in a practical nation. His most powerful idea was that working for the spiritual and material happiness of others was to increase one's own chances for salvation.

Finney's career emphasized the great change that had taken place in America since the American Revolution. Although the Civil War later created a crisis of dual identity similar to that of the colonial era, early nineteenth-century Americans actively sought a single identity that included an American religion. They were successful, and Finney was one reason for this success. In 1832 he established a church in New York City, thus ending his revival days, but his influence was just beginning. Three years later he accepted an offer to create a theology department at the newly established Oberlin (Ohio) College. His first students were the Lane Rebels, abolitionist radicals dismissed from Lane Seminary in Cincinnati for following the dictates of Theodore Dwight Weld.

Finney's impact on his age, first as a professor and then as president of Oberlin College, was comparable to that of Andrew Jackson. The Lane Rebels, who formed the nucleus of the Oberlin student body, and those who followed in their footsteps included many who became the most influential revivalists and abolitionists in America. The doctrine the Oberlin evangelist preached became the most persistent religious theme of ante-bellum America. Armed with Finney's theology, the Oberlinites created a hunger for holiness which became the touchstone for every reform movement concerned with the establishment of a meaningful Christian society. Their teachings, known as "Oberlin Perfectionism," swept across the northern section of the nation from 1835 to 1860.

Basically, Perfectionism was an outgrowth of Finney's concept that anyone who patterned his or her life after Jesus, walked in his steps, and made all decisions just as Christ would have, could achieve sanctification, and thus perfection, in this life. Sanctification was not considered highly probable, but in an egotistical and utopian era, it was considered possible. At that time, there were many millennialists — people who advocated that the Kingdom was at hand — but Finney's millennium was of this world, not the next. Through revitalizing and reforming society, the Perfectionists hoped to establish the Kingdom of Christ here on earth.

Finney's disciples were not puppets. Nearly all of them clashed with the master on one major point: they set out to right all societal wrongs to achieve the millennium and most of them became abolitionists. Finney thought this was a grave mistake; revitalize the church and the individual Christian, he argued, and they will change society. But his disciples were too impatient. As the modern idiom goes, they "wanted to do it themselves."

Possibly Finney was correct. As the success of the evangelicals grew, their energies were more and more directed into one channel: abolitionism. They were so successful that they put themselves out of jobs and then watched as the Civil War destroyed most of the brotherly love they had established and halted most reform movements. The next generation of reformers would turn to Darwin, not Christ, for their ideas, and the next generation of evangelists — Billy Sunday and Dwight Moody — fought Finney's idea that the Kingdom was of this world.

But while the Perfectionist movement was so all-consuming that it destroyed itself, its impact upon America was great. Its relation to the Civil War is made obvious by the hundreds of thousands converted by Finney or his disciples becoming oriented toward anti-slavery ideas. Later liberal religious movements, like the Social Gospel and the Salvation Army, drew openly upon Finney's ideas. But possibly the greatest impact Finney had was on Calvinism. His doctrines destroyed the hold Calvinism had upon the American mind, and created a distinctly American religion, based on the belief that people can achieve anything. His doctrines also suggested that Americans, as they assumed responsibility for their own salvation, were also responsible for whatever authority their government exercised over them.

Issue

The Nature of Authority

The times call upon us to return to the egalitarianism of the Founders and once and for all to strip away the pernicious mystique with which we ourselves have surrounded the President. We too must regard him as but a man . . . and firmly maintain that he is subject to the law.

Raoul Berger, 1974

In framing a government which is to be administered by men over men, the great difficulty lies in this: You must first enable the government to controul the governed; and in the next place, oblige it to controul itself.

James Madison, 1788

The problem of authority is intrinsic to all human relationships. Parents exert control over their children; education relies on the acquiescence of the student; the culture itself elevates talented, useful, attractive, or notorious individuals and groups into positions of influence and power; a market economy rewards the successful with profits and opportunities which the less successful do not enjoy; a system of justice and law must constantly alleviate the powerlessness of the weak and protect the property of the well-to-do. To be effective, authority must serve the needs of the person exerting it and the one over whom it is extended. To be more than raw force, authority must be closely related to trust.

The question of the nature of authority has arisen again and again in American history because the United States has a constitutional government founded on the basic assumption that the authority of government is derived from the consent of the governed. That consent must be continually renewed, and the purposes for which the people's power is used must be frequently reexamined.

◆ DOCUMENTS ◆

The Sources of National Authority

GEORGE WASHINGTON

At the moment of victory in the War for Independence, George Washington implores his fellow Americans to construct and support a strong national government. Why did he regard national unity as a test of the moral character of the people? In what ways had history given the people, at this point, the rare opportunity to exercise control over their own destiny?

The Citizens of America, placed in the most enviable condition, as the sole Lords and Proprietors of a vast Tract of Continent, comprehending all the various soils and climates of the World, and abounding with all the necessaries and conveniencies of life, are now by the late satisfactory pacification, acknowledged to be possessed of absolute freedom and Independency; They are, from this period, to be considered as the Actors on a most conspicuous Theatre, which seems to be peculiarly designated by Providence for the display of human greatness and felicity; Here, they are not only surrounded with every thing which can contribute to the completion of private and domestic enjoyment, but Heaven has crowned all its other blessings, by giving a fairer oppertunity for political happiness, than any other Nation has ever been favored with. . . .

Such is our situation, and such are our prospects: but notwithstanding the cup of blessing is thus reached out to us, notwithstanding happiness is ours, if we have a disposition to seize the occasion and make it our own; yet, it appears to me there is an option still left to the United States of America, that it is in their choice, and depends upon their conduct, whether they will be respectable and prosperous, or contemptable and miserable as a Nation; This is the time of their political probation, this is the moment when the eyes of the whole World are turned upon them, this is the moment to establish or ruin their national Character forever, this is the favorable moment to give such a tone to our Federal Government, as will enable it to answer the ends of its institution, or this may be the ill-fated moment for relaxing the powers of the Union, annihilating the cement of the Confederation, and exposing us to become the sport of European politics, which may play one State against another to prevent their growing importance, and to serve their own interested purposes. For, according to the system of Policy

From John C. Fitzpatrick, ed., *The Writings of George Washington* (Washington, D.C.: U.S. Government Printing Office, 1938), XXVI, 484–486.

the States shall adopt at this moment, they will stand or fall, and by their confirmation or lapse, it is yet to be decided, whether the Revolution must ultimately be considered as a blessing or a curse: a blessing or a curse, not to the present age alone, for with our fate will the destiny of unborn Millions be involved.

Restraining the People's Authority

ALEXANDER CONTEE HANSON

The Revolution affirmed that power belonged to the people and was to be exercised by their representatives, but in such partnership, which side was to be dominant? In a fierce controversy in Maryland over paper money in 1787–1788, Alexander Contee Hanson ("Aristides") attacked the contention of William Paca ("Publicola") that legislators should be bound to obey the instructions drafted by their constituents. Why were legislators better qualified than their constituents to make public policy decisions? What benefits would the community derive from being governed by an enlightened elite? Why was such a political system the very essence of constitutional government?

I did not, at first, take notice of an essay under the signature of Publicola; but I understand that the author's confident assertions, and the great names he has mentioned for authorities, have even staggered men in the right faith. He has informed you, as I collect from the whole of his piece, that Mr. Locke, lord Molesworth, and Mr. Trenchard, have maintained with their pens the right of binding by instructions; that Mr. Hambden and lord John Russel have maintained it with their blood, and that Mr. Algernon Sydney has maintained it with both. In a popular harangue, this assertion might not surprise. Committed to writing, published to the world, and open for examination, there is no excuse or palliation for it, except that which Publicola would disdain to offer.

In Mr. Locke's two celebrated treatises of government, I can find nothing to countenance the opinion, that in a government by representation the people have a right to prescribe a particular law. He considers the natural unalienable right of interfering, when the ends of government are perverted or liberty manifestly endangered, in the same light as I have done, except that he does not go quite so far with respect to the legislature's gratifying the wishes and sentiments of the people. . . .

From the *Maryland Journal*, April 1, 1787.

It is agreed on all hands, that men in a remote corner of the state cannot so well judge, what will suit the society, as when they are convened at the capital from every part, and hear all that can be urged on every side. It is agreed likewise, that men in general, cannot, in any place, so well judge as those, who are selected from their fellow-citizens, on account of superior talents, and devote their attention to the public affairs. It cannot be denied, that undue influence will ever be exerted in obtaining what is called the people's sense; and it is impossible, that every man can be qualified to decide nice questions of policy.

It is alleged, that, if your representatives are independent in their votes, they will become your masters. — Strange it is, that no medium can be found between implicit obedience and arbitrary sway! The several constitutional restrictions on the power of the legislature, and the mode of appointing your representatives, have not surely been attended to. For violating their duty, they cannot expect, at the end of the year, otherwise than to be dismissed with disgrace; and, as a part of the people, they are themselves to sustain, in the beginning, the mischiefs originating from the bad laws they enact. There is no power in the state capable of corrupting either branch of the legislature — Whilst left at perfect freedom to act as a check upon each other, your liberties can incur no risk, unless you can suppose them guilty of undue combination; and then that fatal period has arrived which demands your interference. I should not be surprised if the patriots in England, beholding the baneful influence of the ministry, obtained by barefaced bribery and corruption, should sometimes contend for a doctrine, which might if established by law prevent some of the evils, arising from the improper duration of parliaments; but there is no good reason whatever for establishing this doctrine in Maryland.

The most certain way of examining all propositions is to trace the consequences of their admission. *My* proposition cannot be wicked, because, if admitted, it will promote ORDER and GOOD GOVERNMENT, and can do no harm. It cannot be slavish; because it will tend to preserve unimpaired our free and happy constitution. There is however enough to justify my calling the opposite doctrine wicked, slavish and absurd. It is wicked, because if established, it must introduce disorder, riot and arbitrary sway — It is slavish, because it tends to confer the height of power on a single branch, and thereby to encourage the most fatal designs. — And it is absurd, because it would render the constitution a jumble of inconsistency and contradictions.

ARISTIDES

Restraining Legislative Authority

WILLIAM PACA

Paca sharply retorted that the power of the people to instruct their representatives was "essential" to the preservation of "liberty." Why was this democratic concept deeply rooted in English and American history? Was a high degree of public participation in politics a threat to public tranquillity and political stability? Was it necessary to restrain the authority of government?

To ARISTIDES

In your last address to the people of Maryland, you have been pleased to take some notice of Publicola. The right of the people to instruct their delegates, had always appeared to me an essential safe guard of public liberty. I not only read of it as a speculative opinion, of individuals in their closets; but history told me of its being actually exercised in all countries, and all governments, where the people had a share in legislation, by delegates or representatives, and when I found you and a few others among us, asserting a different doctrine, I considered it as a dangerous attack upon the rights of my fellow-citizens, and therefore made some animadversions upon it.

But it was your duty, you say, as a *guardian* of the constitution, to protest against what you conceived a most dangerous innovation. This, Sir, seems to me to be another new-fangled doctrine. I wonder what it is that has made you a *guardian* of the constitution, to *protest* in *news papers* against what you may conceive to be *innovations.* I can find nothing of it in your commission as a judge, nor can I find it in your oath of office. But you may tell me, the oath of allegiance, which you also take, binds you to defend the government, against all conspiracies and combinations. If this be the ground on which you rest your title, to be the *guardian* of the constitution, to *protest* in news papers, why then every constable in the state, and every cryer of the courts, and the very door-keepers of the general assembly, are equally with you *guardians* of the constitution; for they all take the same oath of allegiance. In the exercise of your *judicial* authority, upon subjects *judicially* before you, no doubt you have great and extensive powers; but as to questions not before you *judicially,* you are only a *private* citizen. If however the title flatters and pleases you of being a *guardian* of the constitution, to *protest* in *news papers,* you may take it, and so may the cryer of your court, for what I care about it. . . .

You collect, you say, from the whole of my publication, that I asserted that "Mr. Locke, lord Molesworth, and Mr. Trenchard, maintained with their pens *the right of binding by instructions;* that Mr. Hambden and lord Russel

From the *Maryland Gazette,* May 10, 1787.

maintained it with their blood; and Mr. Algernon Sydney with both." This collection of yours, Sir, is nothing more than the work of a prolific fancy; indeed there is so little ground for it, that I am almost led to think it a *wilful* misrepresentation. . . .

I cited the illustrious names of Locke, Molesworth, Trenchard, Hambden, Russel, and Sydney, to maintain the following positions.

1st. That all legislative power is a *grant* of the people, and a *trust* for their welfare and happiness.

2dly. That the people are the *judges* whether this trust was properly or improperly executed.

3dly. That if they were of opinion it was not properly executed, they might go even to the extreme of resuming the powers of government, if *other* means of redress were ineffectual.

The great object of my publication, was to prove the propriety of the assembly's adjourning to take the *sense* and *judgment* of the people, upon the measures proposed by the house of delegates and rejected by the senate. It therefore became material to establish the principle, that the people are the *rightful judges* of the good or bad tendency of all public measures. To maintain this principle, I cited the above authorities, and I hope you will admit they are directly in point. I afterwards shewed, that the right of interference by *instructions,* was a natural and necessary result from the principle or *right of judgment.* Not that these patriots employed their pens and blood in defence of the *particular right of instructing,* but in defence of principles, from which I contended, the right of instructing resulted as a plain and natural consequence. And before I have done, Sir, I think I shall oblige you to confess it by fair argument. . . .

Whenever the people think the powers of government are improperly exercised, they may interfere two ways.

1st. By memorial and remonstrance.

2dly. By instruction and demand.

And their application or direction may be enforced two ways.

1st. By discontinuing the members on a future election.

2dly. By resuming the power of government.

The one or other mode of coertion may be adopted according to the exigency of the case.

But my doctrine, you say is *wicked,* and tends to introduce *riot* and *disorder.* Other partizans of power have said the same thing before you. But the principles, which I contend for, are established upon foundations too strong to be shaken by the feeble efforts of a judge, who, if we may believe his writings, neither knows nor feels what liberty is.

The *binding force* of instructions, you assert, has no connexion with the principles of the English and American revolutions. I never read a writer so confident in his assertions, and yet so often mistaken. The binding force, Sir, of instructions is entirely founded upon the principles of both these revolutions. The principles were, that all rightful power is derived from the people, that it is to be exercised for their welfare and happiness, that the people are the judges, and when they think it is not so employed they may speak and announce it by memorials, remonstrances, or instructions; and if they are disregarded they may right themselves by discontinuing their members at a future election, or if the magnitude of the case requires it, by resuming the powers of government. It was upon these principles the people of England struck off the head of king Charles the first; it was upon these principles that America broke her connexion with Great-Britain, and became an independent empire; and it is upon these principles that we see you, Sir, a *judge* of the *general court* of Maryland, with a salary of £.500 per annum; and like a *blessed guardian* employing all the powers and faculties of your soul to destroy the best guard which the people have for their liberty, safety and happiness.

PUBLICOLA

Balancing Political Authority

JAMES MADISON

In the Federalist Papers, *numbers 10 and 51, James Madison responds to the anti-Federalist argument that the Constitution will encourage greedy political factions to flourish and that federal officials will face irresistible temptations to abuse their extensive power. Why does Madison regard factionalism and the abuse of power as an unavoidable part of all societies and political systems? How did a subtle appreciation of human nature and psychology enable the framers of the Constitution to guard against such antisocial behavior? How can the Constitution "enable government to control the governed" and at the same time "oblige it to control itself"?*

From [Alexander Hamilton, John Jay, and James Madison] "The Federalist." *The Independent Journal of New York,* October 27, 1787–April 2, 1788. [Later published in 2 volumes, 1788.]

No. 10

Among the numerous advantages promised by a well constructed Union, none deserves to be more accurately developed than its tendency to break and control the violence of faction. The friend of popular governments, never finds himself so much alarmed for their character and fate, as when he contemplates their propensity to this dangerous vice. He will not fail therefore to set a due value on any plan which, without violating the principles to which he is attached, provides a proper cure for it. The instability, injustice and confusion introduced into the public councils, have in truth been the mortal diseases under which popular governments have every where perished; as they continue to be the favorite and fruitful topics from which the adversaries to liberty derive their most specious declamations. . . .

By a faction I understand a number of citizens, whether amounting to a majority or minority of the whole, who are united and actuated by some common impulse of passion or of interest, adverse to the rights of other citizens, or to the permanent and aggregate interests of the community.

There are two methods of curing the mischiefs of faction: the one, by removing its causes; the other, by controling its effects.

There are again two methods of removing the causes of faction: the one by destroying the liberty which is essential to its existence; the other, by giving to every citizen the same opinions, the same passions, and the same interests.

It could never be more truly said than of the first remedy, that it is worse than the disease. Liberty is to faction, what air is to fire, an ailment without which it instantly expires. But it could not be a less folly to abolish liberty, which is essential to political life, because it nourishes faction, than it would be to wish the annihilation of air, which is essential to animal life, because it imparts to fire its destructive agency.

The second expedient is as impracticable, as the first would be unwise. As long as the reason of man continues fallible, and he is at liberty to exercise it, different opinions will be formed. As long as the connection subsists between his reason and his self-love, his opinions and his passions will have a reciprocal influence on each other; and the former will be objects to which the latter will attach themselves. . . .

The latent causes of faction are thus sown in the nature of man; and we see them everywhere brought into different degrees of activity, according to the different circumstances of civil society. . . . So strong is this propensity of mankind to fall into mutual animosities, that where no substantial occasion presents itself, the most frivolous and fanciful distinctions have been sufficient to kindle their unfriendly passions, and excite their most violent conflicts. But the most common and durable source of factions, has been the various and unequal distribution of property. Those who hold, and those who are without property, have ever formed distinct interests in society. Those who are creditors, and those who are debtors, fall under a like discrimination. . . . The regulation of these various and interfering interests forms the principal task of modern Legislation, and involves the spirit of party and faction in the necessary and ordinary operations of Government. . . .

No man is allowed to be a judge in his own cause because his interest would certainly bias his judgment, and, not improbably, corrupt his integrity. With equal, nay with greater reason, a body of men, are unfit to be both judges and parties, at the same time; yet, what are many of the most important acts of legislation, but so many judicial determinations, not indeed concerning the rights of single persons, but concerning the rights of large bodies of citizens; and what are the different classes of legislators, but advocates and parties to the causes which they determine? . . .

The apportionment of taxes on the various descriptions of property, is an act which seems to require the most exact impartiality; yet, there is perhaps no legislative act in which greater opportunity and temptation are given to a predominant party, to trample on the rules of justice. . . .

The inference to which we are brought, is, that the *causes* of faction cannot be removed; and that relief is only to be sought in the means of controling its *effects*.

If a faction consists of less than a majority, relief is supplied by the republican principle, which enables the majority to defeat its sinister views by regular vote: It may clog the administration, it may convulse the society; but it will be unable to execute and mask its violence under the forms of the Constitution. When a majority is included in a faction, the form of popular government on the other hand enables it to sacrifice to its ruling passion or interest, both the public good and the rights of other citizens. To secure the public good, and private rights, against the danger of such a faction, and at the same time to preserve the spirit and the form of popular government, is then the great object to which our enquiries are directed. Let me add that it is the great desideratum, by which alone this form of government can be rescued from the opprobrium under which it has so long labored, and be recommended to the esteem and adoption of mankind.

By what means is this object attainable? Evidently by one of two only. Either the existence of the same passion or interest in a majority at the same time, must be prevented; or the majority, having such co-existent passion or interest, must be rendered, by their number and local situation, unable to concert and carry into effect schemes of oppression. . . .

No. 51

To what expedient then shall we finally resort for maintaining in practice the necessary partition of power among the several departments, as laid down in the constitution? . . . The great security against a gradual concentration of the several powers in the same department, consists in giving to those who administer each department, the necessary constitutional means, and personal motives, to resist encroachments of the others. The provision for defence must in this, as in all other cases, be made commensurate to the danger of attack. Ambition must be made to counteract ambition. The interest of the man must be connected with the constitutional rights of the place. It may be a reflection on human nature, that such devices should be necessary to controul the abuses of government. But what is government itself but the greatest of all reflections on human nature? If men were angels, no government would be necessary. If angels were to govern men, neither external nor internal controuls on government would be necessary. In framing a government which is to be administered by men over men, the great difficulty lies in this: You must first enable the government to controul the governed; and in the next place, oblige it to controul itself. A dependence on the people is no doubt the primary controul on the government; but experience has taught mankind the necessity of auxiliary precautions.

The Character of Authority
JAMES WILSON

The way that a government punishes lawbreakers reveals the character of its authority. Justice James Wilson of the Supreme Court in a charge to a Virginia Grand Jury in 1791 explains how the authority of the law should operate to make people respect and obey it. Why does Wilson reject harsh punishment as a proper use of authority? Why should punishment be "mild, swift and sure"?

Gentlemen of the grand jury, to prevent crimes is the noblest end and aim of criminal jurisprudence. To punish them is one of the means necessary for the accomplishment of this noble end and aim. The impunity of an offender encourages him to repeat his offences. The witnesses of his impunity are tempted to become his disciples in his guilt. These considerations form the strongest — some view them as the sole argument for the infliction of punishments by human laws.

There are, in punishments, three qualities, which render them the fit preventives of crimes. The first is their moderation. The second is their speediness. The third is their certainty.

We are told by some writers, that the number of crimes is unquestionably diminished by the severity of punishments. If we inspect the greatest part of the criminal codes; their unwieldy bulk and their ensanguined hue will force us to acknowledge, that this opinion may plead, in its favour, a very high antiquity, and a very extensive reception. On accurate and unbiassed examination, however, it will appear to be an opinion unfounded and pernicious,

From Bird Wilson, ed., *The Works of James Wilson* (Philadelphia, 1804), III, 357–365, 391–393.

inconsistent with the principles of our nature, and, by a necessary consequence, with those of wise and good government.

So far as any sentiment of generous sympathy is suffered, by a merciless code, to remain among the citizens, their abhorrence of crimes is, by the barbarous exhibitions of human agony, sunk in their commiseration of criminals. These barbarous exhibitions are productive of another bad effect — a latent and gradual, but a powerful, because a natural, aversion to the laws. Can laws, which are a natural and just object of aversion, receive a cheerful obedience, or secure a regular and uniform execution? The expectation is forbidden by some of the strongest principles in the human frame. Such laws, while they excite the compassion of society for those who suffer, rouse its indignation against those who are active in the steps preparatory to their sufferings. . . .

True it is, that, on some emergencies, excesses of a temporary nature may receive a sudden check from rigorous penalties: but their continuance and their frequency introduce and diffuse a hardened insensibility among the citizens; and this insensibility, in its turn, gives occasion or pretence to the farther extension and multiplication of those penalties. Thus one degree of severity opens and smooths the way for another, till, at length, under the specious appearance of necessary justice, a system of cruelty is established by law.

Such a system is calculated to eradicate all the manly sentiments of the soul, and to substitute, in their place, dispositions of the most depraved and degrading kind. It is the parent of *pusillanimity*. A nation broke to cruel punishments becomes dastardly and contemptible. For, in nations, as well as individuals, cruelty is always attended by cowardice. It is the parent of *slavery*. In every government, we find the genius of freedom depressed in proportion to the sanguinary spirit of the laws. It is hostile to the prosperity of nations, as well as to the dignity and virtue of men. . . .

The principles both of utility and of justice require, that the commission of a crime should be followed by a speedy inflection of its punishment.

The association of ideas has vast power over the sentiments, the passions, and the conduct of men. When a penalty marches close in the rear of the offence, against which it is denounced; an association, strong and striking, is produced between them: and they are viewed in the inseparable relation of cause and effect. When, on the contrary, the punishment is procrastinated to a remote period; this connexion is considered as weak and precarious; and the execution of the law is beheld and suffered as a detached instance of severity, warranted by no cogent reason, and springing from no laudable motive.

It is just, as well as useful, that the punishment should be inflicted soon after the commission of the crime. It should never be forgotten, that imprisonment, though often necessary for the safe custody of the person accused, is, nevertheless, in itself, a punishment — a punishment galling to some of the finest feelings of the heart — a punishment too, which, since it precedes conviction, may be as undeserved as it is distressing. But imprisonment is not the only penalty, which an accused person undergoes before his trial. He undergoes also the corroding torment of suspense — the keenest agony, perhaps, which falls to the lot of suffering humanity. This agony is by no means to be estimated by the real probability or danger of conviction: it bears a compound proportion to the delicacy of sentiment and the strength of imagination possessed by him, who is doomed to become its prey. . . .

But the certainty of punishments is that quality, which is of the greatest importance in order to constitute them fit preventives of crimes. This quality is, in its operation, most merciful as well as most powerful. When a criminal determines on the commission of a crime, he is not so much influenced by the lenity of the punishment, as by the expectation that, in some way or other, he may be fortunate enough to avoid it. This is particularly the case with him, when this expectation is cherished by examples or by experience of impunity. It was the saying of Solon, that he had completed his system of laws by the combined energy of justice and strength. By this expression he meant to denote, that laws, of themselves, would be of very little service, unless they were enforced by a faithful and an effectual execution of them. The strict execution of every *criminal* law is the dictate of humanity as well as of wisdom. . . .

We have already seen, that the noblest end and aim of criminal jurisprudence is to prevent crimes: and we have already seen that punishments, mild, speedy, and certain, are means calculated for preventing them. But these are not the only means. Crimes may be prevented by the genius as well as by the execution of the criminal laws. Let them be few: let them be clear: let them be simple: let them be concise: let them be consummately accurate. Let the punishment be proportioned — let it be analogous — to the crime. Let the reformation as well as the punishment of offenders be kept constantly and steadily in view; and, while the dignity of the nation is vindicated, let reparation be made to those, who have received injury. Above all, let the wisdom, the purity, and the benignity of the civil code supersede, for they are well calculated to supersede, the severity of criminal legislation. Let the law diffuse peace and happiness; and innocence will walk in their train. . . .

Slavery's Corrosive Authority
THOMAS JEFFERSON

In Jefferson's Notes on Virginia, *published in 1785, the future president confronted directly the issue of how slavery corrupted those in authority. Why did the absolute power of the masters produce abuse of authority? How does the*

From A. L. Lipscomb, ed., *The Writings of Thomas Jefferson* (Washington, D.C.: Thomas Jefferson Memorial Association, 1903), II, 225–230.

exercise of complete control by whites over blacks endanger self-government? How are the personal ethics of rulers connected to the success of self-government?

Query XVIII

It is difficult to determine on the standard by which the manners of a nation may be tried, whether *catholic* or *particular*. It is more difficult for a native to bring to that standard the manners of his own nation, familiarized to him by habit. There must doubtless be an unhappy influence on the manners of our people produced by the existence of slavery among us. The whole commerce between master and slave is a perpetual exercise of the most boisterous passions, the most unremitting despotism on the one part, and degrading submissions on the other. Our children see this, and learn to imitate it; for man is an imitative animal. This quality is the germ of all education in him. . . . The man must be a prodigy who can retain his manners and morals undepraved by such circumstances. And with what execration should the statesman be loaded, who, permitting one half the citizens thus to trample on the rights of the other, transforms those into despots, and these into enemies, destroys the morals of the one part, and the *amor patriæ* of the other. For if a slave can have a country in this world, it must be any other in preference to that in which he is born to live and labor for another. . . . With the morals of the people, their industry also is destroyed. For in a warm climate, no man will labor for himself who can make another labor for him. This is so true, that of the proprietors of slaves a very small proportion indeed are ever seen to labor. And can the liberties of a nation be thought secure when we have removed their only firm basis, a conviction in the minds of the people that these liberties are of the gift of God? That they are not to be violated but with His wrath? Indeed I tremble for my country when I reflect that God is just; that his justice cannot sleep forever; that considering numbers, nature and natural means only, a revolution of the wheel of fortune, an exchange of situation is among possible events; that it may become probable by supernatural interference! The Almighty has no attribute which can take side with us in such a contest. But it is impossible to be temperate and to pursue this subject through the various considerations of policy, of morals, of history natural and civil. We must be contented to hope they will force their way into every one's mind. I think a change already perceptible, since the origin of the present revolution. The spirit of the master is abating, that of the slave rising from the dust, his condition mollifying, the way I hope preparing, under the auspices of heaven, for a total emancipation, and that this is disposed, in the order of events, to be with the consent of the masters, rather than by their extirpation.

God and the People's Authority

CHARLES G. FINNEY

Charles G. Finney emphasizes the ability of individuals to focus their thoughts and lives on the authority of God. Does this suggest that they have the moral capacity to restrain the authority of government? How can "the fallow ground of the heart" become the material for the redemption of society? How would Washington, Madison, Wilson, or Jefferson react to the view that God is the source of political and social authority in American life?

There are great errors on the subject of the laws which govern the mind. People talk about religious feeling, as if they thought they could, by direct effort, call forth emotion. But this is not the way the mind acts. No man can make himself feel in this way, merely by *trying* to feel. The *emotions* of the mind are not *directly* under our control. We cannot by willing, or by direct volition, call forth our emotions. We might as well think to call spirits up from the deep. The emotions are purely involuntary states of mind. They naturally and necessarily exist in the mind under certain circumstances calculated to excite them. But they can be controlled *indirectly*. Otherwise there would be no moral character in our emotions, if there were not a way to control them. We cannot say, "Now I will feel so and so towards such an object." But we can command our *attention* to it, and look at it intently, till the proper feeling arises. . . . So if a man thinks of God, and fastens his mind on any parts of God's character, he will feel — emotions will come up, by the very laws of mind. If he is a friend of God, let him contemplate God as a gracious and holy being, and he will have emotions of friendship kindled up in his mind. If he is an enemy of God, only let him get the true character of God before his mind, and look at it, and fasten his attention on it, and his enmity will rise against God.

If you wish to break up the fallow ground of your hearts, and make your minds feel on the subject of religion, you must go to work just as you would to feel on any other subject. Instead of keeping your thoughts on every thing else, and then imagine that by going to a few meetings you will get your feelings enlisted, go the common sense way to work, as you would on any other subject. It is just as easy to make your minds feel on the subject of religion as it is on any other subject. God has put these states of mind just as absolutely under your control, as the motions of your limbs. If people were as

From Charles G. Finney, *Lectures on Revivals of Religion* . . . (Boston, 1835), Chap. III, Sect. II.

unphilosophical about moving their limbs, as they are about regulating their emotions, you would never have gotten here to meeting to-night.

If you mean to break up the fallow ground of your hearts, you must begin by looking at your hearts — examine and note the state of your minds, and see where you are. Many never seem to think about this. They pay no attention to their own hearts, and never know whether they are doing well in religion or not — whether they are gaining ground or going back — whether they are fruitful, or lying waste like fallow ground. Now you must draw off your attention from other things, and look into this. Make a business of it. Don't be in a hurry. Examine thoroughly the state of your hearts, and see where you are — whether you are walking with God every day, or walking with the devil — whether you are serving God or serving the devil most — whether you are under the dominion of the prince of darkness, or the Lord Jesus Christ.

◆ MODERN ESSAY ◆

Controlling Corrupt Authority

RAOUL BERGER

At the height of the Watergate crisis — as the president still refused to turn subpoenaed documents over to the House Judiciary Committee — legal historian Raoul Berger placed the whole controversy in historical perspective. In what ways did the framers of the Constitution clearly anticipate actions and arguments such as President Nixon's? How did their understanding of human nature equip them to deal with the problem of future presidential misconduct? What role does the Constitution play today in energizing and restraining authority? Do conscience and a knowledge of history make people more responsible citizens?

The American people must be alerted: By refusing to comply with the subpoenas of the House Judiciary Committee, President Nixon is setting himself above the Constitution. He would nullify the constitutional provision for Presidential accountability that was designed to prevent dictatorial usurpations.

The issue far transcends a confrontation between the President and the House; it is a confrontation with the nation. "All officers of the Government,

From Raoul Berger, "Mr. Nixon's Refusal of Subpoenas: A Confrontation with the Nation," *New York Times,* July 8, 1974. © 1974 by The New York Times Company. Reprinted by permission.

from the highest to the lowest," said the United States Supreme Court in 1882, "are creatures of the law and are bound to obey it"; "no officer of the law may set that law at defiance with impunity." A people that tolerate such defiance by the President is sowing the seeds of its own destruction.

The Presidential claim of constitutional right to withhold information from Congress is labeled "executive privilege." A limited power of secrecy was given to Congress, not to the President. No word about "executive privilege" or "confidentiality" is to be found either in the Constitution or its history. On the other hand, the Supreme Court recognized that parliamentary inquiry was an established "attribute" of legislative power and held that it was conferred upon Congress by the grant of "legislative power." No minister challenged the right of Parliament to inquire into executive conduct; no member of the executive branch has ever summoned a pre-1789 "precedent" for executive refusal to honor legislative subpoena; and so far as my own search of parliamentary record goes, there are none.

James Wilson, second only to James Madison as an architect of the Constitution, wrote admiringly that in "the character of grand inquisitors of the realm," the House of Commons "have checked the progress of arbitrary power," and that the "proudest ministers . . . have appeared at the bar of the house, to give an account of their conduct." This inquisitorial function was known as the "Grand Inquest of the Nation;" and the Grand Inquest alone, said Lord Justice Coleridge, was entrusted with the determination of what falls within the limits of its power of investigation. References to that function were made in four or five of the United States Constitution's ratifying conventions, with never a word that the power must be cut down for the protection of the President. The absence of such remarks is but another example of the pervasive distrust and fear of executive usurpation that found expression in convention after convention, and that lies at the root of Congressional power to impeach the President.

Thus, the President's reiterated incantation — the separation of powers — lays claim to a power that was not given to him. The purpose of the separation of powers, said John Adams, was to prevent encroachment by one branch on the powers of another. Before separation of powers comes into play, therefore, it is first necessary to demonstrate that a power was granted to the President to withhold information that a legislature traditionally could demand. Such proof simply cannot be made; Mr. Nixon's claims are merely based on self-serving assertions.

The case for Congressional inquiry as a prelude to impeachment stands even stronger, for arguments that impeachment violated the separation of powers were summarily brushed aside by the Framers themselves. In the Convention, Rufus King and Charles Pinckney protested that the proposed impeachment provision would destroy the independence of the President and violate the separation of powers — the very arguments Mr. Nixon now interposes to the subpoenas. Notwithstanding, they were voted down, 8 to 2, because, as George Mason said, "No point is of more importance than that the right of impeachment should be continued." Note that Mason took for granted that it was the familiar, established "right of impeachment" that would thus be "continued."

Apart from the total lack of historical warrant for the President's attempt to set the bounds of inquiry by the House Judiciary Committee, Mr. Nixon insists on a prerogative to which no other suspect can lay claim before any investigative body. His insistence that he can dictate the rules of the inquiry exhibits contempt for the common sense of the American people. A series of Presidents, from Washington through Polk and Buchanan to Mr. Nixon himself, have recognized the paramountcy of the Grand Inquest of the Nation. Polk put the matter most forcibly; given an inquiry into executive misconduct, the "power of the House . . . would penetrate into the most secret recesses of the Executive Departments."

The House's need for all the facts surrounding suspected Presidential offenses cannot of course be circumscribed by an executive determination of what is relevant. Long since, Chief Justice Marshall declared that what is relevant cannot be left to the determination of the executive. The Constitution does not change according to whose ox is gored.

In the discussion of the alternatives open to the House and the people, there has been a sense of helplessness that does not benefit a great people. The starting point is that Mr. Nixon is in violation of the Constitution, that he "shall take care that the laws be faithfully executed," of which the Constitution is the "supreme law." Just as the sole power of impeachment conferred on the House is not subject to limitation by the President, so he cannot lay down the ground rules for the preliminary investigation that is required for the informed and effective exercise of the power. If the people understand that, then they must exercise the right that John Adams enshrined in the 1780 Massachusetts Constitution, the "right to require of their lawgivers and magistrates an exact and constant observance" of the "fundamental principles of the Constitution." Let the people require of Congress and the President that a halt be called to Presidential attempts to thwart the investigatory function of the House. President Nixon can understand the voice of the people, as his retreat in open court after the Archibald Cox firestorm illustrated. In acting as Grand Inquest, the House is no less entitled to respect than the courts; indeed the powers to impeach and convict the President are perhaps the most important powers conferred by the Constitution. Defiance of the Constitution, the people must tell Mr. Nixon, is intolerable.

It is open to the House Judiciary Committee to ask the House to cite and hold Mr. Nixon for contempt in disobeying the subpoenas of the committee. Such a contempt is plainly an impeachable offense; on a number of occasions the House of Commons brought impeachments for encroachments upon its prerogatives or for thwarting its orders.

When Representative Don Edwards of California stated that the committee cannot force its will upon Mr. Nixon because "he's got the Army, Navy and Air Force and all we've got is Ken Harding" (the sergeant-at-arms) he did not say that the Supreme Court also does not have the ability to call on the armed forces.

The Supreme Court has always assumed that its decrees would be obeyed, and they have been, as when President Truman surrendered the steel plants during the Korean war. If we pursue the Edwards approach, it may be asked what reason there is to believe that Mr. Nixon will surrender his office if he is impeached and convicted.

The Commander in Chief was not given command of the armed forces in order to defy the law but to enforce it. In 1788 James Wilson assured the Pennsylvania Ratification Convention that "not a single privilege is annexed" to the President. And in 1791, Wilson, then a Justice of the Supreme Court, stated: "the most powerful magistrates should be amenable to the law. . . . No one should be secure while he violates the Constitution and the laws." We are not yet a banana republic; the American people will not allow Mr. Nixon to defy the law.

The times call upon us to return to the egalitarianism of the Founders and once and for all to strip away the pernicious mystique with which we ourselves have surrounded the President. We too must regard him as but a man, all the more when he is suspected of impeachable offenses, even of crimes, and firmly maintain that he is subject to the law in all its manifestations, including, if need be, arrest. Finally, I would recall to the nation the words of a great statesman, Edward Livingston, in the early days of the Republic: "No nation ever yet found any inconvenience from too close an inspection into the conduct of its officers, but many have been brought to ruin and . . . slavery . . . only because the means of publicity had not been secured." That was a lesson the Founders had learned.

Issue

The Character of Political Responsibility

Discriminatory laws, doctrines, attitudes, and practices are set deep in our legal system. They are not easily dislodged.

Barbara Brown et al., 1971

Many of our rich men have not been content with equal protection and equal benefits, but have besought us to make them richer by act of Congress. By attempting to gratify their desires we have . . . arrayed

> *section against section, interest against interest, and man against man, in a fearful commotion which threatens to shake the foundations of our Union.*
>
> Andrew Jackson, 1832

The study of political history is much richer than a recitation of presidential administrations, laws, wars, elections, and viewpoints on issues. Politics is a drama with characters who speak movingly, glibly, or desperately about the interests and passions which concern large groups of people. Politics involves the use of language and images and individual leadership to mobilize large numbers of people to enact laws, elect candidates, and vindicate ideas.

For these reasons politics is not very precise in the goals it sets out to achieve, and political achievements fall short of the expectations of those who struggle to bring them to fruition. The tactics and the compromises which are the essence of politics are invariably tainted by the weaknesses of the people who strive to gain and utilize political power.

Little wonder, then, that government is usually the butt of criticism and derision, and that people feel cynical about influencing public affairs. The first half-century of American independence was a period in which the pressures on government to meet certain public expectations were not as severe as they are today. A simpler age and less rapid communication gave politicians more time to maneuver. But because political parties and issues were so new, and because democracy was just beginning to be realized, the drama of politics in a democratic republic was intense.

◆ DOCUMENTS ◆

Government Responsibility vs. Popular Will

FISHER AMES

In a bitter debate over implementation of the Jay Treaty and restoration of normal relations with Great Britain in 1796, Federalist Congressman Fisher Ames of Massachusetts calls for national unity under Federalist leadership, and he condemns Republican attacks on that leadership. Why should government operations, like congressional debates, be insulated from the emotions

From the *Annals of Congress, 1795–1796* (Washington, D.C., 1849), pp. 1239–1256 passim.

felt by the populace? How can such detached, unemotional deliberation serve
the public interest? Why do human passions inject themselves into political
controversy and what dangers do they pose for republican government?

In my judgment, a right decision will depend more on the temper and manner
with which we may prevail on ourselves to contemplate the subject, than upon
the development of any profound political principles, or any remarkable skill
in the application of them. If we should succeed to neutralize our inclinations
[for rancor], we should find less difficulty than we have to apprehend in sur-
mounting all our objections.

The suggestion, a few days ago, that the House manifested symptoms
of heat and irritation, was made and retorted as if the charge ought to create
surprise, and would convey reproach. Let us be more just to ourselves, and
to the occasion. Let us not affect to deny the existence and the intrusion of
some portion of prejudice and feeling into the debate, when, from the very
structure of our nature, we ought to anticipate the circumstance as a probability, and when we are admonished by the evidence of our senses that it is a
fact.

How can we make professions for ourselves, and offer exhortations to
the House, that no influence should be felt but that of duty, and no guide
respected but that of the understanding, while the peal to rally every passion
of man is continually ringing in our ears.

Our understandings have been addressed, it is true, and with ability and
effect; but, I demand, has any corner of the heart been left unexplored? It
has been ransacked to find auxiliary arguments, and, when that attempt failed,
to awaken the sensibilities that would require none. Every prejudice and feeling have been summoned to listen to some particular style of address; and
yet we seem to believe, and to consider a doubt as an affront, that we are
strangers to any influence but that of unbiassed reason.

It would be strange that a subject which has roused in turn all the passions
of the country, should be discussed without the interference of any of our own.
We are men, and, therefore, not exempt from those passions; as citizens and
Representatives, we feel the interest that must excite them. The hazard of
great interests cannot fail to agitate strong passions: we are not disinterested,
it is impossible we should be dispassionate. The warmth of such feelings may
becloud the judgment, and, for a time, pervert the understanding; but the
public sensibility and our own, has sharpened the spirit of inquiry, and given
an animation to the debate. The public attention has been quickened to mark
the progress of the discussion, and its judgment, often hasty and erroneous on
first impressions, has become solid and enlightened at last. Our result will, I
hope, on that account, be the safer and more mature, as well as more accordant
with that of the nation. The only constant agents in political affairs are the
passions of men — shall we complain of our nature? Shall we say that man
ought to have been made otherwise? It is right already, because He, from
whom we derive our nature, ordained it so; and because thus made, and thus

acting, the cause of truth and the public good is the more surely promoted. . . .

Is there anything in the prospect of the interior state of the country, to encourage us to aggravate the dangers of a war? Would not the shock of that evil produce another, and shake down the feeble and then unbraced structure of our Government? Is this the chimera? Is it going off the ground of matter of fact to say, the rejection of the appropriation proceeds upon the doctrine of a civil war of the departments! Two branches have ratified a Treaty, and we are going to set it aside. How is this disorder in the machine to be rectified? While it exists, its movements must stop, and when we talk of a remedy, is that any other than the formidable one of a revolutionary interposition of the people? And is this, in the judgment even of my opposers, to execute, to preserve the Constitution, and the public order? Is this the state of hazard, if not of convulsion, which they can have the courage to contemplate and to brave, or beyond which their penetration can reach and see the issue? They seem to believe, and they act as if they believed, that our Union, our peace, our liberty, are invulnerable and immortal — as if our happy state was not to be disturbed by our dissensions, and that we are not capable of falling from it by our unworthiness. Some of them have no doubt better nerves and better discernment than mine. They can see the bright aspects and happy consequences of all this array of horrors. They can see intestine discords, our Government disorganized, our wrongs aggravated, multiplied and unredressed, peace with dishonor, or war without justice, union or resources, in "*the calm lights of mild philosophy.*" . . .

Government Responsibility to Popular Will

JAMES MADISON

In direct contrast to Ames's exclusion of "warmth" and "passion" from the halls of government, James Madison speaks in the Virginia Resolutions in behalf of an outraged populace opposing the Alien and Sedition acts and other Federalist attempts to stifle political opposition. Why are the Republicans "conscious of the purity of [their] motives"? Why is such "purity" an important qualification for politicians engaged in criticism of government policy? Why is a defensive, self-righteous, manipulative government "vicious" and "artful"?

From Gaillard Hunt, ed., "Address of the General Assembly to the People of the Commonwealth of Virginia," *The Writings of James Madison* (New York: G. P. Putnam's Sons, 1906), VI, 332–340 passim.

Fellow-Citizens, — Unwilling to shrink from our representative responsibility, conscious of the purity of our motives, but acknowledging your right to supervise our conduct, we invite your serious attention to the emergency which dictated the subjoined resolutions. Whilst we disdain to alarm you by ill-founded jealousies, we recommend an investigation, guided by the coolness of wisdom, and a decision bottomed on firmness but tempered with moderation.

It would be perfidious in those entrusted with the guardianship of the State sovereignty, and acting under the solemn obligation of the following oath, "I do swear that I will support the Constitution of the United States," not to warn you of encroachments which, though clothed with the pretext of necessity, or disguised by arguments of expediency, may yet establish precedents which may ultimately devote a generous and unsuspicious people to all the consequences of usurped power. . . .

The acquiescence of the States under infractions of the federal compact, would either beget a speedy consolidation, by precipitating the State governments into impotency and contempt; or prepare the way for a revolution, by a repetition of these infractions, until the people are roused to appear in the majesty of their strength. It is to avoid these calamities that we exhibit to the people the momentous question, whether the Constitution of the United States shall yield to a construction which defies every restraint and overwhelms the best hopes of republicanism.

Exhortations to disregard domestic usurpation, until foreign danger shall have passed, is an artifice which may be forever used; because the possessors of power, who are the advocates for its extension, can ever create national embarrassments, to be successively employed to soothe the people into sleep, whilst that power is swelling, silently, secretly, and fatally. Of the same character are insinuations of a foreign influence, which seize upon a laudable enthusiasm against danger from abroad, and distort it by an unnatural application, so as to blind your eyes against danger at home.

The sedition act presents a scene which was never expected by the early friends of the Constitution. It was then admitted that the States sovereignties were only diminished by powers specifically enumerated, or necessary to carry the specified powers into effect. Now, Federal authority is deduced from implication; and from the existence of State law, it is inferred that Congress possess a similar power of legislation; whence Congress will be endowed with a power of legislation in all cases whatsoever, and the States will be stripped of every right reserved, by the concurrent claims of a paramount Legislature.

The sedition act is the offspring of these tremendous pretensions, which inflict a death wound on the sovereignty of the States. . . .

It is vicious in the extreme to calumniate meritorious public servants; but it is both artful and vicious to arouse the public indignation against calumny in order to conceal usurpation. Calumny is forbidden by the laws, usurpation by the Constitution. Calumny injures individuals, usurpation, States. Calumny may be redressed by the common judicatures; usurpation can only be controlled by the act of society. Ought *usurpation,* which is most mischievous, to be rendered less hateful by *calumny,* which, though injurious, is in a degree less pernicious? But the laws for the correction of calumny were not defective. Every libellous writing or expression might receive its punishment in the State courts, from juries summoned by an officer, who does not receive his appointment from the President, and is under no influence to court the pleasure of Government, whether it injured public officers or private citizens. Nor is there any distinction in the Constitution empowering Congress exclusively to punish calumny directed against an officer of the General Government; so that a construction assuming the power of protecting the reputation of a citizen officer will extend to the case of any other citizen, and open to Congress a right of legislation in every conceivable case which can arise between individuals.

In answer to this, it is urged that every Government possesses an inherent power of self-preservation, entitling it to do whatever it shall judge necessary for that purpose.

This is a repetition of the doctrine of implication and expediency in different language, and admits of a similar and decisive answer, namely, that as the powers of Congress are defined, powers inherent, implied, or expedient, are obviously the creatures of ambition; because the care expended in defining powers would otherwise have been superfluous. Powers extracted from such sources will be indefinitely multiplied by the aid of armies and patronage, which, with the impossibility of controlling them by any demarcation, would presently terminate reasoning, and ultimately swallow up the State sovereignties.

So insatiable is a love of power that it has resorted to a distinction between the freedom and licentiousness of the press for the purpose of converting the third amendment of the Constitution, which was dictated by the most lively anxiety to preserve that freedom, into an instrument for abridging it. Thus usurpation even justifies itself by a precaution against usurpation; and thus an amendment universally designed to quiet every fear is adduced as the source of an act which has produced general terror and alarm. . . .

These are solemn but painful truths; and yet we recommend it to you not to forget the possibility of danger from without, although danger threatens us from within. . . .

Legal Responsibility and Racial Inequality

NORTH CAROLINA SUPERIOR COURT

In 1797, the justices of the North Carolina Superior Court met in regular conference to hear the appeal of a man indicted for murdering a slave. Why did the task of prescribing justice in the case of an innocent slave and an accused free white man involve the justices in such tortuous reasoning? What balance should government, including the courts, strike in weighing the interests and opinions of the people against the requirements of morality and justice?

State v. Boon

The act of 1791 relative to the killing of slaves is too uncertain to warrant the court in passing sentence of death upon prisoner convicted under it.

The prisoner was indicted on the third sec. of the act passed in 1791, the words of which are, "that if any person shall be hereafter guilty of wilfully and maliciously killing a slave, such offender shall upon the first conviction thereof be adjudged guilty of murder, and shall suffer the same punishment as if he had killed a free man, any law, usage or custom to the contrary notwithstanding."

The prisoner was found guilty by a Jury in Hillsborough Superior Court, and being brought up to receive judgment, several exceptions were taken in arrest, by his counsel, upon which the presiding judge directed the case to be sent up to obtain the opinion of this Court. . . .

Justice John Hall: The prisoner has been found guilty of the offence charged in the indictment; whether any, or what punishment, can be inflicted upon him, in consequence thereof, is now to be decided. I will first consider, whether we have any authority to inflict punishment upon him, from any Act of Assembly. . . .

It may be thought that the words "shall suffer the same punishment as if he had killed a free man," from the connexion in which they stand with the words preceding them in the same clause, viz., "that if any person shall hereafter be guilty of wilfully and maliciously killing a slave" should be allowed to have this meaning, and "shall suffer the same punishment, as if he had wilfully and maliciously killed a free man." I cannot agree to this construction; because it is a rule, that penal statutes should be construed strictly. Much

---

From *"State v. Boon," North Carolina Reports* (Winston, 1896), I, 103–114.

latitude of construction ought not to be permitted to operate against life; if it operate at all, it should be in favor of it. Punishments ought to be plainly defined and easy to be understood; they ought not to depend upon construction or arbitrary discretion. . . .

But it has been also contended, on behalf of the State, that the offence with which the prisoner is charged, is a felony at common law, and that having been found guilty by the jury, he ought to be punished, independently of any Act of Assembly on the subject. This question arises out of the peculiarity of our situation; slavery not being known to the laws of England, from them we cannot derive our usual information. Sir William Blackstone says, liberty is so deeply implanted in the English Constitution, that the moment a slave lands there, he falls under the protection of the laws, and so far becomes a free man; though the master's right to his service may possibly continue. . . . From this expression, I understand the author's meaning to be, that the reason why the laws extend their protection to a slave is, because the moment he lands in England he undergoes a change, his condition is ameliorated, and in contemplation of law, at least, he is no longer a slave, but a free man. . . .

Slaves in this country possess no such rights; their condition is more abject; . . . they are not parties to our constitution; it was not made for them. What the powers of a master were over his slave, in this country, prior to the year 1774, have not been defined. I have not heard, that any convictions and capital punishments took place before that period, for killing of negroes. . . .

Justice Samuel Johnston: The murder of a slave, appears to me, a crime of the most atrocious and barbarous nature; much more so than killing a person who is free, and on an equal footing. It is an evidence of a most depraved and cruel disposition, to murder one, so much in your power, that he is incapable of making resistance, even in his own defense: and if, at any time, his conduct becomes so obnoxious that it cannot be longer borne by his master, he has it in his power to dispose of him and remove him to any distance he thinks proper. It is unnecessary to consider what punishment was annexed to the murder of slaves in other countries, either in ancient or modern times; the definition of murder, as laid down in our books, applies as forcibly to the murder of a slave as to the murder of a free man; and had there been nothing in our acts of Assembly, I should not hesitate on this occasion to have pronounced sentence of death on the prisoner.

But the act of 1791, after enacting "that if any person hereafter be guilty of wilfully and maliciously killing a slave, such offender shall, upon the first conviction thereof, be adjudged guilty of 'MURDER;' " had the act of Assembly stopped here, there could have been no doubt in the present case; but, when it goes on further to assign the punishment, it enacts in these words: "and shall suffer the same punishment as if he had killed a free man." The killing of a free man is punished in different ways, and, in some cases, no punishment is annexed to. . . .

Homicide, under the laws of this State, is divided into three classes: I. Murder, which is punishable with death and always attended with malice, express or implied: II. Manslaughter, which is done on a sudden provocation, unaccompanied with malice; for this offence the offender is entitled to his clergy: III. Simple homicide which is either justifiable or excusable, and for which the law of this State has inflicted no kind of punishment: the person charged being deemed unfortunate and not criminal. This is an offence first legislated upon by the act of 1774, and finally by this act of the General Assembly of 1791, which has not affixed either the punishment of murder or manslaughter to it, but that of killing a free man. The killing of a free man under such circumstances as amounts neither to murder or manslaughter, is no crime; no punishment can be inflicted; the person charged is to be acquitted and discharged on his payment of costs. Therefore judgment must be stayed and the prisoner discharged.

Judgment arrested.

Personal Character and Political Responsibility
NILES' WEEKLY REGISTER

The Constitution provided elections as a principal means of making government responsive and responsible to the people. Identifying potential candidates of appeal and ability proved to be a complex and difficult task. This Virginia editorial in support of General Andrew Jackson uses language, imagery, and values which would recommend Jackson to a wide audience. What moral traits qualify a person for public office? What sort of testing and adversity separate the ordinary person from the leader of a society? What evidence does Jackson give from his behavior that he will heed the concerns of his fellows and that he will lead the nation toward its true destiny?

MAJOR-GENERAL JACKSON

From the Richmond Enquirer

Some notice of the life and character of general Jackson will be desirable at this time to the readers of your columns — The distinguished post he at present occupies, the honorable manner in which he has brought the Creek war

From *Niles' Weekly Register,* March 18, 1815.

to a termination, the unexampled enthusiasm which he has instilled into his army in defence of the nation — and the confidence which he has every where obtained, through this vast country, has excited much curiosity on the part of the public, to become more intimately acquainted with him. . . . General Andrew Jackson was, as I am told, born in North Carolina, where he received a liberal education, and at an early age commenced the practice of the law. He was esteemed eminent in his profession — His speeches at the bar were always considered nervous and admired for the perspecuity of the style; he was pointed out to me, in Knoxville, as an elegant scholar. In early life he was poor, his industry soon made him rich — generous and brave in his disposition, he was esteemed by all who knew him — and his influence soon became extensive; he was elected a member of the Tennessee convention, and had a large share in the formation of the constitution of that state. On the admission of Tennessee into the union as a sister state, he was elected to the house of representatives, from which he was subsequently transferred by the legislature of Tennessee to the senate of the United States. This last station he occupied until he was appointed a judge of the supreme court of law and equity of Tennessee, which last named office he held for several years. On giving up this appointment which he filled with honor to himself and advantage to his country — he turned his attention to the military art and soon rose to the rank of major-general of militia. . . . His person remains to be noticed. He is tall, thin and spare, but muscular and hardy, with an eye quick and penetrating — I have frequently seen gen. Jackson, such was the impression his appearance made in my mind, that I have said to myself he is a man of iron — Adversity can make no impression on a bosom braced by such decision and firmness as is visible in his face and manners. Let not the reader conclude from this that he is haughty, distant and imperious — quite the contrary. It is true he sports not with the feelings of others — and no one is permitted to wound his with impunity; but then he is gay, communicative and liberal, and the more you know him, the more you admire and indeed love him. To be a patriot, a soldier and a gentleman, is sufficient to secure the inviolable friendship of this highly distinguished citizen. To the poor he is liberal, to the unfortunate charitable, to the humblest private he is mild and tender, to the base and disaffected to his country stern and unbending and yet just. He is now about fifty-five, but he has a juvenility of appearance that would make him ten years younger. The general is married, but has no children. If in the field and at the head of armies in battles we admire the dauntless soldier; we love the man who at home, and in retirement, is hospitable and friendly, and in this particular the general is pre-eminently conspicuous.

Private Will and Public Responsibility

ANDREW JACKSON

President Jackson vetoes the bill to recharter the Bank of the United States. To what public sentiments does Jackson respond? What overriding principles of political morality dictate his veto? Which factor is more important to Jackson? As president of a democratic republic, does he sense any conflict between the will of the people and his own conscience? If so, does he conceive of the presidency as an institution designed to reconcile such tensions?

Washington, July 10, 1832.

To the Senate:

The bill "to modify and continue" the act entitled "An act to incorporate the subscribers to the Bank of the United States" was presented to me on the 4th July instant. Having considered it with that solemn regard to the principles of the Constitution which the day was calculated to inspire, and come to the conclusion that it ought not to become a law, I herewith return it to the Senate, in which it originated, with my objections.

A bank of the United States is in many respects convenient for the Government and useful to the people. Entertaining this opinion, and deeply impressed with the belief that some of the powers and privileges possessed by the existing bank are unauthorized by the Constitution, subversive of the rights of the States, and dangerous to the liberties of the people, I felt it my duty at an early period of my Administration to call the attention of Congress to the practicability of organizing an institution combining all its advantages and obviating these objections. I sincerely regret that in the act before me I can perceive none of those modifications of the bank charter which are necessary, in my opinion, to make it compatible with justice, with sound policy, or with the Constitution of our country.

The present corporate body, denominated the president, directors, and company of the Bank of the United States, will have existed at the time this act is intended to take effect twenty years. It enjoys an exclusive privilege of banking under the authority of the General Government, a monopoly of its favor and support, and, as a necessary consequence, almost a monopoly of the foreign and domestic exchange. The powers, privileges, and favors bestowed upon it in the original charter, by increasing the value of the stock far above its par value, operated as a gratuity of many millions to the stockholders. . . .

Suspicions are entertained and charges are made of gross abuse and vio-

From James D. Richardson, ed., *Messages and Papers of the Presidents* (Washington, D.C., 1905–1909), II, 576–591 passim.

lation of its charter. An investigation unwillingly conceded and so restricted in time as necessarily to make it incomplete and unsatisfactory discloses enough to excite suspicion and alarm. In the practices of the principal bank partially unveiled, in the absence of important witnesses, and in numerous charges confidently made and as yet wholly uninvestigated there was enough to induce a majority of the committee of investigation — a committee which was selected from the most able and honorable members of the House of Representatives — to recommend a suspension of further action upon the bill and a prosecution of the inquiry. As the charter had yet four years to run, and as a renewal now was not necessary to the successful prosecution of its business, it was to have been expected that the bank itself, conscious of its purity and proud of its character, would have withdrawn its application for the present, and demanded the severest scrutiny into all its transactions. In their declining to do so there seems to be an additional reason why the functionaries of the Government should proceed with less haste and more caution in the renewal of their monopoly. . . .

Experience should teach us wisdom. Most of the difficulties our Government now encounters and most of the dangers which impend over our Union have sprung from an abandonment of the legitimate objects of Government by our national legislation, and the adoption of such principles as are embodied in this act. Many of our rich men have not been content with equal protection and equal benefits, but have besought us to make them richer by act of Congress. By attempting to gratify their desires we have in the results of our legislation arrayed section against section, interest against interest, and man against man, in a fearful commotion which threatens to shake the foundations of our Union. It is time to pause in our career to review our principles, and if possible revive that devoted patriotism and spirit of compromise which distinguished the sages of the Revolution and the fathers of our Union. If we can not at once, in justice to interests vested under improvident legislation, make our Government what it ought to be, we can at least take a stand against all new grants of monopolies and exclusive privileges, against any prostitution of our Government to the advancement of the few at the expense of the many, and in favor of compromise and gradual reform in our code of laws and system of political economy.

Public Responsibility vs. Private Will

DANIEL WEBSTER

Daniel Webster denounces Jackson's veto of the Bank recharter bill. Why is Jackson's moralistic language a threat to the very survival of republican government? How does Webster's view of human nature compare with Madison's? How has Jackson betrayed the special function of the presidency?

Mr. President, we have arrived at a new epoch. We are entering on experiments, with the government and the Constitution of the country, hitherto untried, and of fearful and appalling aspect. This message calls us to the contemplation of a future which little resembles the past. Its principles are at war with all that public opinion has sustained, and all which the experience of the government has sanctioned. It denies first principles; it contradicts truths, heretofore received as indisputable. It denies to the judiciary the interpretation of law, and claims to divide with Congress the power of originating statutes. It extends the grasp of executive pretension over every power of the government. But this is not all. It presents the chief magistrate of the Union in the attitude of arguing away the powers of that government over which he has been chosen to preside; and adopting for this purpose modes of reasoning which, even under the influence of all proper feeling towards high official station, it is difficult to regard as respectable. It appeals to every prejudice which may betray men into a mistaken view of their own interests, and to every passion which may lead them to disobey the impulses of their understanding. It urges all the specious topics of State rights and national encroachment against that which a great majority of the States have affirmed to be rightful, and in which all of them have acquiesced. It sows, in an unsparing manner, the seeds of jealousy and ill-will against that government of which its author is the official head. It raises a cry, that liberty is in danger, at the very moment when it puts forth claims to powers heretofore unknown and unheard of. It affects alarm for the public freedom, when nothing endangers that freedom so much as its own unparalleled pretenses. This, even, is not all. It manifestly seeks to inflame the poor against the rich; it wantonly attacks whole classes of the people, for the purpose of turning against them the prejudices and the resentments of other classes. It is a state paper which finds no topic too exciting for its use, no passion too inflammable for its address and its solicitation.

Such is this message. It remains now for the people of the United States to choose between the principles here avowed and their government. These can-

From Edward Everett, ed., *The Writings and Speeches of Daniel Webster* (Boston: Little, Brown and Co., 1903), VI, 179–180.

not subsist together. The one or the other must be rejected. If the sentiments of the message shall receive general approbation, the Constitution will have perished even earlier than the moment which its enemies originally allowed for the termination of its existence. It will not have survived to its fiftieth year.

◆ MODERN ESSAY ◆

Sex Discrimination and Expanding Political Responsibility

BARBARA BROWN, THOMAS I. EMERSON, GAIL FALK, and
ANN E. FREEDMAN

A legal brief in support of the Equal Rights Amendment to the Constitution insists that government is not, and cannot be, responsive to the claims of women for equality of opportunity, treatment, and protection. Why is the Constitution itself the central mechanism for correcting injustice, and why is constitutional amendment preferable to any other alternatives? How would Ames or Webster have reacted to the tone and argumentative style of this essay? What are the inescapable limits of those who would establish justice in a pluralistic society? Do the authors of this essay acknowledge such limitations and, if so, how do they deal with them? Is the task of defending human rights in American society significantly more difficult today than it was during the late eighteenth and early nineteenth centuries? Why?

American society has always confined women to a different and, by most standards, inferior status. The discrimination has been deep and pervasive. Yet in the past the subordinate position of more than half the population has been widely accepted as natural or necessary or divinely ordained. The women's rights movement of the late nineteenth and early twentieth centuries concentrated on obtaining the vote for women; only the most radical of the suffragists called into question the assumption that woman's place was in the home and under the protection of man. Now there has come a reawakening and a widespread demand for change. This time the advocates of women's rights are insisting upon a broad reexamination and redefinition of "woman's place."

From Barbara Brown, Thomas I. Emerson, Gail Falk, and Ann E. Freedman, "The Equal Rights Amendment: A Constitutional Basis for Equal Rights for Women." Reprinted by permission of The Yale Law Journal Company and Fred B. Rothman & Company from *The Yale Law Journal*, Vol. 80, 1971, pp. 872–880.

Historically, the subordinate status of women has been firmly entrenched in our legal system. At common law women were conceded few rights. Constitutions were drafted on the assumption that women did not exist as legal persons. Courts classified women with children and imbeciles, denying their capacity to think and act as responsible adults and enclosing them in the bonds of protective paternalism. Over the last century, it is true, the legal status of women has gradually improved. Common law rules have been altered in many states and some additional rights conferred by legislation. A marked advance was made in 1920 with the adoption of the Nineteenth Amendment granting suffrage to women. Since then, there has been other progress. But the development has been slow and haphazard. Major remnants of the common law's discriminatory treatment of women persist in the laws and institutions of all states. In addition, efforts during the past century to protect working women have created a new set of laws which turn out to discriminate against women rather than secure equality.

In the present legal structure, some laws exclude women from legal rights, opportunities, or responsibilities. Some are framed as legislation conferring special benefits, or protection, on women. Others create or perpetuate a separate legal status without indicating on their face whether the position of women ranks below, or above, the position of men. Many of the efforts to create a separate legal status for women stem from a good faith attempt to advance the interests of women. Nevertheless, the preponderant effect has been to buttress the social and economic subordination of women.

Our legal structure will continue to support and command an inferior status for women so long as it permits *any* differentiation in legal treatment on the basis of sex. This is so for three distinct but related reasons. First, discrimination is a necessary concomitant of any sex-based law because a large number of women do not fit the female stereotype upon which such laws are predicated. Second, all aspects of separate treatment for women are inevitably interrelated; discrimination in one area creates discriminatory patterns in another. Thus a woman who has been denied equal access to education will be disadvantaged in employment even though she receives equal treatment there. Third, whatever the motivation for different treatment, the result is to create a dual system of rights and responsibilities in which the rights of each group are governed by a different set of values. . . .

There are three methods of making changes within the legal system to assure equal rights for women. One is by extending to sex discrimination the doctrines of strict judicial review under the Equal Protection Clause of the Fourteenth Amendment. A second is by piecemeal revision of existing federal and state laws. The third is by a new constitutional amendment. These alternatives are not, of course, mutually exclusive. The basic question is what method, or combination of methods, will be most effective in eradicating sex discrimination from the law.

In past years many proponents of equal rights for women believed that the goal could be achieved through judicial interpretation of the Equal

Protection Clause, as applied to both state and federal governments. Thus the President's Commission on the Status of Women argued in 1963 that "the principle of equality [could] become firmly established in constitutional doctrine" through use of the Fourteenth and Fifth Amendments, and concluded that "a constitutional amendment need not now be sought." At the present time that viewpoint has been abandoned by active supporters of women's rights. The shift in position is fully justified. An examination of the decisions of the Supreme Court demonstrates that there is no present likelihood that the Court will apply the Equal Protection Clause in a manner that will effectively guarantee equality of rights for women. More important, equal protection doctrines, even in their most progressive form, are ultimately inadequate for that task.

Over the years, some proponents of women's rights have thought sex discrimination could be ended most effectively if legislatures prepared women and men gradually for equality by a series of step-by-step reforms. There is no constitutional obstruction to the elimination of discrimination in our legal system by the piecemeal revision or repeal of existing federal and state laws. However such suggestions unrealistically assume a delicacy and precision in the legislative process which has no relationship to actual legislative capability. More importantly, the process is unlikely to be completed within the lifetime of any woman now alive. Such a method requires multiple actions by fifty state legislatures and the federal congress, by the courts and executive agencies in each one of these jurisdictions, and by similar government authorities in numerous political subdivisions as well. This government machinery would have to be mobilized to repeal or modify the statutes and practices in scores of different areas where unequal treatment now prevails. To be comprehensive such efforts would require a tremendously expensive, sophisticated, and sustained political organization, both nationally and within every state and locality. Campaigns to change the laws one by one could drag on for many years, and perhaps in some areas never be finished. . . .

If expansion of the Equal Protection Clause and piecemeal legislation will not result in effective action, there remains the third alternative: a new constitutional amendment. Passage of a new amendment is a serious and difficult step, but we believe that it is a sensible, necessary means of achieving equal rights for women. A major reform in our legal and constitutional structure is appropriately accomplished by a formal alteration of the fundamental document. Claims of similar magnitude, such as the right to be free from discrimination on account of race, color, national origin, and religion, rest on a constitutional basis. The amending process is designed to elicit national ratification for changes in basic governing values, and those who feel that the Supreme Court has gone too far in recent years in effectuating constitutional change through interpretation should especially welcome the amending process.

Many of the reasons why piecemeal legislation is inadequate are also positive advantages in proceeding by amendment. The major political action — passage and ratification of the Amendment — can be accomplished by a single strong nationwide campaign of limited duration. Once passed, the

Amendment will provide an immediate mandate, a nationally uniform theory of sex equality, and the prospect of permanence to buttress individual and political efforts to end discrimination. The political and psychological impact of adopting a constitutional amendment will be of vital importance in actually realizing the goal of equality. Discriminatory laws, doctrines, attitudes and practices are set deep in our legal system. They are not easily dislodged. The expression of a national commitment by formal adoption of a constitutional amendment will give strength and purpose to efforts to bring about a far-reaching change which, for some, may prove painful.

There are likewise strong reasons for developing a consistent theory and program for women's equality under the aegis of an independent Equal Rights Amendment, rather than by judicial extension of the Equal Protection Clause. An amendment that deals with all sex discrimination, and only sex discrimination, corresponds roughly to the boundaries of a distinct and interrelated set of legal relationships. As already noted, woman's status before the law in one area, such as employment, relates both practically and theoretically to her status in other areas, such as education or responsibility for family support. Coming to grips with the dynamics of discrimination against women requires that we recognize the indications of, the excuses for, and the problems presented by women's inferior status. An understanding of these dynamics in any one field informs and enlightens understanding of sex bias elsewhere in the law. This is because, in the past, the legal and social systems have been permeated with a sometimes inchoate, but nevertheless pervasive, theory of women's inferiority. . . .

The basic principle of the Equal Rights Amendment is that sex is not a permissible factor in determining the legal rights of women, or of men. This means that the treatment of any person by the law may not be based upon the circumstance that such person is of one sex or the other. The law does, of course, impose different benefits or different burdens upon different members of the society. That differentiation in treatment may rest upon particular characteristics or traits of the persons affected, such as strength, intelligence, and the like. But under the Equal Rights Amendment the existence of such a characteristic or trait to a greater degree in one sex does not justify classification by sex rather than by the particular characteristic or trait. Likewise the law may make different rules for some people than for others on the basis of the activity they are engaged in or the function they perform. But the fact that in our present society members of one sex are more likely to be found in a particular activity or to perform a particular function does not allow the law to fix legal rights by virtue of membership in that sex. In short, sex is a prohibited classification. . . .

. . . Only an unequivocal ban against taking sex into account supplies a rule adequate to achieve the objectives of the Amendment.

From this analysis it follows that the constitutional mandate must be absolute. The issue under the Equal Rights Amendment cannot be different but equal, reasonable or unreasonable classification, suspect classification, fundamental interest, or the demands of administrative expediency. Equality of rights means that sex is not a factor. This at least is the premise of the Equal Rights Amendment. And this premise should be clearly expressed as the intention of Congress in submitting the Amendment to the states for ratification. . . .

The fundamental legal principle underlying the Equal Rights Amendment, then, is that the law must deal with particular attributes of individuals, not with a classification based on the broad and impermissible attribute of sex. This principle, however, does not preclude legislation (or other official action) which regulates, takes into account, or otherwise deals with a physical characteristic unique to one sex. In this situation it might be said that, in a certain sense, the individual obtains a benefit or is subject to a restriction because he or she belongs to one or the other sex. Thus a law relating to wet nurses would cover only women, and a law regulating the donation of sperm would restrict only men. Legislation of this kind does not, however, deny equal rights to the other sex. So long as the law deals only with a characteristic found in all (or some) women but *no* men, or in all (or some) men but *no* women, it does not ignore individual characteristics found in both sexes in favor of an average based on one sex. Hence such legislation does not, without more, violate the basic principle of the Equal Rights Amendment.

This subsidiary principle is limited to *physical* characteristics and does not extend to psychological, social or other characteristics of the sexes. The reason is that, so far as appears, it is only physical characteristics which can be said with any assurance to be unique to one sex. . . .

The transformation of our legal system to one which establishes equal rights for women under the law is long overdue. Our present dual system of legal rights has resulted, and can only result, in relegating half of the population to second class status in our society. What was begun in the Nineteenth Amendment, extending to women the right of franchise, should now be completed by guaranteeing equal treatment to women in all areas of legal rights and responsibilities. . . .

. . . There is a broad consensus in the women's movement that, within the sphere of governmental power, change must involve equal treatment of women with men. Moreover, the increasing nationwide pressure for passage of an Equal Rights Amendment, among women both in and out of the active women's movement, makes it clear that most women do not believe their interests are served by sexual differentiation before the law. Legal distinctions based upon sex have become politically and morally unacceptable.

In this context the Equal Rights Amendment provides a necessary and a particularly valuable political change. It will establish complete legal equality without compelling conformity to any one pattern within private relationships. Persons will remain free to structure their private activity and association without governmental interference. Yet within the sphere of state activity, the Amendment will establish fully, emphatically, and unambiguously the proposition that before the law women and men are to be treated without difference.

PART III

Manifest Destiny and Reform

Introduction

America's Mission
and How to Achieve It

In the past ten years Americans have clashed in lunchrooms in Atlanta and Birmingham; ghettos in New York, Chicago, Detroit and Los Angeles; suburbs of Pontiac, Michigan; Boston's settled Irish neighborhoods; Chicago's downtown loop; the wide malls and avenues of Washington, D.C.; the plains of Wounded Knee; campuses in Berkeley, California; Kent, Ohio; Orangeburg, South Carolina; Lawrence, Kansas; Madison, Wisconsin; and New York City.

The sources of these clashes ranged from minor campus inequities to the anguish of the Vietnam War and the nation's racial crisis. But underlying these specific issues, protestors and their opponents were asking a fundamental question, one as old as America itself: What should America be? How may it achieve the ideals which it has always claimed to cherish? Does the nation's role require it to secure democracy throughout the world, to create at home a society which will be an example to the world, or to achieve both these goals?

Americans have always worried about the mission of this nation in the world. The first colonists were told by their leaders that they had come not just to satisfy themselves, but to be an example to the world of the way in which God's people should live. They saw that their way of life, therefore, had a meaning for the world — it was the way that people everywhere might emulate. This feeling was undiminished when our Revolution declared to the world not only our independence, but the fact that this new nation would be founded on self-evident truths, laws of nature. Again, we announced that there was something special about this country. It was not just a nation with its own peculiar ways of doing things, no better or worse than other countries with different ideals and customs. We were first God's nation and then Nature's nation. We were, to use Carl Sandburg's words, "the greatest city and the greatest nation. Nothing like us ever was."

This self-idealization has had great power in shaping our character and activities as a people. We are the world's most energetic reformers, constantly urging each other to end all evils, yet our achievements belie our hopes: poverty in the midst of wealth, monopoly in an allegedly free market economy, discrimination where all people are supposed to be born equal, authoritarian manipulation of what we believe should be the people's institutions. Our high ideals have generated the desire to reform and to improve our nation in every era.

In addition to provoking internal reform, our ideals produce immense pressures on our foreign policy. If we are truly the greatest nation in the world, if every person in the world secretly prefers to live as we do, if our institutions offer the greatest hope for liberty, wealth, stability, and individual happiness, shouldn't Americans reach out and help the world be like America? Don't we have a responsibility because of our many blessings to promote, protect, and energize democracy abroad? Perhaps we should even use our wealth and power to expand our way of life in other countries. If we were not a great power, these questions would not be asked, but because of our power as a nation, we face them daily.

This belief in the mission of America has an aspect other than expansionism. Opponents of expansionism have invoked the idea in support of noninvolvement in the world. They argue that America's influence must be exerted by example, not by force. Our influence must arise from creating an admirable society within our borders. We must be a city on the hill, not an expanding empire. Creating a humane, egalitarian, open, and free society is the strongest insurance that what we believe in will help shape the world. Although the argument between these two viewpoints shows itself most often in disputes over our foreign policy, it appears also in questions about domestic spending priorities. Should we spend money to go to the moon, or to save our cities? Should we expand into space, or expand the possibilities and opportunities of racial minorities and the poor?

In the years 1824–1848, America squarely faced the question of her mission. Two dominant issues became entangled, and in so doing, shaped the ways in which this nation perceived itself and how it would face the crises ahead. The issues were the existence of slavery in what was claimed to be the world's freest society, and the ways in which we should expand our influence in the western hemisphere.

Agitation against slavery had begun as early as 1688, and had gained influence during the American Revolution under the credo, "All men are created equal." But as decades passed and this ideal remained theoretical only, opposition to slavery gained intensity. In 1831, William Lloyd Garrison trumpeted a new era in antislavery tactics — immediate abolition passionately proclaimed in language "as harsh as truth, and as uncompromising as justice." Citing the realization of the principles of the Declaration of Independence as his goal, Garrison claimed that the time for moderation and cautious advance toward these ideals had passed. Slavery corrupted the nation's purpose, destroyed the lives of blacks, and turned whites into hypocrites. It was time to abandon restraints and leap toward a free society. "On this subject," Garrison continued, "I do not wish to think or speak or write with moderation. No! No! Tell a man whose house is on fire to give a moderate alarm; tell him to moderately rescue his wife from the hands of the ravisher; tell the mother to gradually extricate her babe from the fire into which it has fallen — but urge me not to use moderation in a cause like the present."

Few people disagreed with Garrison's ideals. If the nation was serious about its mission, if it sought to live the ideals it asserted, then slavery was in fact an evil to be eliminated. What made people reluctant to embrace Garrison's call was its stridency — its uncompromising nature — and its militance. His opponents argued that he made enemies for the antislavery cause by his extremism, that he would have been more effective working for change within the system than shouting outside of it. They insisted that he magnified the evils of slavery beyond reality and that he discredited his cause by the unrestrained heat with which he called the nation to its goals. His answer was simple and direct, "I have need to be on fire, for I have mountains of ice around me to melt."

In 1964, Republican presidential candidate Barry Goldwater was attacked for the extremism of his rhetoric in calling for changes in the United States. His answer was similarly direct, "Extremism in defense of liberty is no vice. Moderation in pursuit of justice is no virtue." Four years later, protest movements, violence, and agitation swept across the country with demands for black power, gay liberation, an end to the Vietnam War, student power. The beginnings of the Women's Liberation Movement began to emerge, as did militant agitation for the rights of Indians. In 1976, the People's Bicentennial Movement continued the tradition of insisting that the evils of the system were grotesque and that the time to end them was *now*. Though campuses have quieted and cities no longer burn, though the voices of minority protest are muted and only occasionally do blood and fire and bullets shatter the rather placid scene, the tradition of agitation obviously endures. Questions about the best way to awaken a nation to reform abide: In calling a nation to live up to its goals, what are the best tactics? extreme language? marches in the street? private acts of civil disobedience? political organization? violence? The second part of this section is an attempt to involve students and faculty in a discussion of this issue.

First, however, we want to direct attention to an aspect of the search for mission in America which touches more directly on the role of America in the world. As we withdraw from our involvement in Vietnam, it is tempting to think that we can divert attention from such issues, but an end to military engagement in Southeast Asia does not eliminate the fact that we are the strongest nation in the world and thus have interests in almost every corner of the globe. The crucial issue is not whether we should be involved with the world: there is no escaping from such involvement. The true issue is what emphasis our involvement should have — physical participation in the affairs of other nations, or concentration on building a great society in our own country. Of course, neither of these alternatives can be adopted to the exclusion of the other. What is of concern in these pages is the question of degree. It is a question with which mid-nineteenth-century Americans also were very familiar.

In the early 1840s, the nation was in an expansionist mood. Americans were in the Northwest disputing with English traders the right to the lands of Oregon. Texas, which had successfully revolted from Mexico in 1836, was asking to be admitted to the Union. In California, our citizens were deploring Mexico's misrule and neglect of the territory which now comprises all of the southwestern United States. There was a general feeling that this nation had come of age and was ready to flex its muscles. Andrew Jackson's election signaled the triumph of democratic America. Intellectuals like Ralph Waldo Emerson, William Cullen Bryant, and James Fenimore Cooper began to extol the unique, vital, and promising qualities of the nation. The personal success of individuals seeking their fortunes endorsed such claims, and reformers promised to eliminate any evils that might remain. In such an atmosphere it was almost impossible to avoid believing in the special mission of America, and perhaps even in its manifest destiny to reach out its arms and embrace the less fortunate people of the whole western hemisphere. A lusty, boisterous, and proud nation, the kind exemplified in the careers of self-made men such as Thomas Hart Benton, was clearly ready to assert itself.

But how to do so? Senators, editors, legislators, presidents, and average citizens debated the question. And they did not agree. Daniel Webster exemplified the argument of those who insisted that we should be an example, not a conqueror: "You have a Sparta," he said. "Embellish her!" But other ideas prevailed. When the dispute with England over the Oregon boundary broke into the open, many men endorsed the militant cry, "Fifty-four forty, or fight." There was no fight in this case, though there was no 54°40′ either. The present forty-nine-degree boundary was agreed to. But Mexico gave us the fight we seemed to be spoiling for, and here the debate over expansion or example reached its peak. So compelling was the insistence on expanding U.S. interest and influence that Americans would argue the question into the 1850s regarding Hungary, southern Mexico, and Yucatan. The events of the current decade, particularly the role of moralism in American foreign policy, suggest that the debate goes on, and that it should.

One person who contributed to this debate in the nineteenth century, and who lived a life linked to its resolution, was Thomas Hart Benton. As both an ambitious and successful politician and as a private citizen, he had a large personal stake in the destiny of America. His personal star was tied to the rise of this nation in the world. He believed that the God-given superiority of Americans promised them a noble future. Like most Americans of his age, Benton tried to avoid the question of what the existence of slavery in this country meant to such optimistic hopes. His most frequent response when he dealt with the issue was to attack those who agitated about it.

But the issue could not be avoided. Benton was forced to wonder how mission and slavery might be linked, about the meaning of the nation and its people, about their ability to fulfill their potential, and about the obstacles that stood in the way. His biography allows us to see how such concerns were interwoven with the life and personality of a truly striking man.

Personalizing the Issues

Thomas Hart Benton:
The Roman Gladiator
of the American West

"What then is this new man, this American?" J. Hector St. John de Crèvecoeur asked this provocative question in 1780, and students of the American character have been trying to answer it ever since. If we look for a man whose life and accomplishments might have symbolized the answer to this question during the ante-bellum era, we would look no further than the floor of the Senate of the United States between 1821 and 1851. There, the towering presence of a western giant, Thomas Hart Benton, would be found addressing — or haranguing — his fellow senators.

Clay, Webster, and Calhoun, the three most famous senators of the era, were great men. But their contemporaries considered the senator from Missouri their equal, or superior, in many ways. Little wonder. With the possible exception of Andrew Jackson, no man symbolized the contemporary concept of democracy better than Thomas Hart Benton. Unlike the famous triumvirate, he did not represent special interests, such as planters or businessmen; indeed, he was the greatest proponent of the worth of the common man and woman in his era. Long before it became fashionable to do so, he championed the cause and spread of democracy. Accepting the Greek definition of the word — "the people, the majority" — he often stated, "Benton and the people, Benton and democracy, are one and the same, sir. Synonymous terms."

Since Benton lived in an egalitarian age, it is possible that he stated "democracy" and "Benton" as synonymous terms for political reasons. A careful study of his political life, however, illustrates that he believed what he said. But one should not confuse Benton's concept of democracy with the modern version. As Whig leader Henry Clay often noted, Jacksonian Democracy ignored many minority groups and sat firmly entrenched upon the institution of chattel slavery. The Jacksonians considered abolitionists dangerous radicals; Mexicans as incapable of political responsibility; Indians as a barrier to the achievement of the national mission; they argued strenuously that English-speaking peoples had a genius for government. This last view, however, did not stop Benton from declaring that the Oregon dispute with England could be settled by letting the American "emigrants go on" to Oregon. When there were "thirty thousand rifles in the valley," he declared, "they will make all quiet there. . . ." The militant nature of his democracy was even clearer when he spoke on the Indian question. While he admitted they were the "victims of the American Destiny," their fate was foreordained because the "White race" had a superior right to the land since they "used it according to the intentions of the CREATOR."

Obviously, Benton was a product of his era, but as such, he gained the admiration and respect of both contemporaries and historians for his great moral courage. While Webster, once the great sectionalist became the great nationalist, and Calhoun, once the great nationalist became the great sectionalist, each in response to the changing mood of their constituents, Benton seldom vacillated. He stood against his constituents, his senatorial colleagues, his party, his president, and his family whenever he thought them in error. In 1856, for example, he campaigned for the Democratic candidate, James Buchanan, whom he despised, against the candidate of the Republican party, his son-in-law John C. Fremont, because Benton believed a victory for a sectional party would lead to a civil war. Considering his intense devotion to his favorite daughter, Jessie Benton Fremont, one can only imagine the agonizing price of his convictions.

But if any single factor epitomized his claim to being a representative man of his age, it was Benton's fanatical devotion to the concept that America was the great noble experiment in democracy which would stand as a beacon light to a misguided world. He devoted his life to bringing about the legal and political reforms that would make the United States the "City Upon a Hill" that the Puritans had tried to create. In most of these political battles, Thomas Hart Benton, as the Democratic floor leader in the Senate, and not his more famous colleagues, was victorious.

Born in the hills of North Carolina in 1782, Benton grew up on the Tennessee frontier and migrated to Missouri, where he established the second newspaper west of the Mississippi River. In 1830, he became the state's first senator. But his path to fame — only fame, never fortune — was not an easy one, and en route he had to overcome a great personal disgrace and a public scandal.

The disgrace occurred at the age of sixteen when he was expelled from the University of North Carolina for stealing. He vowed at that point to redeem himself and learn as much as any college man. He achieved both goals. As a senator he refused to accept the many gratuities which were offered him. While these subsidies were not considered bribes or conflicts of interest as they are today, his behavior was in sharp contrast to that of Daniel Webster. The Massachusetts senator, for example, calmly reminded the president of the Bank of the United States, shortly before Webster was to defend the Bank in Congress, that "as yet I have not received my retainer." Certainly if Benton had accepted a few such retainers he would not have lost his house for failure to pay a $2,000 mortgage. His integrity was so above dispute that the University of North Carolina later bestowed an honorary degree upon him. As to his other goal, self-education, he became one of the most knowledgeable men of his era. Even his opponents admitted that he seemed to walk around with the Congressional Library tucked away comfortably in his head.

The scandal occurred during the War of 1812. Having moved to Tennessee after his youthful disgrace, Benton worked hard as a farmer, teacher, and self-educated lawyer, and became a respected member of the community. When the War of 1812 started, he was appointed a Colonel of the Volunteers under Andrew Jackson. As such, Benton earned great respect for his organizational abilities. "Old Hickory" often sent him on missions to procure supplies. Once when Benton was off on such a mission, his younger brother, Jesse, became involved in a duel with another of Jackson's officers, William Carroll. In an effort to convince both men of their folly, Jackson agreed to be Carroll's second. But the general's attempt at peacemaking failed, and the two men engaged in a duel which left poor Jesse Benton wounded in the buttocks which, of course, is not the usual place for a dueling scar. Just how it came about is not clear. Carroll insisted that Jesse Benton shot, panicked, and swerved, leaving his *derrière* exposed. The legend grew in the Benton family, however, that due to Billy Carroll's poor eyesight, Jackson had arranged for the duel to be fought from a crouch, and Carroll supposedly swung around too soon.

Whichever version was correct, Benton believed his brother's story, and through letters and intermediaries he let his anger be known. At first Jackson denied any wrongdoing, but then he fired back as many angry words as his subordinate. When their tempers reached the kindling point, the two men, now earnest adversaries, met in a Nashville hotel. Each man was well armed and accompanied by several friends who eagerly anticipated the encounter. When Jackson saw Thomas Hart Benton he reportedly screamed, "Now defend yourself, you damned rascal!" But for once Jackson came off second best. Thomas's bullet wounded him badly, and in the heat of the ensuing battle "Old Hickory" almost bled to death. The eagerly awaited duel soon degenerated into a brawl as Thomas Hart Benton, dueling with several of Jackson's men, stumbled down a flight of stairs, while Jesse was saved from death only when his opponent's sword broke on the metal button of Jesse's overcoat. As the perplexed man stood over his opponent with his broken sword, Jesse Benton stuck a pistol in his opponent's face and pulled the trigger, but the gun misfired.

At this juncture, someone noticed Jackson's plight and carried him downstairs. The victorious Benton picked up Jackson's sword and broke it over his knee. But this was the angry gesture of an otherwise defeated man. With an enemy like Jackson, there was little future for Benton in Tennessee, so he moved to Missouri, where he became an editor. At first he made no attempt to improve his blustering ways, and once he killed a man in a duel at nine feet. But the sight of the dead man tempered the previously uncontrollable frontiersman. Thereafter, he limited his dueling to words, but he became so brutal with them that many of his opponents would have preferred swords so they would at least have had a chance against the thick-skinned Missourian. While "thick-skinned" usually applies to someone who is insensible to verbal abuse, Benton was also literally "thick-skinned": he followed the practice of the Roman gladiators and brushed his skin daily with a horsehair brush.

As a young lawyer in Tennessee, Benton had fought for equality before the law for all people, even for slaves in cases involving the death penalty. He continued this battle in Missouri and added a new cause, one that was to give him his nickname of "Old Bullion." According to Benton, bullion (hard money) was the only reliable currency. Paper money, then issued by local banks, was often unreliable since its value fluctuated with the stability of each bank. Because so many banks were dishonest, Benton took it upon himself to barge in — uninvited — to investigate their books. This action brought him several lawsuits, but much success. What he found seems incredible by modern standards. In one bank, he kicked over several barrels which were supposed to be full of hard money only to discover that they were full of nails, topped off by coins. In another instance he exposed a bank that added zeroes to its currency when it was reissued, so that a $10 bill instantly became a $100 bill.

His flamboyant behavior made him very popular in Missouri, and in 1821, when the territory became a state, Benton was elected to fill one of Missouri's two Senate seats. He became the first man in American history to serve in the Senate for thirty consecutive years. As such he also became one of the greatest exponents of democracy and political reform in the nation's history. Even before Jackson made it part of his annual appeal, Benton proposed the direct election of the president to make that office more responsible to the will of the people.

His greatest battle, however, was for a democratic land policy. Many politicians, including Webster, Calhoun, and Clay, argued for a high price for land; Webster and Calhoun because that policy protected the interests they represented, and Clay because he wanted money to pay for the internal improvements the West needed so badly. Benton argued, however, that land ownership was a right of all Americans, and that the nation would benefit from widespread economic democracy. For this reason he fought for preemption, graduation, and reduction. Pre-emption, or squatters' rights, as it was called, gave original settlers the opportunity of buying land upon which they had "squatted" before it was legally open to sale. Such land, which was more valuable than unimproved land, often fell into the hands of rich speculators who took advantage of undemocratic land laws. Graduation, a policy dear to Benton, called for the adjustment of the price of land relative to its value. Federal lands, regardless of their value, were sold for the same price, again to the advantage of the speculators. Reduction, of course, was the overall lowering of the price of land. Western historians have noted that these, as well as the programs which were combined to become the Homestead Act shortly after Benton's death, were first proposed by the nationalistic senator from the West. So too were the programs which eventually became the Pony Express, the Sante Fe Road, and the transcontinental railroad.

It is indeed ironic that Benton almost killed Jackson, because they later reestablished their friendship and "Old Bullion" became one of the most typical and effective Jacksonians. The reconciliation occurred in 1825 when the two men, then both senators, were placed on the same committee with "Old Hickory" as the chairman. One day, as the two men sat beside each other in the Senate, Jackson turned to Benton and informed him, "Colonel, we are on the same committee; I will give you notice when to attend." Benton graciously replied that Jackson could "make the time to suit" himself. Shortly after that Jackson left his card at the Benton lodgings and Benton returned the call.

Recent scholars have noted that the passionate beliefs of the two frontiersmen created the false impression that both were unreasonable. Such was not always the case. Jackson could never have played the instrumental role he did in building the Democratic Party if he was not a man of conciliation. Benton, moreover, could not have pushed the Jackson program through the Senate if he treated everyone the way he treated Jackson in the Nashville hotel, or the defenders of slavery late in his life. Indeed, the two men had a great interaction which helped develop Democratic ideology. Benton's zest for democracy in government, and Jackson's for economy in government, significantly changed the political ideals of both men. Under Benton's influence,

Jackson accepted the idea that rotation in office was a democratic reform designed to get the scoundrels out of office. And whatever it became later when it was known as the "Spoils System," it was at first a necessary democratic reform. Conversely, Benton amended his policy on internal improvements to accept only those which were obviously national in nature. Previously, as a western man, Benton welcomed all internal improvements as necessary for national expansion.

Despite the fact that Benton was the successful Senate floor leader for the Democrats against Clay, Webster, and Calhoun, his contemporary image was created during the period of his life in which he independently stood against his section, his constituency, his party, and his president. Before James K. Polk became president in 1845, Benton opposed the annexation of Texas. Like many of his northern colleagues, this great exponent of expansionism considered Texas a "slavery plot hatched by Calhoun." But Benton was not the only southerner who opposed the Calhoun plan for annexing Texas in the spring of 1844 without first negotiating with Mexico. Nine of the twenty southern senators voted against Calhoun's attempt to add Texas to the Union in June of 1844. Only after the election of James K. Polk in November of that year on a militantly expansionist platform did Benton and his colleagues alter their stand. Accepting the election of a "Dark Horse" candidate as a political mandate, they voted to accept annexation in December of 1844.

Eight southern senators stood with Benton in his early opposition to the annexation of Texas, but when he again voted with the North to give Oregon a territorial government without slavery, he had no such support. His vote, along with that of his fellow slaveholder Sam Houston, carried the measure by two votes. His behavior on both issues alienated the South and his party, yet it was not inconsistent with his Democratic ideology nor his idealization of popular rule. The Jacksonians idealistically argued that the "second sober judgment" of the American people could never be wrong. Only a politician who had the courage to stand against public opinion could force his constituents to use that "second sober judgment."

By the late 1840s Benton was a man without a party or president, as he also split with James K. Polk when the latter justifiably upheld the verdict of a court martial that found Benton's son-in-law, John C. Fremont, guilty of insubordination. But his great defection was his refusal to join southerners who wanted to rally around the cause of slavery. His first defection occurred in 1847 when he opposed Calhoun's resolution defending the "peculiar institution" of slavery from northern attacks. Frightened by the rise of political abolitionism, Calhoun not only defended slavery, but also questioned the constitutionality of the Missouri Compromise, which prohibited slavery from those areas of the Louisiana Purchase (except Missouri) above 36°30'. Both Polk and Benton considered the slavery question settled by the Compromise of 1820–1821, but it was the senator who attacked Calhoun. The South Carolinian, Benton said, was "introducing needless firebrands to set the world on fire." He refused to sign Calhoun's resolution, and when his colleague asked him where he stood, he defiantly replied, "With the Union, sir."

Many historians have noted that Benton was a confused mixture of southern agrarianism and western vision. No better illustration of this confused mixture exists than Benton's ambivalent attitude toward expansion. Whenever expansion appeared to him to be a "slavery plot," he opposed such efforts vigorously. But whenever expansion appeared as a natural extension of the concept of Anglo-Saxon manifest destiny, he supported such efforts, and his statements in the *Congressional Globe* in 1846 on the "Superior Race and Divine Command" are strikingly similar to those expressed in the militantly pro-southern *De Bow's Review* on the necessity for the annexation of Mexico.

As a border state senator, however, he dreaded the civil war which extremism could bring about. For these reasons, he not only opposed southern extremists, but abolitionists as well. While he recognized that only the issue of race kept both slavery and sectionalism alive, he denounced what he called the "fanatics" of both sections. In 1835, for example, the great exponent of democracy accepted the "gag rule," which denied the right of petition to abolitionists because "their constitutional right" was dividing the nation on an "abstract issue." He further argued that the abolitionist crusade did great injury to the slaves, as it angered slaveholders and caused the bonds of the slaves "to be drawn tighter around them." Noting the bloody rebellions characteristic of the West Indies (which he attributed to incendiary abolitionists), he pleaded with them to stop their agitation before America was also engulfed in violent rebellion.

While he attacked all "fanatics," Benton made no attempt to defend slavery, saving his most devastating attacks for his southern colleagues. Thus his attack upon Calhoun in 1847 was just one more battle in the Benton–Calhoun duel that started during the early days of Jacksonian Democracy. Benton was contemptuous of Calhoun because of his inconsistent support of the Democratic Party, and referred to him as John "Cataline" (the famous Roman traitor) Calhoun. While Calhoun's behavior was based on principles as deeply felt as Benton's own, "Old Bullion" considered the South Carolinian an opportunist. Thus the battle between the two men continued for a quarter of a century and was so fierce that when Calhoun died someone sarcastically asked Benton if he were planning to continue the vilification of his dead colleague. Equally sarcastic, Benton replied that he would not because, "When the good Lord put his hand upon a man, sir, I take mine off." Furthermore, because he thought most of Calhoun's resolutions were "fungus cancers" that would destroy the nation, he was the only important senator who refused to deliver a eulogy for the departed South Carolinian. Since he had earlier angered the South with his eloquent words for the deceased abolitionist John Quincy Adams, whose integrity "Old Bullion" respected, this refusal was doubly annoying to the South.

Despite his lifelong struggle with Calhoun, his most dramatic encounter occurred with another senator, Henry "Hangman" Foote of Mississippi. Foote unwittingly earned the title of "Hangman" when he offered to hang any abolitionist senator who ever came to Mississippi. A fiery little man who fought four duels and was wounded in three of them, Foote was one of the few senators who verbally abused Benton and tried to provoke him to physical combat. He was aided in this by the southern sympathizer Vice President Millard Fillmore, who ignored the abuse as he presided over the Senate. For some reason Benton refused to respond, possibly because he thought the Congress was spending too much time on the "abstract" issue of slavery. This "abstract issue," he argued, which had been settled by the Missouri Compromise, sidetracked America from its great mission. As he lamented:

> We ... owe a great example to a struggling and agonized world. ... They see us almost in a state of disorganization — legislation paralyzed — distant territories left without government — [and] violent outrage on the floors of Congress. ... Our ancestors ... left us the admiration of the friends of freedom through the world. And are we to spoil this rich inheritance — mar this noble work — discredit this great example — and throw the weight of the republic against the friends of freedom throughout the world?

Once during a furious six-week debate over one part of the Compromise of 1850, Benton lost his temper and fiercely marched down the aisle towards his smaller opponent. Foote pulled a pistol and aimed it at the hulking figure marching toward him, but Benton boldly moved on shouting, "I have no pistols! Let him fire! ... Let the assassin fire!" Fortunately, other senators disarmed Foote, who had retreated, and they also halted Benton's march. "Assassin" Foote, as he was now called by northerners, vowed that he would write a small book in which his fracas with Benton would play a big part; Benton countered by saying that he would write a large book which would not feature the encounter at all. Foote never wrote his book, but Benton completed his two-volume history of the Democratic party, *Thirty Years' View,* which is still an American classic.

The encounter with Foote illustrated many of Benton's strongest characteristics, including his monumental ego. When asked how many copies of *Thirty Years' View* should be published, he replied, "Look to the census," as every "family would want one." He overestimated grossly, but his history sold 70,000 copies, a phenomenal number in that era.

Benton was easily *the* braggart in an era of braggarts. Once when informed that a boy had walked twenty miles barefoot to hear him speak, Benton patted the lad on the head and said, "You done right." In his later years, when asked if he had known General Jackson, he replied, "Yes, sir, I knew him, sir; General Jackson was a great man, sir. I shot him, sir. Afterward he was of great use to me, sir, in *my* battle with the Bank." But the ultimate example of "Old Bullion's" ego occurred when he attended a banquet at which he was toasted first as "the greatest man in the Senate," then "as the greatest man there ever was in the Senate," and finally as "the greatest man there ever will be in the Senate." To these he merely replied, "Friends, you have done me simple justice." While in an insecure age his ego might have been offensive, in the Jackson era it was not. Clay and Webster each thought of themselves as the greatest men of their time; Calhoun doubted them both since all three of them could not share this distinction.

But in his last years in the Senate, Benton's ego, combined with his anger at his isolation, made him a vindictive opponent. He left so many opponents mentally destroyed as he heaped facts from his encyclopedic mind and abuse from his uncontrollable tongue upon them, that they had little sympathy for him when the Missouri state legislature refused to reelect him to the Senate after thirty years of service. Yet as unpopular as he became, his ego, his passionate defense of his beliefs, and his devotion to duty made him as representative a man of his age as then existed. The age was as much his as it was Jackson's. Indeed, it would not be too much to state that the Age of Jackson ended with the failure of Thomas Hart Benton to be reelected to the Senate in 1850 as manifest destiny, the growth of democracy, and the issues of the Jackson era were set aside as the nation concentrated on fulfilling its mission by dealing with a major obstacle to the "City Upon a Hill": the peculiar institution of slavery.

Issue

The Mission of America

[Our] responsibility continues — not only as a task we shoulder for others or in fulfillment of our ideals, but as a responsibility to ourselves — to create a world environment in which America and its values can thrive.

Henry Kissinger, 1976

I should like to see the world redeemed . . . and whilst I feel a devotion, amounting to idolatry, for my country and her institutions and her peculiar form of government . . . I would not impose it upon one single solitary being on earth.

J. C. Jones, 1849

Two themes form the foundation of the argument over America's role in the world: they are the idea of mission and the idea of manifest destiny. Although people who use these terms often do not discriminate between them, historians have found it useful to make a distinction. By *mission* we usually mean activity which has a domestic focus: the establishment of an example at home rather than the foreign expansion of our power. *Manifest destiny* refers to the physical expansion of American power abroad. This expansion is justified as a clearly apparent part of our destiny as a people — thus the use of force is justified in achieving our goal. Indians, blacks, Mexicans, the English, French, Spanish, and Russians — all the people and powers who have contested our alleged duty to control this continent and dominate this hemisphere have felt the power of manifest destiny.

Yet the misdeeds of manifest destiny should not lead us to conclude that our only proper focus of attention is at home. However much Americans may wish to turn their backs on the world, it keeps tapping us on the shoulder. Our nation has interests which transcend its borders. Our wish for continued security and prosperity cannot be satisfied unless we are involved in the international arena.

Security against hostile foreign influence in bordering countries is an obvious requirement for a safe America; access to certain natural resources is an important factor for a prosperous America; the continued survival of friendly nations helps maintain a secure America. Sustaining hope in the hearts of others that liberty and equality may exist wherever people desire them may validate our faith in this nation's ideals. These factors argue for some reconciliation of the concepts implicit in the words *mission* and *manifest destiny*.

As you read the following, consider the sources of both the mission and manifest destiny arguments. Try to determine the strengths and weaknesses of both. Attempt to discover possible compromises between the two. In short, try to determine on what basis this nation should participate in the world.

◆ DOCUMENTS ◆

The Mission of the Anglo-Saxon Race
THOMAS HART BENTON

Senator Thomas Hart Benton asserts American superiority over other nations and races. Why does he believe we are superior? What are the limits of our ability to expand? What respect should we show to the wishes and needs of other races and countries?

From U.S., Congress, Senate, *Congressional Globe,* 29th Cong., 1st sess., May 28, 1846, pp. 917–918.

Since the dispersion of man upon earth, I know of no human event, past or to come, which promises a greater, and more beneficent change upon earth than the arrival of the van of the Caucasian race (the Celtic-Anglo-Saxon division) upon the border of the sea which washes the shore of the eastern Asia. The Mongolian, or Yellow race, is there, four hundred millions in number, spreading almost to Europe; a race once the foremost of the human family in the arts of civilization, but torpid and stationary for thousands of years. It is a race far above the Ethiopian, or Black — above the Malay, or Brown, (if we must admit five races) — and above the American Indian, or Red; it is a race far above all these, but still, far below the White; and, like all the rest, must receive an impression from the superior race whenever they come in contact. It would seem that the White race alone received the divine command, to subdue and replenish the earth! for it is the only race that has obeyed it — the only one that hunts out new and distant lands, and even a New World, to subdue and replenish. Starting from western Asia, taking Europe for their field, and the Sun for their guide, and leaving the Mongolians behind, they arrived, after many ages, on the shores of the Atlantic, which they lit up with the lights of science and religion, and adorned with the useful and the elegant arts. Three and a half centuries ago, this race, in obedience to the great command, arrived in the New World, and found new lands to subdue and replenish. For a long time it was confined to the border of the new field, (I now mean the Celtic-Anglo-Saxon division;) and even fourscore years ago the philosophic Burke was considered a rash man because he said the English colonists would top the Alleganies, and descend into the valley of the Mississippi, and occupy without parchment if the Crown refused to make grants of land. What was considered a rash declaration eighty years ago, is old history, in our young country, at this day. Thirty years ago I said the same thing of the Rocky Mountains and the Columbia: it was ridiculed then: it is becoming history to-day. The venerable Mr. Macon has often told me that he remembered a line low down in North Carolina, fixed by a royal governor as a boundary between the whites and the Indians: where is that boundary now? The van of the Caucasian race now top the Rocky Mountains, and spread down to the shores of the Pacific. In a few years a great population will grow up there, luminous with the accumulated lights of European and American civilization. Their presence in such a position cannot be without its influence upon eastern Asia. The sun of civilization must shine across the sea: socially and commercially, the van of the Caucasians, and the rear of the Mongolians, must intermix. They must talk together, and trade together, and marry together. Commerce is a great civilizer — social intercourse as great — and marriage greater. The White and Yellow races can marry together, as well as eat and trade together. Moral and intellectual superiority will do the rest: the White race will take the ascendant, elevating what is susceptible of improvement — wearing out what is not. The Red race has disappeared from the Atlantic coast: the tribes that resisted civilization, met extinction. This is a cause of lamentation with many. For my part, I cannot murmur at what seems to be the effect of divine law. I cannot repine that this Capitol has replaced the wigwam —

this Christian people, replaced the savages — white matrons, the red squaws — and that such men as Washington, Franklin, and Jefferson, have taken the place of Powhattan, Opechonecanough, and other red men, howsoever respectable they may have been as savages. Civilization, or extinction, has been the fate of all people who have found themselves in the track of the advancing Whites, and civilization, always the preference of the Whites, has been pressed as an object, while extinction has followed as a consequence of its resistance. The Black and the Red races have often felt their ameliorating influence. The Yellow race, next to themselves in the scale of mental and moral excellence, and in the beauty of form, once their superiors in the useful and elegant arts, and in learning, and still respectable though stationary; this race cannot fail to receive a new impulse from the approach of the Whites, improved so much since so many ages ago they left the western borders of Asia. The apparition of the van of the Caucasian race, rising upon them in the east after having left them on the west, and after having completed the circumnavigation of the globe, must wake up and reanimate the torpid body of old Asia. Our position and policy will commend us to their hospitable reception: political considerations will aid the action of social and commercial influences. Pressed upon by the great Powers of Europe — the same that press upon us — they must in our approach hail the advent of friends, not of foes — of benefactors, not of invaders. The moral and intellectual superiority of the White race will do the rest: and thus, the youngest people, and the newest land, will become the reviver and the regenerator of the oldest.

It is in this point of view, and as acting upon the social, political, and religious condition of Asia, and giving a new point of departure to her ancient civilization, that I look upon the settlement of the Columbia river by the van of the Caucasian race as the most momentous human event in the history of man since his dispersion over the face of the earth.

Our Hemispheric Mission

JAMES K. POLK

President Polk reaffirms the United States' commitment to the Monroe Doctrine. What limits does Polk impose on our involvement in South America? Why are we justified in making these claims? If you were the president of Mexico, how would you feel about Polk's message? Does this message support American conquest of the Western Hemisphere?

From James D. Richardson, ed., *Messages and Papers of the Presidents* (Washington, D.C., 1897), IV, 398–399.

The rapid extension of our settlements over our territories heretofore un-
occupied, the addition of new States to our Confederacy, the expansion of free
principles, and our rising greatness as a nation are attracting the attention of
the powers of Europe, and lately the doctrine has been broached in some of
them of a "balance of power" on this continent to check our advancement.
The United States, sincerely desirous of preserving relations of good understanding with all nations, can not in silence permit any European interference
on the North American continent, and should any such interference be attempted will be ready to resist it at any and all hazards.

It is well known to the American people and to all nations that this
Government has never interfered with the relations subsisting between other
governments. We have never made ourselves parties to their wars or their
alliances; we have not sought their territories by conquest; we have not mingled
with parties in their domestic struggles; and believing our own form of government to be the best, we have never attempted to propagate it by intrigues, by
diplomacy, or by force. We may claim on this continent a like exemption from
European interference. The nations of America are equally sovereign and
independent with those of Europe. They possess the same rights, independent
of all foreign interposition, to make war, to conclude peace, and to regulate
their internal affairs. The people of the United States can not, therefore, view
with indifference attempts of European powers to interfere with the independent action of the nations on this continent. The American system of government is entirely different from that of Europe. Jealousy among the different
sovereigns of Europe, lest any one of them might become too powerful for the
rest, has caused them anxiously to desire the establishment of what they term
the "balance of power." It can not be permitted to have any application on the
North American continent, and especially to the United States. We must ever
maintain the principle that the people of this continent alone have the right to
decide their own destiny. Should any portion of them, constituting an independent state, propose to unite themselves with our Confederacy, this will be a
question for them and us to determine without any foreign interposition. We
can never consent that European powers shall interfere to prevent such a union
because it might disturb the "balance of power" which they may desire to
maintain upon this continent. Near a quarter of a century ago the principle was
distinctly announced to the world, in the annual message of one of my predecessors, that —

> The American continents, by the free and independent condition which
> they have assumed and maintain, are henceforth not to be considered as
> subjects for future colonization by any European powers.

This principle will apply with greatly increased force should any European power attempt to establish any new colony in North America. In the
existing circumstances of the world the present is deemed a proper occasion to
reiterate and reaffirm the principle avowed by Mr. Monroe and to state my
cordial concurrence in its wisdom and sound policy. The reassertion of this

principle, especially in reference to North America, is at this day but the promulgation of a policy which no European power should cherish the disposition to resist. Existing rights of every European nation should be respected, but it is due alike to our safety and our interests that the efficient protection of our laws should be extended over our whole territorial limits, and that it should be distinctly announced to the world as our settled policy that no future European colony or dominion shall with our consent be planted or established on any part of the North American continent.

Annexation and Mission

JOHN L. O'SULLIVAN

John O'Sullivan justifies the annexation of Texas. What role have foreign nations played in justifying annexation? Why should Mexican claims be ignored? Do you believe his assurances that the expansion of slavery plays no role in annexation? What activities give the United States better title than the Mexicans have? What limits does O'Sullivan envision on controlling this territory?

Texas is now ours. Already, before these words are written, her Convention has undoubtedly ratified the acceptance, by her Congress, of our proffered invitation into the Union; and made the requisite changes in her already republican form of constitution to adopt it to its future federal relations. Her star and her stripe may already be said to have taken their place in the glorious blazon of our common nationality; and the sweep of our eagle's wing already includes within its circuit the wide extent of her fair and fertile land. She is no longer to us a mere geographical space — a certain combination of coast, plain, mountain, valley, forest and stream. She is no longer to us a mere country on the map. She comes within the dear and sacred designation of Our Country; no longer a *"pays,"* she is a part of *"la patrie,"* and that which is at once a sentiment and a virtue, Patriotism, already begins to thrill for her too within the national heart. It is time then that all should cease to treat her as alien, and even adverse — cease to denounce and vilify all and everything connected with her accession — cease to thwart and oppose the remaining steps for its consummation; or where such efforts are felt to be unavailing, at least to embitter the hour of reception by all the most ungracious frowns of aversion and words of unwelcome. There has been enough of all this. It has had its fitting day during the period when, in common with every other possible question of practical

From John L. O'Sullivan, "Annexation," *United States Magazine and Democratic Review,* (July 1845), XVII, 5–10.

policy that can arise, it unfortunately became one of the leading topics of party division, of presidential electioneering. But that period has passed, and with it let its prejudices and its passions, its discords and its denunciations, pass away too. The next session of Congress will see the representatives of the new young State in their places in both our halls of national legislation, side by side with those of the old Thirteen. Let their reception into "the family" be frank, kindly, and cheerful, as befits such an occasion, as comports not less with our own self-respect than patriotic duty towards them. Ill betide those foul birds that delight to 'file their own nest, and disgust the ear with perpetual discord of ill-omened croak.

Why, were other reasoning wanting, in favor of now elevating this question of the reception of Texas into the Union, out of the lower region of our past party dissensions, up to its proper level of a high and broad nationality, it surely is to be found, found abundantly, in the manner in which other nations have undertaken to intrude themselves into it, between us and the proper parties to the case, in a spirit of hostile interference against us, for the avowed object of thwarting our policy and hampering our power, limiting our greatness and checking the fulfilment of our manifest destiny to overspread the continent allotted by Providence for the free development of our yearly multiplying millions. This we have seen done by England, our old rival and enemy; and by France, strangely coupled with her against us, under the influence of the Anglicism strongly tinging the policy of her present prime minister, Guizot. The zealous activity with which this effort to defeat us was pushed by the representatives of those governments, together with the character of intrigue accompanying it, fully constituted that case of foreign interference, which Mr. Clay himself declared should, and would unite us all in maintaining the common cause of our country against the foreigner and the foe. . . .

It is wholly untrue, and unjust to ourselves, the pretence that the Annexation has been a measure of spoliation, unrightful and unrighteous — of military conquest under forms of peace and law — of territorial aggrandizement at the expense of justice, and justice due by a double sanctity to the weak. This view of the question is wholly unfounded, and has been before so amply refuted in these pages, as well as in a thousand other modes, that we shall not again dwell upon it. The independence of Texas was complete and absolute. It was an independence, not only in fact but of right. No obligation of duty towards Mexico tended in the least degree to restrain our right to effect the desired recovery of the fair province once our own — whatever motives of policy might have prompted a more deferential consideration of her feelings and her pride, as involved in the question. If Texas became peopled with an American population, it was by no contrivance of our government, but on the express invitation of that of Mexico herself; accompanied with such guaranties of State independence, and the maintenance of a federal system analogous to our own, as constituted a compact fully justifying the strongest measures of redress on the part of those afterwards deceived in this guaranty, and sought to be enslaved under the yoke imposed by its violation. She was released, rightfully and absolutely released, from all Mexican allegiance, or duty of cohesion to the Mexican political body, by the acts and fault of Mexico herself, and Mexico alone. There never was a clearer case. It was not revolution; it was resistance to revolution; and resistance under such circumstances as left independence the necessary resulting state, caused by the abandonment of those with whom her former federal association had existed. What then can be more preposterous than all this clamor by Mexico and the Mexican interest, against Annexation, as a violation of any rights of hers, any duties of ours? . . .

Nor is there any just foundation for the charge that Annexation is a great pro-slavery measure — calculated to increase and perpetuate that institution. Slavery had nothing to do with it. Opinions were and are greatly divided, both at the North and South, as to the influence to be exerted by it on Slavery and the Slave States. That it will tend to facilitate and hasten the disappearance of Slavery from all the northern tier of the present Slave States, cannot surely admit of serious question. The greater value in Texas of the slave labor now employed in those States, must soon produce the effect of draining off that labor southwardly, by the same unvarying law that bids water descend the slope that invites it. Every new Slave State in Texas will make at least one Free State from among those in which that institution now exists — to say nothing of those portions of Texas on which slavery cannot spring and grow — to say nothing of the far more rapid growth of new States in the free West and Northwest, as these fine regions are overspread by the emigration fast flowing over them from Europe, as well as from the Northern and Eastern States of the Union as it exists. On the other hand, it is undeniably much gained for the cause of the eventual voluntary abolition of slavery, that it should have been thus drained off towards the only outlet which appeared to furnish much probability of the ultimate disappearance of the negro race from our borders. The Spanish-Indian-American populations of Mexico, Central America and South America, afford the only receptacle capable of absorbing that race whenever we shall be prepared to slough it off — to emancipate it from slavery, and (simultaneously necessary) to remove it from the midst of our own. Themselves already of mixed and confused blood, and free from the "prejudices" which among us so insuperably forbid the social amalgamation which can alone elevate the Negro race out of a virtually servile degradation even though legally free, the regions occupied by those populations must strongly attract the black race in that direction; and as soon as the destined hour of emancipation shall arrive, will relieve the question of one of its worst difficulties, if not absolutely the greatest.

No — Mr. Clay was right when he declared that Annexation was a question with which slavery had nothing to do. The country which was the subject of Annexation in this case, from its geographical position and relations, happens to be — or rather the portion of it now actually settled, happens to be — a slave country. But a similar process might have taken place in proximity to a different section of our Union; and indeed there is a great deal of Annexation yet to take place, within the life of the present generation, along the whole line of our northern border. Texas has been absorbed into the Union in the

inevitable fulfilment of the general law which is rolling our population westward; the connexion of which with that ratio of growth in population which
is destined within a hundred years to swell our numbers to the enormous
population of *two hundred and fifty millions* (if not more), is too evident to
leave us in doubt of the manifest design of Providence in regard to the occupation of this continent. It was disintegrated from Mexico in the natural course
of events, by a process perfectly legitimate on its own part, blameless on ours;
and in which all the censures due to wrong, perfidy and folly, rest on Mexico
alone. And possessed as it was by a population which was in truth but a
colonial detachment from our own, and which was still bound by myriad ties
of the very heart-strings to its old relations, domestic and political, their incor-
poration into the Union was not only inevitable, but the most natural, right and
proper thing in the world — and it is only astonishing that there should be any
among ourselves to say it nay. . . .

California will, probably, next fall away from the loose adhesion which, in
such a country as Mexico, holds a remote province in a slight equivocal kind
of dependence on the metropolis. Imbecile and distracted, Mexico never can
exert any real governmental authority over such a country. The impotence of
the one and the distance of the other, must make the relation one of virtual
independence; unless, by stunting the province of all natural growth, and forbidding that immigration which can alone develope its capabilities and fulfil
the purposes of its creation, tyranny may retain a military dominion which is
no government in the legitimate sense of the term. In the case of California
this is now impossible. The Anglo-Saxon foot is already on its borders. Already
the advance guard of the irresistible army of Anglo-Saxon emigration has
begun to pour down upon it, armed with the plough and the rifle, and marking
its trail with schools and colleges, courts and representative halls, mills and
meeting-houses. A population will soon be in actual occupation of California,
over which it will be idle for Mexico to dream of dominion. They will necessarily become independent. All this without agency of our government, without
responsibility of our people — in the natural flow of events, the spontaneous
working of principles, and the adaptation of the tendencies and wants of the
human race to the elemental circumstances in the midst of which they find
themselves placed. And they will have a right to independence — to self-
government — to the possession of the homes conquered from the wilderness
by their own labors and dangers, sufferings and sacrifices — a better and a
truer right than the artificial title of sovereignty in Mexico a thousand miles
distant, inheriting from Spain a title good only against those who have none
better. Their right to independence will be the natural right of self-government
belonging to any community strong enough to maintain it — distinct in position, origin and character, and free from any mutual obligations of membership of a common political body, binding it to others by the duty of loyalty and
compact of public faith. This will be their title to independence; and by this
title, there can be no doubt that the population now fast streaming down upon
California will both assert and maintain that independence. Whether they will
then attach themselves to our Union or not, is not to be predicted with any cer-

tainty. Unless the projected rail-road across the continent to the Pacific be carried into effect, perhaps they may not; though even in that case, the day is not distant when the Empires of the Atlantic and Pacific would again flow together into one, as soon as their inland border should approach each other. But that great work, colossal as appears the plan on its first suggestion, cannot remain long unbuilt. Its necessity for this very purpose of binding and holding together in its iron clasp our fast settling Pacific region with that of the Mississippi valley — the natural facility of the route — the ease with which any amount of labor for the construction can be drawn in from the overcrowded populations of Europe, to be paid in the lands made valuable by the progress of the work itself — and its immense utility to the commerce of the world with the whole eastern coast of Asia, alone almost sufficient for the support of such a road — these considerations give assurance that the day cannot be distant which shall witness the conveyance of the representatives from Oregon and California to Washington within less time than a few years ago was devoted to a similar journey by those from Ohio; while the magnetic telegraph will enable the editors of the "San Francisco Union," the "Astoria Evening Post," or the "Nootka Morning News" to set up in type the first half of the President's Inaugural, before the echoes of the latter half shall have died away beneath the lofty porch of the Capitol, as spoken from his lips.

Away, then, with all idle French talk of *balances of power* on the American Continent. There is no growth in Spanish America! Whatever progress of population there may be in the British Canadas, is only for their own early severance of their present colonial relation to the little island three thousand miles across the Atlantic; soon to be followed by Annexation, and destined to swell the still accumulating momentum of our progress. And whosoever may hold the balance, though they should cast into the opposite scale all the bayonets and cannon, not only of France and England, but of Europe entire, how would it kick the beam against the simple solid weight of the two hundred and fifty, or three hundred millions — and American millions — destined to gather beneath the flutter of the stripes and stars, in the fast hastening year of the Lord 1945!

Domestic vs. International Mission
ALBERT GALLATIN

Writing during the Mexican War, Albert Gallatin argues for a domestic mission, not an international one. Does Gallatin reject the racism of Benton and O'Sullivan? What would be the cost to the United States should it subjugate

From Henry Adams, ed., "Peace with Mexico," *Writings of Albert Gallatin* (Philadelphia, 1879), III, 581–587.

Mexico? How should Americans carry out their mission? Does Gallatin consider the relationship between domestic and foreign affairs? Is Gallatin making a realistic proposal?

The people of the United States have been placed by Providence in a position never before enjoyed by any other nation. They are possessed of a most extensive territory, with a very fertile soil, a variety of climates and productions, and a capacity of sustaining a population greater in proportion to its extent than any other territory of the same size on the face of the globe.

By a concourse of various circumstances, they found themselves, at the epoch of their independence, in the full enjoyment of religious, civil, and political liberty, entirely free from any hereditary monopoly of wealth or power. The people at large were in full and quiet possession of all those natural rights for which the people of other countries have for a long time contended and still do contend. They were, and you still are, the supreme sovereigns, acknowledged as such by all. For the proper exercise of these uncontrolled powers and privileges you are responsible to posterity, to the world at large, and to the Almighty Being who has poured on you such unparalleled blessings.

Your mission is to improve the state of the world, to be the "model republic," to show that men are capable of governing themselves, and that this simple and natural form of government is that also which confers most happiness on all, is productive of the greatest development of the intellectual faculties, above all, that which is attended with the highest standard of private and political virtue and morality.

Your forefathers, the founders of the republic, imbued with a deep feeling of their rights and duties, did not deviate from those principles. The sound sense, the wisdom, the probity, the respect for public faith, with which the internal concerns of the nation were managed made our institutions an object of general admiration. Here, for the first time, was the experiment attempted with any prospect of success, and on a large scale, of a representative democratic republic. If it failed, the last hope of the friends of mankind was lost or indefinitely postponed; and the eyes of the world were turned towards you. Whenever real or pretended apprehensions of the imminent danger of trusting the people at large with power were expressed, the answer ever was, "Look at America!" . . .

Your mission was to be a model for all other governments and for all other less-favored nations, to adhere to the most elevated principles of political morality, to apply all your faculties to the gradual improvement of your own institutions and social state, and by your example to exert a moral influence most beneficial to mankind at large. Instead of this, an appeal has been made to your worst passions; to cupidity; to the thirst of unjust aggrandizement by brutal force; to the love of military fame and of false glory; and it has even been tried to pervert the noblest feelings of your nature. The attempt is made to make you abandon the lofty position which your fathers occupied, to substitute for it the political morality and heathen patriotism of the heroes and statesmen of antiquity.

I have said that it was attempted to pervert even your virtues. Devotedness to country, or patriotism, is a most essential virtue, since the national existence of any society depends upon it. Unfortunately, our most virtuous dispositions are perverted not only by our vices and selfishness, but also by their own excess. Even the most holy of our attributes, the religious feeling, may be perverted from that cause, as was but too lamentably exhibited in the persecutions, even unto death, of those who were deemed heretics. It is not, therefore, astonishing that patriotism carried to excess should also be perverted. In the entire devotedness to their country, the people everywhere and at all times have been too apt to forget the duties imposed upon them by justice towards other nations. It is against this natural propensity that you should be specially on your guard. The blame does not attach to those who, led by their patriotic feelings, though erroneous, flock around the national standard. On the contrary, no men are more worthy of admiration, better entitled to the thanks of their country, than those who, after war has once taken place, actuated only by the purest motives, daily and with the utmost self-devotedness brave death and stake their own lives in the conflict against the actual enemy. I must confess that I do not extend the same charity to those civilians who coolly and deliberately plunge the country into any unjust or unnecessary war. . . .

In the total absence of any argument that can justify the war in which we are now involved, resort has been had to a most extraordinary assertion. It is said that the people of the United States have an hereditary superiority of race over the Mexicans, which gives them the right to subjugate and keep in bondage the inferior nation. This, it is also alleged, will be the means of enlightening the degraded Mexicans, of improving their social state, and of ultimately increasing the happiness of the masses.

Is it compatible with the principle of democracy, which rejects every hereditary claim of individuals, to admit an hereditary superiority of races? You very properly deny that the son can, independent of his own merit, derive any right or privilege whatever from the merit or any other social superiority of his father. Can you for a moment suppose that a very doubtful descent from men who lived one thousand years ago has transmitted to you a superiority over your fellow-men? . . .

But admitting, with respect to Mexico, the superiority of race, this confers no superiority of rights. Among ourselves the most ignorant, the most inferior, either in physical or mental faculties, is recognized as having equal rights, and he has an equal vote with any one, however superior to him in all those respects. This is founded on the immutable principle that no one man is born with the right of governing another man. He may, indeed, acquire a moral influence over others, and no other is legitimate. The same principle will apply to nations. However superior the Anglo-American race may be to that of Mexico, this gives the Americans no right to infringe upon the rights of the inferior race. The people of the United States may rightfully, and will, if they use the proper means, exercise a most beneficial moral influence over the Mexicans and other less enlightened nations of America. Beyond this they have no right to go.

The allegation that the subjugation of Mexico would be the means of enlightening the Mexicans, of improving their social state, and of increasing their happiness, is but the shallow attempt to disguise unbounded cupidity and ambition. Truth never was or can be propagated by fire and sword, or by any other than purely moral means. By these, and by these alone, the Christian religion was propagated, and enabled, in less than three hundred years, to conquer idolatry. During the whole of that period Christianity was tainted by no other blood than that of its martyrs.

The duties of the people of the United States towards other nations are obvious. Never losing sight of the divine precept, "Do to others as you would be done by," they have only to consult their own conscience. For our benevolent Creator has implanted in the hearts of men the moral sense of right and wrong, and that sympathy for other men the evidences of which are of daily occurrence.

It seems unnecessary to add anything respecting that false glory which, from habit and the general tenor of our early education, we are taught to admire. The task has already been repeatedly performed, in a far more able and impressive manner than anything I could say on the subject. It is sufficient to say that at this time neither the dignity or honor of the nation demand a further sacrifice of invaluable lives, or even of money. The very reverse is the case. The true honor and dignity of the nation are inseparable from justice. Pride and vanity alone demand the sacrifice. Though so dearly purchased, the astonishing successes of the American arms have at least put it in the power of the United States to grant any terms of peace without incurring the imputation of being actuated by any but the most elevated motives. It would seem that the most proud and vain must be satiated with glory, and that the most reckless and bellicose should be sufficiently glutted with human gore.

A more truly glorious termination of the war, a more splendid spectacle, an example more highly useful to mankind at large, cannot well be conceived than that of the victorious forces of the United States voluntarily abandoning all their conquests, without requiring anything else than that which was strictly due to our citizens.

Ideals and Mission

LEWIS CASS

Lewis Cass urges that the United States announce its disapproval of the invasion of Hungary by Russia in 1849. Would such action violate our diplomatic traditions? Would our words without the willingness to fight have any positive effect?

We ought neither to mistake our position, nor neglect the obligations it brings with it. We have at length reached the condition of one of the great Powers of the earth, and yet we are but in the infancy of our career. The man yet lives, who was living, when a primitive forest extended from the Alleghany to the Rocky Mountains, trodden only by the Indian, and by the animals, his co-tenants of a world of vegetation, whom God had given to him for his support. Then a narrow strip upon the sea-coast, thirteen remote and dependent colonies, and less than three millions of people, constituted what is now this vast Republic, stretching across the continent and extending almost from the Northern Tropic to the Arctic Circle. And the man is now living, who will live to see one hundred and fifty millions of people, free, prosperous, and intelligent, swaying the destinies of this country, and exerting a mighty influence upon those of the world. And why not, Mr. President? Is it not likely to be more beneficially exerted, than the influence now exercised by the despotic Powers of the earth? No one can doubt this. Why, sir, even Vattel, enlightened as he was, tells us that "the law of nations is the law of sovereigns. It is principally for them and for their ministers, that it ought to be written," &c. The age has got far beyond this degrading doctrine. That law was made for the great civilized community of the world, and its obligations and their violations will be judged by this high tribunal, and its voice will become, from day to day, louder and more efficacious. Let us aid it by the expression of our views, whenever questions arise interesting to all the members of the great commonwealth of nations. There are no considerations of right or expediency to restrain us from such a course; for, as I have shown, we are just as free to act or forbear, after such a declaration, as before. But it has been asked, why proclaim your opinion, unless you mean to maintain it by the strong hand? For the same reason, that countless representations and remonstrances have been made by independent Powers, when they had reason to apprehend the adoption of measures, hostile to the just principles of national intercommunication. To mark their disapprobation of the act and of the doctrine, that their silence might not be construed into acquiescence, and that when, in the mutation of

From U.S., Congress, Senate, *Congressional Globe,* 32d Cong., 1st sess., February 10, 1852, Appendix, pp. 162–164.

political affairs, the proper time should come, they might interpose effectually, if they should desire it, not concluded by the success of violence nor by the lapse of time, that the Power itself, contemplating the step, might pause and review its position and its pretensions, and the consequences to which it might be led; not knowing, of course, what measures might follow these appeals to its sense of right should they fail to be effectual; and, above all, that the public opinion of the world should be rightly instructed and brought to aid these peaceful efforts to preserve the rights of mankind. And let no man underrate the power of this mighty engine for good. It will go on from conquering to conquer, till its influence is everywhere established and recognized. . . .

It has been said, in condemnation, or in reproach of this effort, that there are many other suffering people and violated principles calling equally for the assertion of this right, and why, it is asked sneeringly, if not triumphantly, why do you not extend your regards and your action to all such cases? And as that is impossible with any useful result, as every one knows, we are, therefore, to sit still and do nothing, because we cannot do everything. Such is no dictate of wisdom or duty, either in political or ethical philosophy. The prudent states-man looks to what is practicable, as well as what is right. The principle im-bodied in the substitute is general and applies to all cases of armed intervention in the internal affairs of other countries; and if our discussion and our immediate action have reference to the attack upon Hungary, the reason is obvious and justifiable. There are conditions of the public mind, arising out of passing events, favorable to the consideration of particular questions, while others are cast into the shade, and command no attention. The former is the state of things in relation to Hungary; to her rights and her wrongs; and the principles thus brought up are attracting the attention of the world, and are discussed in conversation, in legislative assemblies, in the public journals, and in diplomatic correspondence, and they thus commend themselves to general consideration. And the facts have been of a nature to impart deep interest to the whole sub-ject, and without some degree of interest it were vain to endeavor to engage the public attention.

Mr. President, what earthly tribunal has a better right than the Congress of the American people to pronounce the opinion of that people upon such subjects? I do not speak, lest I should be accused of patriotic exaggeration, of those qualities, intellectual and moral, which are found here, and which are essential to a sound decision; but I speak of its representative capacity, as the depository of much of the power of a people, whose interest and feelings are intimately connected with the broadest principles of freedom and inde-pendence. . . .

Many objections, more or less plausible, have been presented to deter us from any action in this matter, but not one of them, with more confidence or pertinacity, nor with less regard to the true circumstances of our position, than that which warns us, that by such a proceeding we should violate alike the traditions of our policy and the advice of our wisest statesmen, and especially the injunctions of Washington and Jefferson. Never were just recommendations more inappropriately applied, than in this attempt to apply the views of those great men to the circumstances in which we are placed.

Non-intervention, it is said, was the policy they maintained, and the legacy they bequeathed to us; but is it possible that a single American can be found, who believes that either of those patriots would condemn the declaration of his country's opinion upon a great question of public law, because they condemned its interference with the affairs of other nations? Why, this is our affair, sir; an affair as interesting to us as to any other community on the face of the globe; one which involves the safety of independent States, and the true intent and obligation of the code, that regulates their intercourse. . . .

Mr. President, it has often been said, that we have a mission to fulfill, and so, indeed, has every nation; and the first mission of each is to conduct its own affairs honestly and fairly, for its own benefit; but after that, its position and institutions may give to it peculiar influence in the prevailing moral and political controversies of the world, which it is bound to exert for the welfare of all. While we disclaim any crusading spirit against the political institutions of other countries, we may well regard with deep interest the struggling efforts of the oppressed through the world, and deplore their defeat, and rejoice in their success. And can any one doubt, that the evidences of sympathy which are borne to Europe from this great Republic will cheer the hearts, even when they do not aid the purposes, of the downtrodden masses, to raise themselves, if not to power, at least to protection? Whatever duties may be ultimately imposed on us by that dark future which overshadows Europe, and which we cannot foresee, and ought not to undertake to define, circumstances point out our present policy, while, at the same time, they call upon us to exert our moral influence in support of the existing principles of public law, placed in danger, not merely by the ambition, but still more by the fear of powerful monarchs — the fear lest the contagion of liberty should spread over their dominions, carrying destruction to the established systems of oppression. But I repeat emphatically what I said upon a former occasion, when this subject was before us, and what upon no occasion have I since contradicted or unsaid, and I may add, what I distinctly stated to the martyr of the struggles of his own country, now the honored guest of ours, in the first conversation I had with him upon this subject — that the people of the United States were not prepared to maintain the rights of Hungary by war; that the only influence we could exert was a moral, and not a physical one.

Realism and Mission

J. C. JONES

Senator J. C. Jones disputes Cass's argument about the benefits of protesting Russia's invasion of Hungary. What will be lost if we speak out against oppression without the will to back up our words? What should our focus be, if not tyranny and oppression throughout the world? Can we live up to our ideals at home if we don't assert them in the world?

The Senator from Michigan, in his able and learned speech, which was filled with beauty, made a declaration to which I freely assent. It is this, in substance: That every nation has a right to determine for itself when its safety demands that it shall interpose. Now, if that be true, (and I am not disposed to controvert it,) I ask, upon what pretext is Russia arraigned at the bar of the enlightened judgment of the world? I am no eulogist of Russia. I am not her advocate. I despise her cruelty; I scorn and condemn her wrongs and outrages; but if that principle which is asserted by the Senator from Michigan be true, then Russia had a right to intervene. If that is the law of nations, and if each nation has a right to judge for itself, then Russia had that right; and judging for herself, and acting upon that judgment, I want to know how the honorable Senator can get up here and arraign her. I believe there was no necessity for the interposition of Russia, but, according to the principles laid down by the Senator from Michigan, she must be the judge of that. She put it upon that express ground, and used the express words that her safety depended upon it.

But have we a right to interfere at all, and is it proper and expedient that we should interfere? My doctrine is, that our best interests would be subserved by having nothing to do with this matter. If we have a right to speak out at all, we have a right to speak boldly, to speak freely, and to speak authoritatively. If it is the policy of this government to interfere in the affairs of foreign countries, though I shall oppose it at every step, I want to see gentlemen come up and speak boldly, fearlessly, frankly, independently, and authoritatively, and when we have spoken, then, to borrow the language of a distinguished gentleman of your party, let us maintain it, "at all hazards, and to the last extremity." Suppose you make this protest, and it goes to Russia, and Russia receives it, and treats it with scorn and contempt, tramples it under foot, sends back an indignity and an insult, what do you propose to do then? The Senator from Michigan says that the man who is in favor of an armed intervention is a madman. The Senator from New York says we must not go to war except in self-defense. Then your protest is received with scorn and contempt, and a

From U.S., Congress, Senate, *Congressional Globe,* 32d Cong., 1st sess., March 18, 1852, Appendix, pp. 305–306, 308.

re-protest is sent back here, full of insolence. How will you receive it? I can speak for you, Mr. President: You would not pocket the insult, you would not submit to the indignity. Now, if we take this step at all, I want to know from the learned Senators from Michigan, and from New York, whether they are ready to take the next step? If Russia treat us with scorn and contempt, and heap odium upon our Government and nation, are we ready to vindicate it? Are we ready to stand up to it, and to vote the men and the money necessary to vindicate the honor of the Government? If they are not ready to do this, in the name of God, in the name of liberty, in the name of the honor of this country, let us stop before we take another step. They have no right to involve the pride and the honor of this country, unless they are willing also to take the necessary steps to vindicate and maintain them. My policy is to let them alone; to let them manage their own affairs in their own way. But if we speak at all, speak like men; speak like Americans; speak as Senators ought to speak. Let us say to Russia, "Hands off; a clear field and a fair fight;" and if she disregards it, and treats it with contempt, we know where duty points the way. I shall oppose it; but if this Government takes the step, if she madly forgets her best interests, for one — though I shall have no agency in it, it may be carried by a majority of the Senate and House — "I am for my country, right or wrong"; and if it should take the last ship that floats upon our seas, the last American ship upon all seas, and every American soldier that wears the insignia of his country's arms, and every dollar in the American Treasury, I would bring them all and lay them down at the footstool of my country, to vindicate the honor of the nation.

But the gentlemen say they will not fight over this. Well, if you do not mean to fight about it, just let it alone. [Laughter.] I am opposed to fighting as much as you are; but if you mean to get us into a quarrel, in which our honor will be at stake, in which our pride will be involved, I want you to stand up and fight it out, and have no dodging.

But, I would like to know why we should go out upon this crusade? This is a wonderful age, Mr. President. Oh! it is a stupendous age! We are to go out upon a crusade for the liberties of the whole world? There is not enough in this broad Union of ours — "ocean bound," I believe my friend from Illinois calls it — to engage the time and the intellect of Senators; but the redemption, the political redemption of the whole world is brought up, and we are to march out upon that grand crusade. I should like to see the world redeemed; but I am no propagandist; and whilst I feel a devotion, amounting to idolatry, for my country and her institutions, and her peculiar form of government, deeply as I am devoted to it, high and holy as I conceive it to be, I would not impose it upon one single, solitary being upon earth. If a man chooses to be a slave, let him be so. I would not force him from any position he might occupy. Let every people choose their own government; and let us choose ours, and take care of it, and guard it, and protect it, and defend it.

But the very distinguished Senator from Michigan claims that the chief virtue which is to be found in his resolution — his protest, I believe, it is called, though I do not know what notary public has signed it; I suppose when you sign it, Mr. President, it will be — is the moral influence it is to exert upon Russia and the world. Do you remember, Mr. President and Senators, the speech of that learned gentleman, in which he inveighed with such touching and powerful eloquence against the cruelties, the enormities, and the outrages of the Czar of Russia? Why, sir, the veriest monster that ever disgraced the image of his God is an angel transformed into the brightness of light, compared with that miserable wretch, and yet the Senator from Michigan thinks there is virtue enough in this protest to rouse the moral sensibilities of such a devil. It may be so. I cannot tell, but it does seem to me that there is some mistake about the moral influence of such a protest. What amount of moral power and influence is to attach to it? How is it to arise? It must arise either from the inherent virtue and justice of the thing said, the manner of saying it, or the source from which it comes. Now, if that be so, let us see how it would work. The distinguished Senator has said it as strongly as it can be said; but would that give it weight and influence with his royal highness the Emperor of Russia? If there is virtue in the thing said, and that is the moral influence which it is to exert, why, sir, coming from the distinguished Senator, and said in terms so beautiful and classical, and coming from so high a source, it would be entitled to all the moral influence which could attach to it. Yet, with the profoundest respect for that Senator, how do you suppose such a protest, going to the Czar of Russia, would be received? The distinguished Senator from Michigan protests, in the presence of his Majesty, against this outrage upon the rights of humanity and justice. But, going a little further, suppose the little republic of San Marino should publish just such a protest as this, and send it to the Russian court, what moral influence would it possess? I do not suppose it would disturb the quietude of the Emperor for a single moment. Then, I apprehend, the moral influence of a legislative declaration or government edict is to be found in the virtue and merit of the thing said, and the physical power and force possessed, to constrain obedience to it. I would not give a straw for all the moral influences of your declarations, unless there be a power behind the throne greater than the throne. There must be physical power, and force, and will, to execute and require obedience to the protest. . . .

Sir, I love this Union — love of the Union is idolatry with me; and it is because I love and cherish it with the fondness of devoted affection, that I am against any of those Utopian schemes, any of those modern doctrines of progress, or manifest destiny, or higher or lower law, come from what sources they may. Why should we go abroad? Have we not enough to do at home? Have we not a field broad enough for the sympathies of Senators? Are all our sympathies to be exhausted on Hungary? Weep over her wrongs to your heart's content; I will join you in the holy office; but I ask you to come back in the hours of quietude, and look to your own country. Have you not enough here to engage your time, to enlist your talents, to enlist the talents of the loftiest intellect of the age? See your country, with twenty-five millions of population, extending from ocean to ocean; a territory of empires in extent, and yet not enough for the enlarged capacity of some gentlemen. The world itself seems scarcely large enough to contain their boundless sympathies. It is enough for me to know that there are interests here that command and demand my attention. Look at the interests of this country! You have a territory almost boundless; unnumbered millions and hundreds of millions of public domain, that might be made the basis upon which the hopes, the prosperity, the happiness, the grandeur, and the glory of the mightiest nation upon earth might be established. And yet, sir, that is a small matter, that concerns nobody. We must go and weep over Hungary. If your sympathies are so large, go into the valley of the Mississippi, that I have the honor in part to represent. I see the honored representative of my district here now. Go there, and see the unnumbered and numberless lives that are constantly sacrificed to the imbecility and weakness of this Government of ours. There is a hecatomb of living spirits carried down into the deep and angry waters of the Mississippi and its tributaries. There is no sympathy for them. We must go abroad, and shed tears of blood and compassion for the sufferings of Hungary. Better come home, and weep over widows and orphans, left husbandless and fatherless by the neglect of the Government to give protection, and to improve her inland and her external commerce. That is enough to engage the time and the talents of the whole Senate — of the loftiest genius that ever lived. Yet these are very small matters — we may forget them all! We have a sea-coast almost boundless, with harbors to improve, interests to protect, thousands and tens of thousands of American citizens languishing for the want of that paternal regard which the Government ought to extend them, in giving protection to the honest labor of the country. All that moves no sympathetic cord in those hearts that sympathise with the oppressed of all nations. Come home, gentlemen, come home, and let us see if we cannot do something here. When we shall have made our own people happy and prosperous, when the Treasury shall be overflown, when the Navy shall find nothing to do, when the Army shall be a burden upon our hands, then you may go out and fight the battles of other people. But first let us establish ourselves upon a basis, not only honorable, but safe and perpetual.

Intervention and Mission

SAM HOUSTON

Sam Houston urges American intervention to protect the white people of Yucatan from an Indian uprising. What humanitarian principles does Houston invoke to justify U.S. involvement? What will be the role of foreign nations

From U.S., Congress, Senate, *Congressional Globe,* 30th Cong., 1st sess., May 8, 1848, Appendix, p. 604.

in Yucatan if we stay out? How long does Houston propose that the United States stay in the area? How easy will it be for us to get out?

No case can possibly arise that will more directly appeal to the true policy of the country or the humanity of a nation than that which is now under discussion. Yucatan has appealed to this country for relief. She has offered to us in return her "dominion and sovereignty." Her existence is dependent upon our action. We are to decide in favor of civilization or barbarism. The war raging in Yucatan is not only one of desolation and rapine, but of unheard-of cruelty and extermination. It seems to me if any circumstance independent of the true policy of this Government could claim our consideration, it would be the sufferings of the unhappy Yucatecos. Laying aside their appeals to our humanity, the highest political considerations present themselves to the patriot's mind. In the desperation of the affairs of those people, they have not only appealed to the Government of the United States, and made a tender of their dominion and their sovereignty, but they have made a similar tender to England and to Spain. They have first appealed to us, and we are now discussing the propriety of interposing in their behalf. Some Power must interpose. It is true, they are not entitled to our consideration as a recognized member of the family of nations, for they have been abandoned by their natural ally, with whom we are at war. If we refuse aid, and England or Spain or any other Power should interpose in their behalf, how can we say to them, you have no right to interpose? If England should acquire peaceable possession, with the right of dominion and sovereignty, will we not be precluded from all interference hereafter in relation to that territory? If, in consequence of delay on the part of this Government, or a want of action, a foreign Power should take possession of it, we are precluded forever from all interference with that country, unless by an act of open war, nor will we have a right to question their title to it. No matter whether they are prompted by a love of dominion or feelings of humanity, if they acquire possession of it owing to delinquency on the part of this Government, we never can question their right, as connected with the affairs of this continent, as embraced in the declaration of Mr. Monroe. That declaration either meant something or it meant nothing; and if this Government does not take action in behalf of Yucatan, we must regard that proud sentiment of a revolutionary patriot as idle gasconade. It was no idle threat, nor has it been so understood. The history given of that declaration by the Senator from Indiana [Mr. Hannegan] upon this floor, derived from a distinguished member of the cabinet of Mr. Monroe, leads the mind to a clear conclusion that it was the avowal of a great principle, upon which this Government would act in all future time. If we do not aid Yucatan in this emergency, it will be an abandonment of all pretext for resisting any encroachment that may be made upon this continent upon any territory not within the defined boundary of the United States. Hence, I believe the true policy of this country, aside from motives of humanity, should induce us to act promptly and efficiently. The course which we ought to pursue is consistent with the safety and well-being of our country. No time would be more propitious than the present for the practical application of the principle inhibitory of the intervention of foreign Powers upon this continent. When again will the state of Europe be found so auspicious to the upbuilding of free institutions upon this continent? Since the existence of this Government no such opportunity has been afforded to us in the establishing of our free institutions as the present. Europe is convulsed. England has to guard her own position. She has perplexities at home. Her complicated colonial system must be kept in operation, and will call in requisition all the ability of her most enlightened statesmen. Under these circumstances, we are left to the accomplishment of the great object of our mission here, if she were even disposed to raise objections to our taking possession of Yucatan. But she can have no ground of complaint. Our intervention has been invoked, and I can apprehend no reason why we should withhold it. But gentlemen have discovered imaginary dangers. They apprehend that it may be a cause of war with France or England. A cause of war, if we choose to assist a neighboring people overwhelmed by calamity! Would it be a just cause? Would the community of nations countenance such a pretext? I cannot believe that there is a nation of the earth that would raise its voice against the interference of this country for the protection of Yucatan. If we were to usurp her territory for self-aggrandizement — if we were seeking to conquer them for spoil, then there would be some pretext for supposing that any foreign Power might interpose to prevent the extension of our dominion. I cannot believe that the Executive contemplates any object, unless it is to prevent the intervention of a foreign Power, and to interfere in behalf of humanity. He has not the power to assist Yucatan, or to arrest the carnage now carrying on in that country, and he has presented the measure for the consideration of Congress. Whilst the United States are engaged in a war with Mexico, and necessarily occupying her territory, until a peace, with all the available forces of the army, it would be unwise in him to withdraw any portion of the forces from the service in which they are now engaged.

It is to be regretted that obstacles are thrown in the way of the proposition to supply a force and means necessary for the alleviation of the sufferings of Yucatan. The President requests this aid and support from Congress. Is it to annex Yucatan to the United States? No, sir. It is to render such aid as may be necessary to defend the white population of that country against the savages, and to enable them to maintain their position until the Indians can be repulsed, or peace is restored, and then to leave the country in the enjoyment of liberty, after making such arrangements as will reimburse the United States for the aid rendered. This I understand to be the object of the President; and whether it be his meaning or not, it is the design which I would entertain myself. . . .

Gentlemen have expressed apprehensions and fears lest this subject should enter into the Presidential election, as I understand them. Sir, I discover that everything here, to the minds of some gentlemen, enters into the Presidential election. Nothing is exempt from its influence, nor is it exempt from other influences in their estimation. Are we to avoid the discharge of our duty, and abandon an object of national policy, or the cause of humanity, because, in its prosecution, a Presidential election may be incidentally involved? I should be sorry to participate in the legislation of this Hall, if honorable Senators were to so far forget themselves as to huckster in a Presidential canvass, or render aid to the aspirations of any candidate for that high office. This is not the appropriate sphere for electioneering. These Halls are dedicated to a higher and nobler object. The legislators who meet here are expected to promote the public weal, but not to minister to personal ambition. Elections appropriately belong to the people. Their intelligence enables them to bestow their suffrages aright. The present is a subject in which the whole nation is either to be benefited or involved. It is a national interest, and rises far above all the influences of party. I trust we shall never be so chained down to party that we cannot legislate for the whole American people. Ill-fated would we be, if we could not avoid the influence of cliques, and legislate independently for the whole community, and, rising above every consideration which is unworthy of a proud mind, never stoop; but making rectitude our standard, be governed by intelligence and patriotism. We should proceed boldly, firmly, and promptly, until we had relieved the people of Yucatan from their fearful adversaries. Our aid could then be withdrawn from that country, after making such regulations and securing such commercial privileges as would repay us for the benefits which we had conferred upon them. I would not desire to act either upon the principle of annexation or absorption; but I would have a just care for our interests. The Balize is already in possession of England. It is a portion of the peninsula of Yucatan. I do not see any possible objection which can arise on the part of any government to the course suggested. Mexico cannot object, for if it be an integral part of that Republic, it must acknowledge itself to be under obligations to us for defending a portion of their country which they cannot protect.

Mission vs. Intervention

JOHN DAVIS

Senator John Davis opposes U.S. involvement in Yucatan. Can the United States bring republican principles when it intervenes militarily? What are the costs to the United States of military expansion abroad? What will happen to those we seek to protect when we intervene? What will be the position of foreign nations?

From U.S., Congress, Senate, *Congressional Globe,* 30th Cong., 1st sess., May 8, 1848, Appendix, pp. 622–623.

We are a responsible Government, ruling under the authority of the people of the country. They appoint their own agents or delegates to Congress, and invest whomsoever they think proper with a practical exercise of the constitutional provisions for legislation. Now, sir, such a Government as this, wherein public opinion is supreme, demands a state of peace. A sagacious, enlightened, comprehensive public mind can alone be its only safe guide, as it is the soul of public liberty, its breath, its vitality, and this soul must be nursed in the lap of peace. It is not a Government that is to flourish under the old idea of the monarchical and despotic States of Europe, that true fame consists in a long and brilliant history of military achievements. They spread their principles, both political and religious, by the sword, literally living and dying by it. But, sir, what is such propagandism worth? What will it come to? We may, by unparalleled bravery and skill, raise our flag in foreign countries, and, like the Romans, establish what we call free governments; but all seed thus sown by violence and bloodshed will, I fear, fail to produce the peaceful fruits of public liberty.

I would ask, Mr. President, if it is not infinitely better to rely for success upon the convictions of men, upon the dissemination of just and equitable principles, upon the doctrines of peace, upon the practical fulfillment of doctrines of equal rights and equal privileges? These are not the doctrines of the bayonet, sir. You may carry the name of the Republic to South America; you may plant your standard entirely around the Gulf of Mexico; you may hold, through your great power, possession of Yucatan; you may assert your authority to Cuba, and even as far as the West India and Bahama Islands; but what have you gained when you have done all this? If you have not carried free principles there, and respected in others those rights which we demand for ourselves, of what avail are all your efforts — all your achievements? None at all. Oppression is not the less odious because it is done in the name of a republic. Violation of rights is not the less painful to endure because inflicted in the name of a free people. All this must be obvious. And now, Mr. President, I earnestly desire the Senator to consider what the peace of the last thirty years has done for us and for mankind? That period of peace, sir, has done more for the human race — more to elevate and improve the condition of man, than all the wars that have raged from the days of Alexander down to the present time. I reflect with amazement upon the progress of free and enlightened principles in a state of peace, when I see in a despotism like that of Austria a mere volition of public sentiment crushing the overshadowing powers of a great and ancient dynasty. This is the work of peace, sir; and does any one believe that if war had been continued moral power could have attained this ascendency? This is what belongs to free institutions; to mind left to freedom of action; to mind which finds repose to deliberate. Every act of wrong done, sir, by us upon a neighboring nation, brings ignominy not only upon us but upon our principles. We should stop, then, Mr. President, and consider what we do before we carry our bayonets into Yucatan for the purpose of uniting that country to this. Again, we should consider, sir, whether, if we administer our Government in the spirit which belongs to our Constitution, and fully demonstrate to mankind, whose friends we profess to be, the justice and equality it asserts; the privileges to the person and to property which it secures; its tolerance of opinion on all subjects; the enterprise to which it gives birth, and the unexampled prosperity which it secures; whether all these countries will not, from witnessing our example of moderation, justice, equality, and security, drop into our arms, seeking of their own free will our friendship, association, and protection. Sir, the time will come, if we so conduct our affairs, when they will eagerly embrace us, and desire to belong to a family of States where such principles find root and grow to maturity. My word for it, sir, this is the way to conquer nations, and vastly more effective than the bayonet. What has England done in the six hundred years she has held possession of Ireland to harmonize and reconcile the people? Has she conquered and subdued their free spirit? Has she reconciled them to their condition? Is Ireland not hostile and rebellious to her authority at this day? Does she not remember that she was subjugated by conquest, and feel the degradation now? Will Poland forget, even if her condition is or should be improved, to feel that she is the victim of ambition? No, sir, the sword is the most dangerous of all ties of union; the disgrace belonging to defeat and subjugation is seldom effaced.

. . . Nothing can be more incompatible with the genius of free institutions than the interposition of military force. It has at all times been the deadly enemy of popular liberty. I say, therefore, that every proposal to extend our territory or principles by force is greatly to be deprecated. Whoever does it labors under a great mistake, if, as the friend of public liberty, he attempts to ingraft upon us the feudal notion, the ancient idea, that power is to be obtained and principles propagated by force of arms, by the shedding of blood. That idea, sir, does not belong to our institutions; it does not belong to a generous, but to a selfish spirit. It does not belong to freedom of conscience, or to a philanthropy which aims to elevate and improve mankind, and we ought to repudiate it. Give us peace, Mr. President, so that men may pause, reflect, and examine into their rights, and consider the means by which they are to be maintained, and the methods by which the grievous burdens which have been loaded upon them by wars and by an unnatural social organization, may be mitigated or totally removed. It has already been demonstrated, sir, that all you need to do, is to let the human mind become acquainted with its own condition and high destiny. What has already taken place in many parts of Europe will be repeated elsewhere. We beheld there but recently the arms fall from the hands of the soldier, the sword from the hands of the officer, because the people have been wise enough to see where their common prosperity lies; and that the means by which to secure it are not to be found in arms or the shedding of each other's blood. Never was there a greater mistake made than when this country took that attitude. Gentlemen are congratulating themselves on our increasing power and glory, the result of the bravery of our citizens. Who, sir, ever doubted the valor and courage of our citizens in a cause which demands patriotic sacrifice? In such a cause, it is not too much to say that they are invincible. They are always strong when they act from convictions of right; but whatever success may attend us in prosecuting wars of conquest, the result will as certainly ruin us as it did Rome.

Sir, there is another difficulty which seems to trouble the minds of many gentlemen. England, say they, is ambitious; England is strong and powerful; England is for clustering together nations and establishing in them her power and her principles. I shall do no more than justice to my own feelings when I say, that I am often pained in reflecting upon these considerations when I call to mind England's history. I am not unmindful of her aggressions, and of the pretexts by which she has often possessed herself of the territory of others, nor of the manner in which she has demonstrated her power when she has obtained possession. All this is too obvious to admit of any doubt or mistake. When she is about to commit an aggression, what does she do? She sets up some plausible pretext, claims she has been wronged some way or other, and thus she justifies not only the infliction of punishment, but conquests which she makes perpetual. She begins just as we are preparing to begin with Yucatan, by helping the weaker party. Rome did that, sir, and it was a favorite policy by which she overran Asia, Africa, and Europe. Who does not know that a very large portion of the Roman Empire was annexed by this process? A party or faction, incapable of protecting itself, sent to her for assistance, offering, perhaps, the sovereignty as a consideration for her aid. Of course the aid was given, and the sovereignty claimed as the reward, whether offered or not; and thus kingdom after kingdom were brought into subjection to her power. England has spread her empire in the east by precisely the same process. The Senator from Michigan pertinently inquired when England puts her foot down in any place, does she voluntarily take it away? I fear she has seldom if ever yielded territory which she thought to be useful to herself. When Rome interfered to aid a weaker faction, did she ever subsequently find a state of things existing which induced her to relinquish her misnamed protection? Never. If remonstrance was made, what was the answer? It was, that the condition of the people was improved, and Roman institutions were better than their own, and remonstrance was of no avail. And what is the answer of England when remonstrance is made concerning such aggressions? Her reply is of the same tenor. We give you a better Government; you have greater security to your persons; larger liberty than before: what have you to complain of? That is the course of reasoning adopted, sir; and although it implies a violation of every principle of liberty, and an utter disregard of the opinions and happiness of others, yet, in ambitious minds, it is a justification even of bloodshed. Are we not falling gradually into this same process, and bringing odium both upon our name and our principles? When we wish to advance our frontier a little, do we not find some plausible pretext which we set up as an argument wherewith to satisfy the world? But does it satisfy our own judgment? If we were to be placed in the condition of those we undertake to annex to us, whether they will or not, would we be satisfied with the same course — with a declaration that our condition would be improved? Of this we prefer to be our own judges. We do not desire to have even happiness thrust upon us against our will, nor do we admit that others have the right to decide questions for us, and to compel our acquiescence. Sir, the great principle of safety everywhere is nonintervention. The great and fundamental principle which lies at the very root of public liberty, is the right of a people to judge for themselves and maintain such institutions as they please, and in the way they please, provided they do not interfere wrongfully with others. They may appear absurd to us, but if they find happiness in maintaining them, no means of violence employed to demonstrate such an error can be justified. It is a privilege of the free to act from conviction; but to force opinions or views of policy upon others, is a violation of the first principles of freedom.

◆ MODERN ESSAY ◆

Mission and International Survival

HENRY KISSINGER

The international arena of the 1970s is more complex than that of the nineteenth century. Intercontinental nuclear missiles eliminate the security from massive attack that the United States had in the past. Errors in judgment made in this century can be fatal for the entire human race. But we cannot hide from decision making. Henry Kissinger outlines the future of this nation in international relations. Does he pay enough attention to the relationship between our ideals and our role in the world? Where would Kissinger stand in the debate between Cass and Jones on the value of proclaiming our ideals abroad? What is the role of ideals in dealing with Third World countries, in dealing with hostile foreign countries, in dealing with our allies? Where and when should we assert our ideals? What is the mission of America in the world today?

There could be no better moment for the "dispassionate public discussion and national self-examination" in foreign policy for which you, Mr. Chairman [Senator John J. Sparkman], have called these hearings.

The moment is propitious not primarily because of the numerical happenstance of our 200th year, or of the political milestone of this Presidential election campaign, but because of the era we have entered in international affairs. It is a moment to take stock of our country's record and consider our future

From Henry Kissinger, "The Future and United States Foreign Policy," *Department of State Bulletin,* April 12, 1976, pp. 481–493.

course, to reflect about the transformations of the international order which we can perceive from this vantage point — some already completed and some still in train — that have altered many of the circumstances in which American foreign policy is conducted.

Today I want to focus on what lies ahead of us: the international issues that will confront the American public, the President, and the Congress, regardless of party, as we enter our third century. For we must remember, amid all our debates, that this nation has permanent interests and concerns in the world that must be preserved through and beyond this election year. This nation faces objective conditions in the world that are not the result of the machinations of personalities nor even, often, the product of our national decisions. They are realities brought by the ebb and flow of history. The issues they raise must be addressed with seriousness, understanding, and objectivity if we as a people are to remain masters of events and of our own destiny.

As President Ford has said:

> America has had a unique role in the world since the day of our independence 200 years ago. And ever since the end of World War II we have borne successfully a heavy responsibility for insuring a stable world order and hope for human progress.

That responsibility continues — not only as a task we shoulder for others or in fulfillment of our ideals, but as a responsibility to ourselves — to create a world environment in which America and its values can thrive.

Mr. Chairman, in foreign policy we stand on the firm ground of America's strength and clear purpose. We face the future with confidence. We have made considerable progress in strengthening partnership with our allies, in managing the global issues of peace and security, and in beginning a new era of cooperation on the global problems of interdependence. The potential for further advance is great.

But today the world looks anxiously to America to gauge whether we will choose to build upon this progress. They ask whether America will use its strength to respond to today's challenges. One of the greatest factors of uncertainty in the world today is concern about America's will and constancy. These doubts are not caused by statements made in the heat of a political campaign but, rather, by a decade of convulsions culminating in a serious question as to the basic direction of American foreign policy. These doubts must be dispelled. I am convinced that they will be dispelled — not by public statements, but by demonstrations of the purposefulness of national policy, the vigor of the American economy, and the renewed unity of the American people, on which all else depends. We are going through a period of adjustment and reappraisal. We must all work together, so that we are the stronger for it when it is completed.

The American people, and the Congress as their elected representatives, have a central part to play in the enterprise of national reaffirmation. Their contribution is essential as a matter of constitutional principle in the making of foreign policy, and as a matter of practical necessity in the implementation of any successful long-term course. As Senator Case has pointed out:

> Congress has an important role in helping voters make known their concerns and to guide the executive branch in its conduct of foreign policy. A democracy such as ours cannot hope to successfully carry out for any length of time a foreign policy which does not have firm domestic roots.

These hearings have already provided much insight into the American public's perceptions of foreign policy, which we have found extremely useful.

The International Environment

Through most of our history, Mr. Chairman, our peace and security were provided for us. The successful growth of our democratic society at home, and the absence of direct threat from abroad, nourished our sense of uniqueness and the belief that it was our own choice whether and when we would participate in the world. We entered wars only when overwhelming danger threatened. We identified exertion in foreign affairs as a temporary interruption of our domestic tranquillity. Once aroused, we were implacable, fighting "the war to end all wars," or until "unconditional surrender."

We had margin for error. Our history, except for the Civil War, was without tragedy, and our resources and good fortune left us without the sense of external limits that so colored the experience of almost every other nation. Our successes seemed to teach us that any problem could be solved — once and for all — by determined effort. The qualities on which all other nations in history depended to insure their survival in a hostile or ambiguous environment — subtlety, maneuver, imagination, consistency — were disparaged in America as cynical or immoral. The equilibrium of power which kept the peace for long periods in the turbulent history of Europe was denounced in this country as a preoccupation with power at the expense of moral principle.

Even in the first 25 years after World War II — an era of great creativity and unprecedented American engagement in foreign affairs — we acted as if the world's security and economic development could be conclusively insured by the commitment of American resources, know-how, and effort. We were encouraged — even impelled — to act as we did by our unprecedented predominance in a world shattered by war and the collapse of the great colonial empires.

At the same time, the central character of moral values in American life always made us acutely sensitive to the purity of means — and when we disposed of overwhelming power we had a great luxury of choice. Our moral certainty made compromise difficult; our preponderance often made it seem unnecessary.

Today, power takes many forms and our circumstances are more complex.

In military power, while we still have massive strength, we no longer enjoy meaningful nuclear supremacy. In economic terms we remain the world's most productive economy; but we must now share leadership with Western Europe, Canada, and Japan; we must deal with the newly wealthy and developing nations; and we must make new choices regarding our economic relations with the Communist countries. Our moral influence, our democratic principles, are still far more valued by the world's millions than we realize; but we must compete with ideologies which assert progressive goals but pursue them by oppressive methods.

All Americans have a right to be proud of what this nation accomplished in our past 30 years of world leadership. We assisted European and Japanese recovery; we built indispensable alliances; we established an international economic system; and we sustained global peace and global progress for a generation.

We have great things yet to do, requiring our unity, our dedication, and our strength. For we live, and our children will live, in a more complex time:

— First, we face the necessity of drawing on the new strength and vitality of our allies and friends to intensify our partnership with them. They have become, again, major centers of power and initiative. This is a lasting success of our foreign policy. And today, our unity with the great industrial democracies is fundamental to all we seek to accomplish in the world. It is we who maintain the global balance of power that keeps the peace. And it is our unmatched economic dynamism that is the best hope for a world of widening prosperity. Above all, our moral unity and commitment to the values of democracy are crucial to the fulfillment of our own dreams as well as to the creative use of man's energies in solving the problems of the future. In a complex world — of equilibrium and coexistence, of competition and interdependence — it is our ideals that give meaning and purpose to our endeavors.

— For we face, secondly, the age-old challenge of maintaining peace, but in the unprecedented dimension of an age of thermonuclear weapons. The Soviet Union, after 60 years of economic and industrial growth, has — inevitably — reached the status of a superpower. As a result, we must conduct a dual policy. We and our allies must restrain Soviet power and prevent its use to upset global stability. At the same time, our generation faces the long-term challenge of putting the U.S.-Soviet relationship on a more secure, constructive, and durable basis.

We must, as well, continue the progress we have made in fashioning a new relationship with the People's Republic of China. We consider the opening to the People's Republic of China one of the key elements of our foreign policy.

Beyond this, global security presents other permanent necessities. There is the continuing need to moderate and resolve regional conflicts which threaten global economic or political stability. And there is the urgent and growing challenge of preventing the proliferation of nuclear weapons, which gravely increases the risks of nuclear holocaust.

— The third central challenge is to build a wider world community out of the turbulent environment of today's nearly 150 independent nations. Two World Wars in this century and the process of decolonization have broken down the international order of previous centuries. For the first time in history the international community has become truly global. The new nations make insistent demands on the global system, testing their new economic power and seeking a greater role and more equitable share in the world's prosperity. A new pattern of relationships must be fashioned out of cooperation for mutual benefit, impelled by the reality of our global interdependence.

Our friendships with nations in Latin America, Asia, and Africa, on the basis of mutual respect and practical cooperation, take on a new importance as the building blocks of world community. We must recognize that no world order will be stable over the last quarter of this century unless all its participants consider that they have a stake in it and that it is legitimate and just.

These are the basic challenges facing this nation as we enter our third century.

In such a world, Mr. Chairman, this country can no longer choose whether or not it is involved in international affairs. On a shrinking planet, there is no hiding place. There are no simple answers. This nation cannot afford to swing recklessly between abdication and confrontation; we must pursue a long-term course. Although we are stronger than any other, we cannot operate primarily by throwing our weight around. Lasting peace is not achievable without an international consensus. We must learn to conduct foreign policy as other nations have had to conduct it for many centuries, without escape and without respite. We must learn patience, precision, perspective — knowing that what is attainable falls short of the ideal, mindful of the necessities of self-preservation, deriving from our moral conviction the courage to persevere. For America finds itself, for the first time in its history, irrevocably and permanently involved in international affairs.

The world needs desperately our strength and our purpose. Without American strength, there can be no security; without American convictions, there can be no progress.

Americans have always regarded challenges as a test, not an obstacle. We have great opportunities for creative diplomacy, to shape from this turbulence and complexity a world community of greater stability and hope. We, more than any other country, are in a position to determine — or have a decisive impact upon — the evolution of the global order.

Forty years ago when the forces of democracy faced a great threat, the United States was waiting in the wings to come to Europe's rescue. Today there is no one waiting in the wings to come to *our* rescue.

Let me discuss at greater length some of the basic long-term challenges we face.

The Unity of the Industrial Democracies

The cornerstone of our foreign policy is — as it has been for a generation — our partnership with our principal allies in the Atlantic community and Japan. These partnerships began three decades ago as a means of collective security against aggression and of cooperation for economic recovery from the devastation of World War II. In the succeeding period our alliances have been the bulwark of the global balance of power. Our cooperation with the great industrial democracies has been the underpinning of the world economic system which has sustained global prosperity and spread it to the far corners of the earth.

Rarely in history have alliances survived as ours have survived, and indeed flourished, through so many vast changes in the international environment. And in the last few years, we and our allies have not only continued to strengthen our common defenses; we have extended our collaboration successfully into new dimensions of common endeavor — in improved political consultation, in coordinating our approaches to negotiations with the Communist countries, in developing a common energy policy and strategy, in reinforcing our respective economic policies for recovery from recession, in environmental cooperation, and in fashioning common approaches for the dialogue with the developing countries.

All these efforts to build peace and promote progress reflect our common belief in freedom and our common hope of a better future for all mankind. These are permanent values of this nation, and therefore our alliances and friendships that are based on them and designed to further them are permanent interests of the United States.

Our cohesion has a more than technical significance. While foreign policy is unthinkable without pragmatism, pragmatism without moral purpose is like a rudderless ship.

Our ties with the great democracies are thus not an alliance of convenience, but a union of principle in defense of democratic values and our way of life. It is our ideals that inspire not only our self-defense but all else that we do. And the resilience of our countries in responding to all our modern challenges is a testimony to the spirit and moral strength of our free peoples.

As we look to the future, there is no higher priority in our foreign policy than sustaining the vitality of democracy and the unity of democracies. The world will become more, not less, complex; our power will grow more, not less, interwoven with others; our values will be more, not less, challenged. In such a world, the solidarity of our relations with those who share our heritage, our way of life, our ideals, takes on more, and not less, importance for as far ahead as we can see. . . .

It is our belief that in an era when our democratic values are under challenge in the world and our societies have been buffeted by economic difficulties at home, the solidarity and cooperation of the great democracies are of crucial importance for giving impetus to all our efforts. We have proved what we can do and vindicated the faith of our people in the values and future of our societies. We have proved that our unity can be as dynamic a force for building a new international order today as it was 30 years ago.

The new solidarity we are building can draw its inspiration from our hopes and ideals, rather than merely our common dangers. A thriving Europe and Japan and North America will not only be secure and prosperous but a magnet to the Communist countries and to the developing world. And so we can enter the last quarter of this century confident that we are masters of our own destiny — and making a decisive contribution to the world's destiny. . . .

Any Administration conscious of the long-term requirements of peace will find itself implementing the same dual approach of firmness in the face of pressure and readiness to work for a more cooperative world. Of course, differences are inevitable as to the practical application of these principles. But as President Kennedy said:

> . . . in the final analysis our most basic common link is that we all inhabit this small planet. We all breathe the same air. We all cherish our children's future. And we are all mortal.

As the United States and Soviet Union have taken important steps toward regulating their own competition, *the problem of local conflicts* persists and indeed, to some extent, increases. The world begins to take for granted the invulnerability of global stability to local disturbances. The world has permitted too many of the underlying causes of regional conflicts to continue unattended until the parties came to believe their only recourse was to war. And because each crisis ultimately has been contained, the world has remained complacent. We cannot forget the ominous lesson of 1914. Tolerance of local conflict tempts world holocaust. We have no guarantee that some local crisis will not explode beyond control. We have a responsibility to prevent such crises.

This must be a permanent preoccupation of statesmen who are concerned for the preservation of peace over the next decades. In the modern era, global communications have shrunk our planet and created a global consciousness. Nations and peoples are increasingly sensitive to events and issues in other parts of the globe. Our moral principle extends our concern for the fate of our fellow men. Ideological conflict respects no boundaries and calls into question even the legitimacy of domestic structures.

We cannot expect stability to continue indefinitely unless determined efforts are made to moderate and resolve local political conflicts peacefully.

The United States is not the world's policeman. But we have learned from bitter experience — as recently as 1973 — that conflicts can erupt and spread and directly touch the interests and well-being of this country. Helping to settle disputes is a longstanding American tradition, in our interest and the world interest. . . .

Shaping a World Community

The upheavals of the 20th century have bequeathed to us another fundamental task: to adapt the international structure to the new realities of our time. We must fashion constructive long-term relationships between the industrial and developing nations, rich and poor, North and South; we must adapt and reinvigorate our friendships in Latin America, Asia, and Africa, taking into account their new role and importance on the world scene; and together with all nations, we must address the new problems of an interdependent world which can only be solved through multilateral cooperation.

A central issue of foreign policy over the next generation will be the relationship between the industrial and developing nations. Decolonization and the expansion of the world economy have given birth to new countries and new centers of power and initiative. The world environment of the next decades can be the seedbed of political instability, ideological confrontation, and economic warfare — or it can become a community marked by international collaboration on an unprecedented scale. The interdependence of nations, the indivisibility of our security and our prosperity, can accelerate our common progress or our common decline.

Therefore, just as we must go beyond maintaining equilibrium if we are to insure peace, so must we transcend tests of strength in North-South relations and seek to build a true world community. In international forums, the United States will resist pressure tactics, one-way morality, and propagandistic assaults on our dignity and on common sense. We will defend our interests and beliefs without apology. We will resist attempts at blackmail or extortion.

We know that world order depends ultimately on cooperative efforts and concrete solutions to the problems in our relations. The price and supply of energy, the conditions of trade, the expansion of world food production, the technological bases for economic development, the protection of the world environment, the rules of law that govern the world's oceans and outer space — these are concerns that affect all nations and that can be satisfactorily addressed only on the basis of mutual respect and in a framework of international collaboration. This is the agenda of an interdependent world.

We have much reason for confidence. It is the West — and overwhelmingly this country — that has the resources, the technology, the skills, the organizational ability, and the good will that are the key to the success of these international efforts. In the global dialogue among the industrial and developing worlds, the Communist nations are conspicuous by their absence and, indeed, by their irrelevance. . . .

Our Debate at Home

This, then, is the design of our foreign policy:

— To promote, together with our allies, the strength and ideals of freedom and democracy in a turbulent world;

— To master the traditional challenges of peace and war, to maintain an equilibrium of strength, but to go beyond balance to a more positive future; and

— To shape a long-term relationship of mutual benefit with the developing countries and to turn all the issues of interdependence into the cement of a new global community.

These are the challenges of our third century.

Since this nation was born in struggle 200 years ago, Americans have never shrunk from challenge. We have never regarded the problems we face as cause for pessimism or despair. On the contrary, America's traditional spirit and optimism have always given millions around the world the hope that the complex issues of today can and will be solved. The world knows full well that no solutions are possible without the active participation and commitment of a united American people. To describe the complex and long-term tasks we face is therefore the greatest expression of confidence in America.

We remain the world's greatest democracy; we are the engine of the global economy; we have been for 30 years the bulwark of the balance of power and the beacon of freedom. The physical strength, the organizational skill, the creative genius of this country make us — as we have always been since our Revolution — the hope of mankind.

What we face today is not a test of our physical strength, which is unparalleled, but a qualitative challenge unlike anything we have ever faced before. It is a challenge to our will and courage and sense of responsibility. We are tested to show whether we understand what a world of complexity and ambiguity requires of us. It is not every generation that is given the opportunity to shape a new international order. If the opportunity is missed, we shall live in a world of increasing chaos and danger. If it is realized, we shall have begun an era of greater peace and progress and justice.

A heavy responsibility lies with us here in Washington. The Congress and the executive owe the American people an end to the divisions of the past decade. The divisive issues are no longer with us. The tasks ahead of us are not partisan or ideological issues; they are great tasks for America in a new century, in a new world that, more than ever, impinges upon our lives and cries out for our leadership. Even more than our resources, the creative vitality of this nation has been a tremendous force for good and continues to be so.

We can accomplish great things — but we can do so only as a united people. Beyond all the special concerns and special interests lies the national interest. Congress and the executive, Republicans and Democrats, have a common stake in the effectiveness and success of American foreign policy. Most of the major initiatives this government has taken on fundamental issues — with our allies, with the People's Republic of China, with the Soviet Union, with the developing nations, in the Middle East — have had broad and deep support in the Congress and in the country.

Therefore, just as we have the capacity to build a more durable international structure, so we have the capacity and opportunity to rebuild the consensus among the executive and legislative branches and among our people that will give new impetus to our responsible leadership in the world in our third century. This is the deepest desire of the President and the strongest commitment of all his Administration.

Mr. Chairman, members of the Committee, I hope that this discussion of what we see as the issues of the future will be helpful in the building of such a consensus. The issues are complex; the degree of public understanding required to deal with them is higher than at any time in our historical experience. And even if we can reach a consensus on objectives and priorities, our resources and options are limited and we cannot hope always to prevail or to be right.

These hearings are a wise and welcome step in promoting the understanding and consensus that are required. Our gift as a people is problem-solving and harnessing the capacities of widely diverse groups of people in large-scale common endeavor. This is exactly what is required of us, both in building a new international structure and in developing the public support needed to sustain our participation in it over the long term.

In the last analysis, we must come together because the world needs us, because the horizons that beckon us in the decades to come are as near, or as far, as we have the courage to seek them.

Issue

Tactics of Reform and Agitation

Here our concern is with the tactic of taking; how the Have-Nots can take power away from the Haves. . . . In a fight almost anything goes.

Saul Alinsky, 1971

For the origin of all reform is in that mysterious fountain of the moral sentiment in man.

Ralph Waldo Emerson, 1841

In dealing with the efforts to force a nation to meet its goals, our focus is on agitation. Agitation is born of reform, in the desire to change the status quo, but it takes a more militant form. We are looking at the activities of people likely to be in the streets protesting, rather than in the library or office, doing planning and administering. We are not looking at the bureaucrats who run a society, but at those who are trying to remind people of the reasons for which their nation exists — justice, liberty, equality. Abolitionist Wendell Phillips described well the role of the agitator:

> Republics exist only on the tenure of being constantly agitated. The antislavery agitation is an important, nay, an essential part of the machinery of the state. . . . Every government is always growing corrupt. Every Secretary of State . . . is an enemy to the people of necessity, because the moment he joins the government he gravitates against that popular agitation which is the life of a republic. A republic is nothing but a constant overflow of lava. . . . The republic which sinks to sleep, trusting to constitutions and machinery, to politicians and statesmen, for the safety of its liberties, will never have any.

The range of agitation tactics is broad. It can extend from violence to peaceful involvement in politics, and can encompass private behavior or groups organized to protest. As you read the following documents, try to decide which tactics are likely to have the greatest effect, what the weaknesses in each are, and why each is advocated.

◆ DOCUMENTS ◆

The Sources and Character of Reform
RALPH WALDO EMERSON

Ralph Waldo Emerson discusses the merits and evils of the spirit of reform and agitation. In what ways do reformers educate society? What public attitudes oppose reform? What does Emerson dislike about reformers? Do you believe that self-reformation must be the foundation of all legitimate reform?

The present age will be marked by its harvest of projects for the reform of domestic, civil, literary, and ecclesiastical institutions. The leaders of the crusades against War, Negro slavery, Intemperance, Government based on force, Usages of trade, Court and Custom-house Oaths, and so on to the agitators on the system of Education and the laws of Property, are the right successors of Luther, Knox, Robinson, Fox, Penn, Wesley, and Whitefield. They

From Ralph Waldo Emerson, "Lecture on the Times," *Nature, Addresses and Lectures* (Boston: Houghton Mifflin, 1903), pp. 269–273, 276–281.

have the same virtues and vices; the same noble impulse, and the same bigotry. These movements are on all accounts important; they not only check the special abuses, but they educate the conscience and the intellect of the people. How can such a question as the Slave-trade be agitated for forty years by all the Christian nations, without throwing great light on ethics into the general mind? The fury with which the slave-trader defends every inch of his bloody deck and his howling auction-platform, is a trumpet to alarm the ear of mankind, to wake the dull, and drive all neutrals to take sides and to listen to the argument and the verdict. The Temperance-question, which rides the conversation of ten thousand circles, and is tacitly recalled at every public and at every private table, drawing with it all the curious ethics of the Pledge, of the Wine-question, of the equity of the manufacture and the trade, is a gymnastic training to the casuistry and conscience of the time. Anti-masonry had a deep right and wrong, which gradually emerged to sight out of the turbid controversy. The political questions touching the Banks; the Tariff; the limits of the executive power; the right of the constituent to instruct the representative; the treatment of the Indians; the Boundary wars; the Congress of nations; are all pregnant with ethical conclusions; and it is well if government and social order can extricate themselves from these alembics and find themselves still government and social order. The student of history will hereafter compute the singular value of our endless discussion of questions to the mind of the period.

Whilst each of these aspirations and attempts of the people for the Better is magnified by the natural exaggeration of its advocates, until it excludes the others from sight, and repels discreet persons by the unfairness of the plea, the movements are in reality all parts of one movement. There is a perfect chain, — see it, or see it not, — of reforms emerging from the surrounding darkness, each cherishing some part of the general idea, and all must be seen in order to do justice to any one. Seen in this their natural connection, they are sublime. The conscience of the Age demonstrates itself in this effort to raise the life of man by putting it in harmony with his idea of the Beautiful and the Just. The history of reform is always identical, it is the comparison of the idea with the fact. Our modes of living are not agreeable to our imagination. We suspect they are unworthy. We arraign our daily employments. They appear to us unfit, unworthy of the faculties we spend on them. . . . For the origin of all reform is in that mysterious fountain of the moral sentiment in man, which, amidst the natural, ever contains the supernatural for men. That is new and creative. That is alive. That alone can make a man other than he is. Here or nowhere resides unbounded energy, unbounded power.

The new voices in the wilderness crying "Repent," have revived a hope, which had well-nigh perished out of the world, that the thoughts of the mind may yet, in some distant age, in some happy hour, be executed by the hands. That is the hope, of which all other hopes are parts. For some ages, these ideas have been consigned to the poet and musical composer, to the prayers and the sermons of churches; but the thought that they can have any footing in real life, seems long since to have been exploded by all judicious persons. . . .

This picture would serve for our times. Religion was not invited to eat or drink or sleep with us, or to make or divide an estate, but was a holiday guest. Such omissions judge the church; as the compromise made with the slaveholder, not much noticed at first, every day appears more flagrant mischief to the American constitution. But now the purists are looking into all these matters. The more intelligent are growing uneasy on the subject of Marriage. They wish to see the character represented also in that covenant. There shall be nothing brutal in it, but it shall honor the man and the woman, as much as the most diffusive and universal action. Grimly the same spirit looks into the law of Property, and accuses men of driving a trade in the great boundless providence which had given the air, the water, and the land to men, to use and not to fence in and monopolize. It casts its eye on Trade, and Day Labor, and so it goes up and down, paving the earth with eyes, destroying privacy and making thorough-lights. Is all this for nothing? Do you suppose that the reforms which are preparing will be as superficial as those we know? . . .

These reforms are our contemporaries; they are ourselves; our own light, and sight, and conscience; they only name the relation which subsists between us and the vicious institutions which they go to rectify. They are the simplest statements of man in these matters; the plain right and wrong. I cannot choose but allow and honor them. The impulse is good, and the theory; the practice is less beautiful. The Reformers affirm the inward life, but they do not trust it, but use outward and vulgar means. They do not rely on precisely that strength which wins me to their cause; not on love, not on a principle, but on men, on multitudes, on circumstances, on money, on party; that is, on fear, on wrath, and pride. The love which lifted men to the sight of these better ends was the true and best distinction of this time, the disposition to trust a principle more than a material force. I think *that* the soul of reform; the conviction that not sensualism, not slavery, not war, not imprisonment, not even government, are needed, — but in lieu of them all, reliance on the sentiment of man, which will work best the more it is trusted; not reliance on numbers, but, contrariwise, distrust of numbers and the feeling that then are we strongest when most private and alone. The young men who have been vexing society for these last years with regenerative methods seem to have made this mistake; they all exaggerated some special means, and all failed to see that the Reform of Reforms must be accomplished without means.

The Reforms have their high origin in an ideal justice, but they do not retain the purity of an idea. They are quickly organized in some low, inadequate form, and present no more poetic image to the mind than the evil tradition which they reprobated. They mix the fire of the moral sentiment with personal and party heats, with measureless exaggerations, and the blindness that prefers some darling measure to justice and truth. Those who are urging with most ardor what are called the greatest benefits of mankind, are narrow, self-pleasing, conceited men, and affect us as the insane do. They bite us, and we run mad also. I think the work of the reformer as innocent as other work that is done around him; but when I have seen it near, I do not like it better. It is done in the same way, it is done profanely, not piously; by management, by tactics and clamor. It is a buzz in the ear. I cannot feel any pleasure in sacrifices which display to me such partiality of character. We do not want actions, but men; not a chemical drop of water, but rain; the spirit that sheds and showers actions, countless, endless actions. You have on some occasion played a bold part. You have set your heart and face against society when you thought it wrong, and returned it frown for frown. Excellent: now can you afford to forget it, reckoning all your action no more than the passing of your hand through the air, or a little breath of your mouth? The world leaves no track in space, and the greatest action of man no mark in the vast idea. To the youth diffident of his ability and full of compunction at his unprofitable existence, the temptation is always great to lend himself to public movements, and as one of a party accomplish what he cannot hope to effect alone. But he must resist the degradation of a man to a measure. I must get with truth, though I should never come to act, as you call it, with effect. I must consent to inaction. A patience which is grand; a brave and cold neglect of the offices which prudence exacts, so it be done in a deep upper piety; a consent to solitude and inaction which proceeds out of an unwillingness to violate character, is the century which makes the gem. Whilst therefore I desire to express the respect and joy I feel before this sublime connection of reforms now in their infancy around us, I urge the more earnestly the paramount duties of self-reliance. I cannot find language of sufficient energy to convey my sense of the sacredness of private integrity. All men, all things, the state, the church, yea, the friends of the heart are phantasms and unreal beside the sanctuary of the heart. With so much awe, with so much fear, let it be respected.

The great majority of men, unable to judge of any principle until its light falls on a fact, are not aware of the evil that is around them until they see it in some gross form, as in a class of intemperate men, or slaveholders, or soldiers, or fraudulent persons. Then they are greatly moved; and magnifying the importance of that wrong, they fancy that if that abuse were redressed all would go well, and they fill the land with clamor to correct it. Hence the missionary, and other religious efforts. If every island and every house had a Bible, if every child was brought into the Sunday School, would the wounds of the world heal, and man be upright?

But the man of ideas, accounting the circumstance nothing, judges of the commonwealth from the state of his own mind. 'If,' he says, 'I am selfish, then is there slavery, or the effort to establish it, wherever I go. But if I am just, then is there no slavery, let the laws say what they will. For if I treat all men as gods, how to me can there be any such thing as a slave?' But how frivolous is your war against circumstances. This denouncing philanthropist is himself a slaveholder in every word and look. Does he free me? Does he cheer me? He is the state of Georgia, or Alabama, with their sanguinary slave-laws, walking here on our northeastern shores. We are all thankful he has no more political power, as we are fond of liberty ourselves. I am afraid our virtue is a little geographical. I am not mortified by our vice; that is obduracy; it colors and palters, it curses and swears, and I can see to the end of it; but I own our virtue makes me ashamed; so sour and narrow, so thin and blind, virtue so vice-like. Then again, how trivial seem the contests of the abolitionist, whilst he aims merely at the circumstance of the slave. Give the slave the least elevation of religious sentiment, and he is no slave; you are the slave; he not only in his humility feels his superiority, feels that much deplored condition of his to be a fading trifle, but he makes you feel it too. He is the master. The exaggeration which our young people make of his wrongs, characterizes themselves. What are no trifles to them, they naturally think are no trifles to Pompey.

We say then that the reforming movement is sacred in its origin; in its management and details, timid and profane. These benefactors hope to raise man by improving his circumstances: by combination of that which is dead they hope to make something alive. In vain. By new infusions alone of the spirit by which he is made and directed, can he be re-made and reinforced.

Reform and the Outraged Conscience
THEODORE DWIGHT WELD

In 1839 Theodore Dwight Weld indicts slavery in a pamphlet that sold over 100,000 copies in the first year. In what ways does Weld seek to persuade his readers? Is he fair to slaveholders? Would the existence of kind masters invalidate the harshness of Weld's argument? How would Emerson's criticism of reformers apply to Weld? What would Weld's answer to Emerson be?

READER, you are empannelled as a juror to try a plain case and bring in an honest verdict. The question at issue is not one of law, but of fact — "What is the actual condition of the slaves in the United States?" A plainer case never went to a jury. Look at it. TWENTY-SEVEN HUNDRED THOUSAND PERSONS in this country, men, women, and children, are in SLAVERY. Is slavery, as a condition for human beings, good, bad, or indifferent? We submit the question without argument. You have common sense, and conscience, and a human heart; — pronounce upon it. You have a wife, or a husband, a child, a father,

From Theodore Dwight Weld, *American Slavery As It Is: Testimony of a Thousand Witnesses* (New York: American Antislavery Society, 1839), pp. 7–9, 132.

a mother, a brother or a sister — make the case your own, make it theirs, and bring in your verdict. The case of Human Rights against Slavery has been adjudicated in the court of conscience times innumerable. The same verdict has always been rendered — "Guilty"; the same sentence has always been pronounced, "Let it be accursed"; and human nature, with her million echoes, has rung it round the world in every language under heaven, "Let it be accursed. Let it be accursed." His heart is false to human nature, who will not say "Amen." There is not a man on earth who does not believe that slavery is a curse. Human beings may be inconsistent, but human *nature* is true to herself. She has uttered her testimony against slavery with a shriek ever since the monster was begotten; and till it perishes amidst the execrations of the universe, she will traverse the world on its track, dealing her bolts upon its head, and dashing against it her condemning brand. We repeat it, every man knows that slavery is a curse. Whoever denies this, his lips libel his heart. Try him; clank the chains in his ears, and tell him they are for *him*. Give him an hour to prepare his wife and children for a life of slavery. Bid him make haste and get ready their necks for the yoke, and their wrists for the coffle chains, then look at his pale lips and trembling knees, and you have *nature's* testimony against slavery.

Two millions seven hundred thousand persons in these States are in this condition. They were made slaves and are held such by force, and by being put in fear, and this for no crime! Reader, what have you to say of such treatment? Is it right, just, benevolent? Suppose I should seize you, rob you of your liberty, drive you into the field, and make you work without pay as long as you live, would that be justice and kindness, or monstrous injustice and cruelty? Now, everybody knows that the slaveholders do these things to the slaves every day, and yet it is stoutly affirmed that they treat them well and kindly, and that their tender regard for their slaves restrains the masters from inflicting cruelties upon them. We shall go into no metaphysics to show the absurdity of this pretence. The man who *robs* you every day, is, forsooth, quite too tenderhearted ever to cuff or kick you! True, he can snatch your money, but he does it gently lest he should hurt you. He can empty your pockets without qualms, but if your *stomach* is empty, it cuts him to the quick. He can make you work a life time without pay, but loves you too well to let you go hungry. He fleeces you of your *rights* with a relish, but is shocked if you work bareheaded in summer, or in winter without warm stockings. He can make you go without your *liberty,* but never without a shirt. He can crush, in you, all hope of bettering your condition, by vowing that you shall die his slave, but though he can coolly torture your feelings, he is too compassionate to lacerate your back — he can break your heart, but he is very tender of your skin. He can strip you of all protection and thus expose you to all outrages, but if you are exposed to the *weather,* half clad and half sheltered, how yearn his tender bowels! What! slaveholders talk of treating men well, and yet not only rob them of all they get, and as fast as they get it, but rob them of *themselves,* also; their very hands and feet, all their muscles, and limbs, and senses, their bodies and minds, their time and liberty and earnings, their free speech and rights of conscience, their right to acquire knowledge, and property, and reputation; — and yet they, who plunder them of all these, would fain make us believe that their soft hearts ooze out so lovingly toward their slaves that they always keep them well housed and well clad, never push them too hard in the field, never make their dear backs smart, nor let their dear stomachs get empty. . . .

As slaveholders and their apologists are volunteer witnesses in their own cause, and are flooding the world with testimony that their slaves are kindly treated; that they are well fed, well clothed, well housed, well lodged, moderately worked, and bountifully provided with all things needful for their comfort, we propose — first, to disprove their assertions by the testimony of a multitude of impartial witnesses, and then to put slaveholders themselves through a course of cross-questioning which shall draw their condemnation out of their own mouths. We will prove that the slaves in the United States are treated with barbarous inhumanity; that they are overworked, underfed, wretchedly clad and lodged, and have insufficient sleep; that they are often made to wear round their necks iron collars armed with prongs, to drag heavy chains and weights at their feet while working in the field, and to wear yokes, and bells, and iron horns; that they are often kept confined in the stocks day and night for weeks together, made to wear gags in their mouths for hours or days, have some of their front teeth torn out or broken off, that they may be easily detected when they run away; that they are frequently flogged with terrible severity, have red pepper rubbed into their lacerated flesh, and hot brine, spirits of turpentine, &c., poured over the gashes to increase the torture; that they are often stripped naked, their backs and limbs cut with knives, bruised and mangled by scores and hundreds of blows with the paddle, and terribly torn by the claws of cats, drawn over them by their tormentors; that they are often hunted with blood hounds and shot down like beasts, or torn in pieces by dogs; that they are often suspended by the arms and whipped and beaten till they faint, and when revived by restoratives, beaten again till they faint, and sometimes till they die; that their ears are often cut off, their eyes knocked out, their bones broken, their flesh branded with red hot irons; that they are maimed, mutilated and burned to death over slow fires. All these things, and more, and worse, we shall *prove*. Reader, we know whereof we affirm, we have weighed it well: *more and worse* WE WILL PROVE. . . .

. . . We know, full well, the outcry that will be made by multitudes, at these declarations; the multiform cavils, the flat denials, the charges of "exaggeration" and "falsehood" so often bandied, the sneers of affected contempt at the credulity that can believe such things, and the rage and imprecations against those who give them currency. We know, too, the threadbare sophistries by which slaveholders and their apologists seek to evade such testimony. If they admit that such deeds are committed, they tell us that they are exceedingly rare, and therefore furnish no grounds for judging of the general

treatment of slaves; that occasionally a brutal wretch in the *free* states bar-
barously butchers his wife, but that no one thinks of inferring from that, the
general treatment of wives at the North and West. . . .

Reform and the Social System

GEORGE FITZHUGH

*George Fitzhugh agitates in defense of slavery and expresses gratitude for
abolitionism. What has been the benefit of abolitionism to the South? How
does Fitzhugh's view of abolitionism compare with Emerson's? What advantages does the southern social system have that the northern system of
competition does not? Is this statement an effective rebuttal to Weld's?*

Equality where are thy monuments? And Echo answers where! Echo deep,
deep, from the bowels of the earth, where women and children drag out their
lives in darkness, harnessed like horses to heavy cars loaded with ore. Or,
perhaps, it is an echo from some grand, gloomy and monotonous factory,
where pallid children work fourteen hours a day, and go home at night to
sleep in damp cellars. It may be too, this cellar contains aged parents too old
to work, and cast off by their employer to die. Great railroads and mighty
steamships too, thou mayest boast, but still the operatives who construct them
are beings destined to poverty and neglect. Not a vestige of art canst thou
boast; not a ray of genius illumes thy handiwork. The sordid spirit of mam-
mon presides o'er all, and from all proceed the sighs and groans of the
oppressed.

Domestic slavery in the Southern States has produced the same results in
elevating the character of the master that it did in Greece and Rome. He is
lofty and independent in his sentiments, generous, affectionate, brave and
eloquent; he is superior to the Northerner in every thing but the arts of
thrift. . . .

But the chief and far most important enquiry is, how does slavery affect
the condition of the slave? One of the wildest sects of Communists in France
proposes not only to hold all property in common, but to divide the profits, not
according to each man's in-put and labor, but according to each man's wants.
Now this is precisely the system of domestic slavery with us. We provide for
each slave, in old age and in infancy, in sickness and in health, not according to
his labor, but according to his wants. The master's wants are more costly and

From George Fitzhugh, *Sociology for the South* (Richmond: A. Morris, 1854), pp.
243–247, 256–258.

refined, and he therefore gets a larger share of the profits. A Southern farm is the beau ideal of Communism; it is a joint concern, in which the slave consumes more than the master, of the coarse products, and is far happier, because although the concern may fail, he is always sure of a support; he is only transferred to another master to participate in the profits of another concern; he marries when he pleases, because he knows he will have to work no more with a family than without one, and whether he live or die, that family will be taken care of; he exhibits all the pride of ownership, despises a partner in a smaller concern, "a poor man's negro," boasts of "our crops, horses, fields and cattle"; and is as happy as a human being can be. And why should he not? — he enjoys as much of the fruits of the farm as he is capable of doing, and the wealthiest can do no more. Great wealth brings many additional cares, but few additional enjoyments. Our stomachs do not increase in capacity with our fortunes. We want no more clothing to keep us warm. We may create new wants, but we cannot create new pleasures. The intellectual enjoyments which wealth affords are probably balanced by the new cares it brings along with it.

There is no rivalry, no competition to get employment among slaves, as among free laborers. Nor is there a war between master and slave. The master's interest prevents his reducing the slave's allowance or wages in infancy or sickness, for he might lose the slave by so doing. His feeling for his slave never permits him to stint him in old age. The slaves are all well fed, well clad, have plenty of fuel, and are happy. They have no dread of the future — no fear of want. A state of dependence is the only condition in which reciprocal affection can exist among human beings — the only situation in which the war of competition ceases, and peace, amity and good will arise. A state of independence always begets more or less of jealous rivalry and hostility. A man loves his children because they are weak, helpless and dependent; he loves his wife for similar reasons. When his children grow up and assert their independence, he is apt to transfer his affection to his grand-children. He ceases to love his wife when she becomes masculine or rebellious; but slaves are always dependent, never the rivals of their master. Hence, though men are often found at variance with wife or children, we never saw one who did not like his slaves, and rarely a slave who was not devoted to his master. "I am thy servant!" disarms me of the power of master. Every man feels the beauty, force and truth of this sentiment of Sterne. But he who acknowledges its truth, tacitly admits that dependence is a tie of affection, that the relation of master and slave is one of mutual good will: Volumes written on the subject would not prove as much as this single sentiment. . . .

. . . Until the last fifteen years, our great error was to imitate Northern habits, customs and institutions. Our circumstances are so opposite to theirs, that whatever suits them is almost sure not to suit us. Until that time, in truth, we distrusted our social system. We thought slavery morally wrong, we thought it would not last, we thought it unprofitable. The Abolitionists assailed us; we looked more closely into our circumstances; became satisfied that slavery was morally right, that it would continue ever to exist, that it was as profitable as it was humane. This begat self-confidence, self-reliance. Since then our improvement has been rapid. Now we may safely say, that we are the happiest, most contented and prosperous people on earth. The intermeddling of foreign pseudo-philanthropists in our affairs, though it has occasioned great irritation and indignation, has been of inestimable advantage in teaching us to form a right estimate of our condition. This intermeddling will soon cease; the poor at home in thunder tones demand their whole attention and all their charity. Self-preservation will compel them to listen to their demands. . . .

In conclusion, we will repeat the propositions, in somewhat different phrascology, with which we set out. First — That Liberty and Equality, with their concomitant Free Competition, beget a war in society that is as destructive to its weaker members as the custom of exposing the deformed and crippled children. Secondly — That slavery protects the weaker members of society just as do the relations of parent, guardian and husband, and is as necessary, as natural, and almost as universal as those relations. Is our demonstration imperfect? Does universal experience sustain our theory? Should the conclusions to which we have arrived appear strange and startling, let them therefore not be rejected without examination. The world has had but little opportunity to contrast the working of Liberty and Equality with the old order of things, which always partook more or less of the character of domestic slavery. The strong prepossession in the public mind in favor of the new system, makes it reluctant to attribute the evil phenomena which it exhibits, to defects inherent in the system itself. That these defects should not have been foreseen and pointed out by any process of *a priori* reasoning, is but another proof of the fallibility of human sagacity and foresight when attempting to foretell the operation of new institutions. It is as much as human reason can do, when examining the complex frame of society, to trace effects back to their causes — much more than it can do, to foresee what effects new causes will produce. We invite investigation.

Agitation and the Sleeping Conscience
WENDELL PHILLIPS

Wendell Phillips defends the tactics of the abolitionists. What justifies extremism? What sort of people are the abolitionists trying to convince? Does his fight to help the helpless justify distortions like "The South is one great brothel"? Are southerners likely to be convinced by Phillips?

From Wendell Phillips, "The Philosophy of the Abolition Movement," *Speeches, Lectures, and Letters* (Boston: James Redpath, 1863), pp. 106–110.

... We are fighting a momentous battle at desperate odds, — one against a thousand. Every weapon that ability or ignorance, wit, wealth, prejudice, or fashion can command, is pointed against us. The guns are shotted to their lips. The arrows are poisoned. Fighting against such an array, we cannot afford to confine ourselves to any one weapon. The cause is not ours, so that we might, rightfully, postpone or put in peril the victory by moderating our demands, stifling our convictions, or filing down our rebukes, to gratify any sickly taste of our own, or to spare the delicate nerves of our neighbor. Our clients are three millions of Christian slaves, standing dumb suppliants at the threshold of the Christian world. They have no voice but ours to utter their complaints, or to demand justice. The press, the pulpit, the wealth, the literature, the prejudices, the political arrangements, the present self-interest of the country, are all against us. God has given us no weapon but the truth, faithfully uttered, and addressed, with the old prophets' directness, to the conscience of the individual sinner. The elements which control public opinion and mould the masses are against us. We can but pick off here and there a man from the triumphant majority. We have facts for those who think, arguments for those who reason; but he who cannot be reasoned out of his prejudices must be laughed out of them; he who cannot be argued out of his selfishness must be shamed out of it by the mirror of his hateful self held up relentlessly before his eyes. We live in a land where every man makes broad his phylactery, inscribing thereon, "All men are created equal," — "God hath made of one blood all nations of men." It seems to us that in such a land there must be, on this question of slavery, sluggards to be awakened, as well as doubters to be convinced. Many more, we verily believe, of the first than of the last. There are far more dead hearts to be quickened, than confused intellects to be cleared up, — more dumb dogs to be made to speak, than doubting consciences to be enlightened. [Loud cheers.] We have use, then, sometimes, for something beside argument.

What is the denunciation with which we are charged? It is endeavoring, in our faltering human speech, to declare the enormity of the sin of making merchandise of men, — of separating husband and wife, — taking the infant from its mother, and selling the daughter to prostitution, — of a professedly Christian nation denying, by statute, the Bible to every sixth man and woman of its population, and making it illegal for "two or three" to meet together, except a white man be present! What is this harsh criticism of motives with which we are charged? It is simply holding the intelligent and deliberate actor responsible for the character and consequences of his acts. Is there anything inherently wrong in such denunciation or such criticism? This we may claim, — we have never judged a man but out of his own mouth. We have seldom, if ever, held him to account, except for acts of which he and his own friends were proud. All that we ask the world and thoughtful men to note are the principles and deeds on which the American pulpit and American public men plume themselves. We always allow our opponents to paint their own pictures. Our humble duty is to stand by and assure the spectators that what they would take for a knave or a hypocrite is really, in American estimation, a Doctor of Divinity or Secretary of State.

The South is one great brothel, where half a million of women are flogged to prostitution, or, worse still, are degraded to believe it honorable. The public squares of half our great cities echo to the wail of families torn asunder at the auction-block; no one of our fair rivers that has not closed over the negro seeking in death a refuge from a life too wretched to bear; thousands of fugitives skulk along our highways, afraid to tell their names, and trembling at the sight of a human being; free men are kidnapped in our streets, to be plunged into that hell of slavery; and now and then one, as if by miracle, after long years, returns to make men aghast with his tale. The press says, "It is all right"; and the pulpit cries, "Amen." They print the Bible in every tongue in which man utters his prayers; and get the money to do so by agreeing never to give the book, in the language our mothers taught us, to any negro, free or bond, south of Mason and Dixon's line. The press says, "It is all right"; and the pulpit cries, "Amen." The slave lifts up his imploring eyes, and sees in every face but ours the face of an enemy. Prove to me now that harsh rebuke, indignant denunciation, scathing sarcasm, and pitiless ridicule are wholly and always unjustifiable; else we dare not, in so desperate a case, throw away any weapon which ever broke up the crust of an ignorant prejudice, roused a slumbering conscience, shamed a proud sinner, or changed, in any way, the conduct of a human being. Our aim is to alter public opinion. Did we live in a market, our talk should be of dollars and cents, and we would seek to prove only that slavery was an unprofitable investment. Were the nation one great, pure church, we would sit down and reason of "righteousness, temperance, and judgment to come." Had slavery fortified itself in a college, we would load our cannons with cold facts, and wing our arrows with arguments. But we happen to live in the world, — the world made up of thought and impulse, of self-conceit and self-interest, of weak men and wicked. To conquer, we must reach all. Our object is not to make every man a Christian or a philosopher, but to induce every one to aid in the abolition of slavery. We expect to accomplish our object long before the nation is made over into saints or elevated into philosophers. To change public opinion, we use the very tools by which it was formed. That is, all such as an honest man may touch.

All this I am not only ready to allow, but I should be ashamed to think of the slave, or to look into the face of my fellow-man, if it were otherwise. It is the only thing which justifies us to our own consciences, and makes us able to say we have done, or at least tried to do, our duty.

Sexual Roles and Reform
ANTISLAVERY CONVENTION OF AMERICAN WOMEN

The Antislavery Convention describes what women can do to oppose slavery. What assumptions are shown about the role of women in nineteenth-century America? Will the tactics advocated actually help the slaves in the South, or will these tactics serve mostly to satisfy the guilty consciences of northerners? What are the similarities between the condition of slaves and the condition of women? What are the differences?

> *The trembling earth, the low murmuring thunders, already admonish us of our danger; and if females can exert any saving influence in this emergency, it is time for them to awake.*
>
> Catharine E. Beecher

BELOVED SISTERS —

The wrongs of outraged millions, and the foreshadows of coming judgments, constrain us, under a solemn sense of responsibility, to press upon your consideration the subject of American Slavery. The women of the North have high and holy duties to perform in the work of emancipation — duties to themselves, to the suffering slave, to the slaveholder, to the church, to their country, and to the world at large; and, above all, to their God. Duties which, if not performed now, may never be performed at all.

Multitudes will doubtless deem such an address ill-timed and ill-directed. Many regard the excitement produced by the agitation of this subject as an evidence of the impolicy of free discussion, and a sufficient excuse for their own inactivity. Others so undervalue the rights and responsibilities of woman, as to scoff and gainsay whenever she goes forth to duties beyond the parlor and the nursery. The cry of such is, that the agitation of this subject has rolled back the cause of emancipation 50 or 100, or it may be 200 years, and that this is a *political* subject with which women have nothing to do. To the first, we would reply, that the people of the South are the *best judges* of the effects of Anti-slavery discussions upon their favorite "domestic institution;" and the universal alarm which has spread through the slave States, is conclusive evidence of *their* conviction that *slavery cannot survive discussion.* . . .

From *An Appeal to the Women of the Nominally Free States Issued by an Antislavery Convention of American Women* (Boston: Isaac Knapp, 1838), pp. 3–6, 58–60, 63, 68–69.

To the second objection, that slavery is a political question, we would say: every citizen should feel an intense interest in the political concerns of the country, because the honor, happiness, and well-being of every class, are bound up in its politics, government and laws. Are we aliens because we are women? Are we bereft of citizenship because we are the *mothers, wives,* and *daughters* of a mighty people? Have *women* no country — no interest staked in public weal — no liabilities in common peril — no partnership in a nation's guilt and shame? — Has *woman* no home nor household altars, nor endearing ties of kindred, nor sway with man, nor power at a mercy seat, nor voice to cheer, nor hand to raise the drooping and to bind the broken? . . .

We come next to the second grand division of our subject: we are now to show you *how* Northern women can help the cause of abolition. That we be not further tedious unto you, we will endeavor to be concise. We would answer, they can organize themselves into Anti-Slavery Societies, and thus add to the number of those beaming stars which are already pouring their cheering rays upon the dreary pathway of the slave. Let the women of the free States multiply these, until a perfect galaxy of light and glory stretches over our Northern hemisphere. By joining an Anti-Slavery Society we assume a responsibility — we pledge ourselves to the cause — we openly avow that we are on the side of the down-trodden and the dumb — we declare that slavery is a crime against God and against man — and we swell the tide of that public opinion which in a few years is to sweep from our land this vast system of oppression and robbery and licentiousness and heathenism. But be not satisfied with merely setting your names to a constitution — this is a very little thing: read on the subject — none of us have yet learned half the abominations of slavery. We wish that every Northern woman could read "Stroud's Sketch of the Slave Laws"; they are as a code worthy of the remark made by Summers of Virginia, when speaking of the laws of that State alone. "How will the provisions of our slave code be viewed in after time? I fear some learned antiquary may use them as a portion of his evidence to prove the *barbarism* of the present enlightened and Christian era; I fear lest *he* may not *understand* the necessity which with us *justifies our attempt to annihilate the mind* of a portion of our race." How monstrous must be those statutes which seek the annihilation of the immortal mind of man! how tremendous the crime!

Anti-Slavery publications abound; and *no intelligent woman ought to be ignorant of this great subject — no Christian woman can escape the obligation now resting upon her, to examine it for herself.* If Anti-Slavery principles and efforts are right, *she is bound* to embrace and to aid them; if they are wrong, as the vestal virgins of her country's honor and safety, and the church's purity and faith, she is bound to oppose them, to crush them if she can. Read, then, beloved sisters; and as many of you as are able, subscribe for one or more Anti-Slavery papers or periodicals, and exert your influence to induce your friends to do the same; and when memory has been stored with interesting facts, lock them not up in her store-house, but tell them from house to house, and strive to awaken interest and sympathy and action in others, who, like Galleo of old, "care for none of these things." The seeds of knowledge must be sown broad-cast over our land — light must be increased a thousand-fold — and woman ought to be in this field: it is *her duty, her privilege* to labor in it "as woman never yet has labored."

By spreading correct information on the subject of slavery, you will prepare the way for the circulation of numerous petitions, both to the ecclesiastical and civil authorities of the nation. Presbyterians ought to petition their Presbyteries and Synods and the General Assembly: Baptists ought to petition their Annual and the Triennial Conventions. Protestant Episcopalians their Conventions, and Methodists their Annual and General Conferences: beseeching and entreating that they would banish slavery from the communion table and the pulpit, and rebuke iron-hearted prejudice from our places of worship. Such memorials must ultimately produce the desired effect.

Every woman, of every denomination, whatever may be her color or her creed, *ought to sign* a petition to Congress for the abolition of slavery and the slave-trade in the district of Columbia, slavery in Florida, and the inter-state slave traffic. Seven thousands of our brethren and sisters are now languishing in the chains of servitude in the capital of this republican despotism: their hands are stretched out to *us* for help; they have heard what the women of England did for the slaves of the West-Indies — 800,000 women signed the petition which broke the fetters of 800,000 slaves; and when there are as many signatures to the memorials sent up by the women of the United States to Congress as there are slaves in our country, oh! then will the prison-doors of the South be opened by the earthquake of public opinion.

We believe you may also help this cause by refraining from the use of slave-grown products. Wives and mothers, sisters and daughters, can exert a very extensive influence in providing for the wants of a family; and those women whose fortunes have been accumulated by their husbands and fathers out of the manufacture and merchandize of such produce, ought to consider themselves deeply indebted to the slave, and be peculiarly anxious to bear a testimony against such participation in the gains of oppression, as well as to aid by liberal donations in spreading Anti-Slavery principles.

Much may be done, too, by sympathizing with our oppressed colored sisters, who are suffering in our very midst. Extend to them the right hand of fellowship on the broad principles of humanity and Christianity, treat them as *equals,* visit them as *equals,* invite them to co-operate with you in Anti-Slavery and Temperance and Moral Reform Societies — in Maternal Associations and Prayer Meetings and Reading Companies. If you regard them as your inferiors, then remember the apostolic injunction to "condescend to men of low estate:" here is a precious opportunity; and if it is improved, dear sisters, we feel assured you will find your own souls watered and refreshed whilst you are watering others. . . .

But there is one thing which above all others we beseech you to do for this glorious cause. *Pray for it.* Pray without ceasing; for unless all your efforts are baptized with prayer, they can never return into your own bosoms with the blessing of Heaven, they can never effectually help forward this work. We have no confidence in *effort without prayer,* and no confidence in *prayer with-*

out effort. We believe them as inseparably connected as are faith and works. And if any woman tell us that she prays but cannot labor for the slave, we must reply to her in the language of James, in reference to faith and works — show me prayers *without* effort, and we will show thee our prayers *by our* efforts. . . .

If our brethren, then, have suffered and dared so much in the cause of bleeding humanity, shall *we* not stand side by side with them in the bloodless contest? Is it true that the women of France often follow their husbands and their brothers to the sanguinary contest, putting on the soldier's armor, and facing the fierceness of war's grim visage of death? And shall American women refuse to follow their husbands, fathers and brothers into the wide field of moral enterprise and holy aggressive conflict with the master sin of the American republic, and the American church? Oh, no! we know the hearts of our sisters too well — we see them already girding on the whole armor of God, already gathering in the plain and on the mountain, in the crowded cities of our seaboard, and the little villas and hamlets of the country; we see them cheering with their smiles and strengthening with their prayers and aiding with their efforts that noble band of patriots, philanthropists and Christians, who have come up to the help of the Lord against the mighty. We see them meekly bowing to the obloquy and uncovering their heads to the curses which are heaped by Southern slaveholders upon all who remember those who are in bonds. Woman is now rising in her womanhood, to throw from her, with one hand the paltry privileges with which *man* has invested her, of conquering by fashionable charms and winning by personal attractions, whilst with the other she grasps the right of woman to unite in holy copartnership with man, in the renovation of a fallen world. She tramples these glittering baubles in the dust, and takes from the hand of her *Creator,* the Magna Charta of her high prerogatives, as a *moral,* an *intellectual,* an accountable being — a *woman,* who, though placed in subjection to the monarch of the world, is still the crown and "the glory of the man."

Private Conscience and Reform
HENRY DAVID THOREAU

Henry David Thoreau advocates civil disobedience. Under what circumstances should a person disobey the law? Is Thoreau speaking to organize a party or to help individuals decide how to act? Why does he deny that voting is a

From Henry David Thoreau, "Civil Disobedience," *A Yankee in Canada with Anti-slavery and Reform Papers* (Boston: Ticknor and Fields, 1866), pp. 127–137.

meaningful act? How are government's actions to remedy unjust laws worse than the laws themselves? Does Thoreau advocate a practical way to reform the state?

How does it become a man to behave toward this American government to-day? I answer, that he cannot without disgrace be associated with it. I cannot for an instant recognize that political organization as *my* government which is the *slave's* government also.

All men recognize the right of revolution; that is, the right to refuse allegiance to, and to resist, the government, when its tyranny or its inefficiency are great and unendurable. But almost all say that such is not the case now. But such was the case, they think, in the Revolution of '75. If one were to tell me that this was a bad government because it taxed certain foreign commodities brought to its ports, it is most probable that I should not make an ado about it, for I can do without them. All machines have their friction; and possibly this does enough good to counterbalance the evil. At any rate, it is a great evil to make a stir about it. But when the friction comes to have its machine, and oppression and robbery are organized, I say, let us not have such a machine any longer. In other words, when a sixth of the population of a nation which has undertaken to be the refuge of liberty are slaves, and a whole country is unjustly overrun and conquered by a foreign army, and subjected to military law, I think that it is not too soon for honest men to rebel and revolutionize. What makes this duty the more urgent is the fact, that the country so overrun is not our own, but ours is the invading army. . . . There are thousands who are *in opinion* opposed to slavery and to the war, who yet in effect do nothing to put an end to them; who, esteeming themselves children of Washington and Franklin, sit down with their hands in their pockets, and say that they know not what to do, and do nothing; who even postpone the question of freedom to the question of free-trade, and quietly read the prices-current along with the latest advices from Mexico, after dinner, and, it may be, fall asleep over them both. What is the price-current of an honest man and patriot to-day? They hesitate, and they regret, and sometimes they petition; but they do nothing in earnest and with effect. They will wait, well disposed, for others to remedy the evil, that they may no longer have it to regret. At most, they give only a cheap vote, and a feeble countenance and God-speed, to the right, as it goes by them. There are nine hundred and ninety-nine patrons of virtue to one virtuous man. But it is easier to deal with the real possessor of a thing than with the temporary guardian of it.

All voting is a sort of gaming, like checkers or backgammon, with a slight moral tinge to it, a playing with right and wrong, with moral questions; and betting naturally accompanies it. The character of the voters is not staked. I cast my vote, perchance, as I think right; but I am not vitally concerned that that right should prevail. I am willing to leave it to the majority. Its obligation, therefore, never exceeds that of expediency. Even voting *for the right* is *doing* nothing for it. It is only expressing to men feebly your desire that it should prevail. A wise man will not leave the right to the mercy of chance, nor wish it to prevail through the power of the majority. There is but little virtue in the action of masses of men. When the majority shall at length vote for the abolition of slavery, it will be because they are indifferent to slavery, or because there is but little slavery left to be abolished by their vote. *They* will then be the only slaves. Only *his* vote can hasten the abolition of slavery who asserts his own freedom by his vote. . . .

It is not a man's duty, as a matter of course, to devote himself to the eradication of any, even the most enormous wrong; he may still properly have other concerns to engage him; but it is his duty, at least, to wash his hands of it, and, if he gives it no thought longer, not to give it practically his support. If I devote myself to other pursuits and contemplations, I must first see, at least, that I do not pursue them sitting upon another man's shoulders. I must get off him first, that he may pursue his contemplations too. See what gross inconsistency is tolerated. I have heard some of my townsmen say, "I should like to have them order me out to help put down an insurrection of the slaves, or to march to Mexico; — see if I would go"; and yet these very men have each, directly by their allegiance, and so indirectly, at least, by their money, furnished a substitute. The soldier is applauded who refuses to serve in an unjust war by those who do not refuse to sustain the unjust government which makes the war; is applauded by those whose own act and authority he disregards and sets at naught; as if the State were penitent to that degree that it hired one to scourge it while it sinned, but not to that degree that it left off sinning for a moment. Thus, under the name of Order and Civil Government, we are all made at last to pay homage to and support our own meanness. After the first blush of sin comes its indifference; and from immoral it becomes, as it were, *un*moral, and not quite unnecessary to that life which we have made. . . .

Unjust laws exist: shall we be content to obey them, or shall we endeavor to amend them, and obey them until we have succeeded, or shall we transgress them at once? Men generally, under such a government as this, think that they ought to wait until they have persuaded the majority to alter them. They think that, if they should resist, the remedy would be worse than the evil. But it is the fault of the government itself that the remedy *is* worse than the evil. *It* makes it worse. Why is it not more apt to anticipate and provide for reform? Why does it not cherish its wise minority? Why does it cry and resist before it is hurt? Why does it not encourage its citizens to be on the alert to point out its faults, and *do* better than it would have them? Why does it always crucify Christ, and excommunicate Copernicus and Luther, and pronounce Washington and Franklin rebels?

One would think, that a deliberate and practical denial of its authority was the only offence never contemplated by government; else, why has it not assigned its definite, its suitable and proportionate penalty? If a man who has no property refuses but once to earn nine shillings for the State, he is put in prison for a period unlimited by any law that I know, and determined only by the discretion of those who placed him there; but if he should steal ninety times nine shillings from the State, he is soon permitted to go at large again.

If the injustice is part of the necessary friction of the machine of government, let it go, let it go: perchance it will wear smooth, — certainly the machine will wear out. If the injustice has a spring, or a pulley, or a rope, or a crank, exclusively for itself, then perhaps you may consider whether the remedy will not be worse than the evil; but if it is of such a nature that it requires you to be the agent of injustice to another, then, I say, break the law. Let your life be a counter friction to stop the machine. What I have to do is to see, at any rate, that I do not lend myself to the wrong which I condemn.

As for adopting the ways which the State has provided for remedying the evil, I know not of such ways. They take too much time, and a man's life will be gone. I have other affairs to attend to. I came into this world, not chiefly to make this a good place to live in, but to live in it, be it good or bad. A man has not everything to do, but something; and because he cannot do *everything,* it is not necessary that he should do *something* wrong. It is not my business to be petitioning the Governor or the Legislature any more than it is theirs to petition me; and, if they should not hear my petition, what should I do then? But in this case the State has provided no way: its very Constitution is the evil. This may seem to be harsh and stubborn and unconciliatory; but it is to treat with the utmost kindness and consideration the only spirit that can appreciate or deserves it. So is all change for the better, like birth and death, which convulse the body.

I do not hesitate to say, that those who call themselves Abolitionists should at once effectually withdraw their support, both in person and property, from the government of Massachusetts, and not wait till they constitute a majority of one, before they suffer the right to prevail through them. I think that it is enough if they have God on their side, without waiting for that other one. Moreover, any man more right than his neighbors constitutes a majority of one already.

Violence, Agitation, and Reform

HENRY DAVID THOREAU

Thoreau endorses John Brown's raid on Harper's Ferry. Brown insisted that it was necessary "to purge this land with blood" in order to get rid of slavery. He was caught and hanged for trying. Do you agree that violence was the quickest way to free the slaves? Is Thoreau right in equating Brown's violence

From Henry David Thoreau, "A Plea for Captain John Brown," *Echoes of Harper's Ferry,* ed. James Redpath (Boston: Thayer and Eldridge, 1860), pp. 37–39.

with the "petty violence" in everyday society? What does Thoreau mean by the violence that is encouraged "not so much by Quaker men as by Quaker women"? Did Brown's act at Harper's Ferry and his death teach us how to live and die when faced with injustice? Is there a difference between Thoreau's position here and that in Civil Disobedience?

It was his peculiar doctrine that a man has a perfect right to interfere by force with the slaveholder, in order to rescue the slave. I agree with him. They who are continually shocked by slavery have some right to be shocked by the violent death of the slaveholder, but no others. Such will be more shocked by his life than by his death. I shall not be forward to think him mistaken in his method who quickest succeeds to liberate the slave. I speak for the slave when I say, that I prefer the philanthropy of Captain Brown to that philanthropy which neither shoots me nor liberates me. At any rate, I do not think it is quite sane for one to spend his whole life in talking or writing about this matter, unless he is continuously inspired, and I have not done so. A man may have other affairs to attend to. I do not wish to kill nor to be killed, but I can foresee circumstances in which both these things would be by me unavoidable. We preserve the so-called peace of our community by deeds of petty violence every day. Look at the policeman's billy and handcuffs! Look at the jail! Look at the gallows! Look at the chaplain of the regiment! We are hoping only to live safely on the outskirts of *this* provisional army. So we defend ourselves and our hen-roosts, and maintain slavery. I know that the mass of my countrymen think that the only righteous use that can be made of Sharpe's rifles and revolvers is to fight duels with them, when we are insulted by other nations, or to hunt Indians, or shoot fugitive slaves with them, or the like. I think that for once the Sharpe's rifles and the revolvers were employed in a righteous cause. The tools were in the hands of one who could use them.

The same indignation that is said to have cleared the temple once will clear it again. The question is not about the weapon, but the spirit in which you use it. No man has appeared in America, as yet, who loved his fellow-man so well, and treated him so tenderly. He lived for him. He took up his life and he laid it down for him. What sort of violence is that which is encouraged, not by soldiers but by peaceable citizens, not so much by laymen as by ministers of the gospel, not so much by the fighting sects as by the Quakers, and not so much by Quaker men as by Quaker women?

This event advertises me that there is such a fact as death — the possibility of a man's dying. It seems as if no man had ever died in America before, for in order to die you must first have lived. I don't believe in the hearses, and palls, and funerals that they have had. There was no death in the case, because there had been no life; they merely rotted or sloughed off, pretty much as they had rotted or sloughed along. No temple's vail was rent, only a hole dug somewhere. Let the dead bury their dead. The best of them fairly ran down like a clock. Franklin — Washington — they were let off without dying; they were merely missing one day. I hear a good many pretend that they are going to die; or that they have died, for aught that I know. Nonsense! I'll defy them to do it. They haven't got life enough in them. They'll deliquesce like fungi, and keep a hundred eulogists mopping the spot where they left off. Only half a dozen or so have died since the world began. Do you think that you are going to die, sir? No! there's no hope for you. You haven't got your lesson yet. You've got to stay after school. We make a needless ado about capital punishment — taking lives, when there is no life to take. *Memento mori!* We don't understand that sublime sentence which some worthy got sculptured on his gravestone once. We've interpreted it in a grovelling and snivelling sense; we've wholly forgotten how to die.

But be sure you do die, nevertheless. Do your work, and finish it. If you know how to begin, you will know when to end.

These men, in teaching us how to die, have at the same time taught us how to live. If this man's acts and words do not create a revival, it will be the severest possible satire on the acts and words that do. It is the best news that America has ever heard. It has already quickened the feeble pulse of the North, and infused more and more generous blood into her veins and heart, than any number of years of what is called commercial and political prosperity could. How many a man who was lately contemplating suicide has now something to live for!

Agitation vs. Reform
THOMAS HART BENTON

In 1854 Thomas Hart Benton published this attack on abolitionism. Whose welfare most concerns Benton? What is the effect of abolitionism on the slaves; on the Union? Is he encouraging violence by opponents of abolition? Does Benton believe that slavery either will or should end?

[T]here was another part whom he could not qualify as good people, seeking benevolent ends by mistaken means, but as incendiaries and agitators, with diabolical objects in view, to be accomplished by wicked and deplorable means. He did not go into the proofs now to establish the correctness of his opinion of this latter class, but he presumed it would be admitted that every attempt to work upon the passions of the slaves, and to excite them to murder their owners, was a wicked and diabolical attempt, and the work of a midnight incendiary. Pictures of slave degradation and misery, and of the white man's

From Thomas Hart Benton, *Thirty Years' View* (New York: D. Appleton & Co., 1889), pp. 587–598.

luxury and cruelty, were attempts of this kind; for they were appeals to the vengeance of slaves, and not to the intelligence or reason of those who legislated for them. He (Mr. B.) had had many pictures of this kind, as well as many diabolical publications, sent to him on this subject, during the last summer; the whole of which he had cast into the fire, and should not have thought of referring to the circumstance at this time, as displaying the character of the incendiary part of the abolitionists, had he not, within these few days past, and while abolition petitions were pouring into the other end of the Capitol, received one of these pictures, the design of which could be nothing but mischief of the blackest dye. It was a print from an engraving (and Mr. B. exhibited it, and handed it to senators near him), representing a large and spreading tree of liberty, beneath whose ample shade a slave owner was at one time luxuriously reposing, with slaves fanning him; at another, carried forth in a palanquin, to view the half-naked laborers in the cotton field, whom drivers, with whips, were scourging to the task. The print was evidently from the abolition mint, and came to him by some other conveyance than that of the mail, for there was no post-mark of any kind to identify its origin, and to indicate its line of march. For what purpose could such a picture be intended, unless to inflame the passions of slaves? And why engrave it, except to multiply copies for extensive distribution? But it was not pictures alone that operated upon the passions of the slaves, but speeches, publications, petitions presented in Congress, and the whole machinery of abolition societies. None of these things went to the understandings of the slaves, but to their passions, all imperfectly understood, and inspiring vague hopes, and stimulating abortive and fatal insurrections. Societies, especially, were the foundation of the greatest mischiefs. Whatever might be their objects, the slaves never did, and never can, understand them but in one way: as allies organized for action, and ready to march to their aid on the first signal of insurrection! . . .

Mr. B. went on to say that these societies had already perpetrated more mischief than the joint remainder of all their lives spent in prayers of contrition, and in works of retribution, could ever atone for. They had thrown the state of the emancipation question fifty years back. They had subjected every traveller, and every emigrant, from the non-slaveholding States, to be received with coldness, and viewed with suspicion and jealousy, in the slaveholding States. They had occasioned many slaves to lose their lives. They had caused the deportation of many ten thousands from the grain-growing to the planting States. They had caused the privileges of all slaves to be curtailed, and their bonds to be more tightly drawn. Nor was the mischief of their conduct confined to slaves; it reached the free colored people, and opened a sudden gulf of misery to that population. In all the slave States, this population has paid the forfeit of their intermediate position; and suffered proscription as the instruments, real or suspected, of the abolition societies. In all these States, their exodus had either been enforced or was impending. In Missouri there was a clause in the constitution which prohibited their emigration to the State; but that clause had remained a dead letter in the book until the agitation produced among the slaves by the distant rumbling of the abolition thunder, led to the knowledge in some instances, and to the belief in others, that these people were the antennæ of the abolitionists; and their medium for communicating with the slaves, and for exciting them to desertion first, and to insurrection eventually. Then ensued a painful scene. The people met, resolved, and prescribed thirty days for the exodus of the obnoxious caste. Under that decree a general emigration had to take place at the commencement of winter. Many worthy and industrious people had to quit their business and their homes, and to go forth under circumstances which rendered them objects of suspicion wherever they went, and sealed the door against the acquisition of new friends while depriving them of the protection of old ones. He (Mr. B.) had witnessed many instances of this kind, and had given certificates to several, to show that they were banished, not for their offences, but for their misfortunes; for the misfortune of being allied to the race which the abolition societies had made the object of their gratuitous philanthropy.

Having said thus much of the abolition societies in the non-slaveholding States, Mr. B. turned, with pride and exultation, to a different theme — the conduct of the great body of the people in all these States. Before he saw that conduct, and while the black question, like a portentous cloud was gathering and darkening on the Northeastern horizon, he trembled, not for the South, but for the Union. He feared that he saw the fatal work of dissolution about to begin, and the bonds of this glorious confederacy about to snap; but the conduct of the great body of the people in all the non-slaveholding States quickly dispelled that fear, and in its place planted deep the strongest assurance of the harmony and indivisibility of the Union which he had felt for many years. Their conduct was above all praise, above all thanks, above all gratitude. They had chased off the foreign emissaries, silenced the gabbling tongues of female dupes, and dispersed the assemblages, whether fanatical, visionary, or incendiary, of all that congregated to preach against evils which afflicted others, not them; and to propose remedies to aggravate the disease which they pretended to cure. They had acted with a noble spirit. They had exerted a vigor beyond all law. They had obeyed the enactments, not of the statute book, but of the heart; and while that spirit was in the heart, he cared nothing for laws written in a book. He would rely upon that spirit to complete the good work it has begun; to dry up these societies; to separate the mistaken philanthropist from the reckless fanatic and the wicked incendiary, and put an end to publications and petitions which, whatever may be their design, can have no other effect than to impede the object which they invoke, and to aggravate the evil which they deplore.

◆ MODERN ESSAY ◆

Agitation, Morality, and Reform

SAUL ALINSKY

Saul Alinsky discusses the tactics used by agitators to move society. Although modern agitators operate in a much more complex society than the abolitionists did, Alinsky's advice might still have been useful for the antislavery agitators. On the other hand, they had advice he might have taken too. Perhaps the major gap between nineteenth- and twentieth-century agitation revealed here is the question of morality of the cause. Is Alinsky as sensitive as the earlier reformers were to moral questions? What might Emerson or Thoreau say to Alinsky on this issue? Does Alinsky concern himself with the nature of the society he is trying to change? Did the abolitionists comply with his twelfth rule? Is there a resolution for either Alinsky or the abolitionists between his third and fourth rule? Can agitators concern themselves with the complexities of the society they confront? Can they concede the humanity of their opponents? If not, do they fall before Emerson's and Benton's critiques?

Tactics means doing what you can with what you have. Tactics are those consciously deliberate acts by which human beings live with each other and deal with the world around them. In the world of give and take, tactics is the art of how to take and how to give. Here our concern is with the tactic of taking; how the Have-Nots can take power away from the Haves.

For an elementary illustration of tactics, take parts of your face as the point of reference; your eyes, your ears, and your nose. First the eyes; if you have organized a vast, mass-based people's organization, you can parade it visibly before the enemy and openly show your power. Second the ears; if your organization is small in numbers, then do what Gideon did: conceal the members in the dark but raise a din and clamor that will make the listener believe that your organization numbers many more than it does. Third, the nose; if your organization is too tiny even for noise, stink up the place.

Always remember the first rule of power tactics:

Power is not only what you have but what the enemy thinks you have.

The second rule is: *Never go outside the experience of your people.* When an action or tactic is outside the experience of the people, the result is confusion, fear, and retreat. It also means a collapse of communication, as we have noted.

The third rule is: *Wherever possible go outside of the experience of the enemy.* Here you want to cause confusion, fear, and retreat.

General William T. Sherman, whose name still causes a frenzied reaction throughout the South, provided a classic example of going outside the enemy's experience. Until Sherman, military tactics and strategies were based on standard patterns. All armies had fronts, rears, flanks, lines of communication, and lines of supply. Military campaigns were aimed at such standard objectives as rolling up the flanks of the enemy army or cutting the lines of supply or lines of communication, or moving around to attack from the rear. When Sherman cut loose on his famous March to the Sea, he had no front or rear lines of supplies or any other lines. He was on the loose and living on the land. The South, confronted with this new form of military invasion, reacted with confusion, panic, terror, and collapse. Sherman swept on to inevitable victory. It was the same tactic that, years later in the early days of World War II, the Nazi Panzer tank divisions emulated in their far-flung sweeps into enemy territory, as did our own General Patton with the American Third Armored Division.

The fourth rule is: *Make the enemy live up to their own book of rules.* You can kill them with this, for they can no more obey their own rules than the Christian church can live up to Christianity.

The fourth rule carries within it the fifth rule: *Ridicule is man's most potent weapon.* It is almost impossible to counterattack ridicule. Also it infuriates the opposition, who then react to your advantage.

The sixth rule is: *A good tactic is one that your people enjoy.* If your people are not having a ball doing it, there is something very wrong with the tactic.

The seventh rule: *A tactic that drags on too long becomes a drag.* Man can sustain militant interest in any issue for only a limited time, after which it becomes a ritualistic commitment, like going to church on Sunday mornings. New issues and crises are always developing, and one's reaction becomes, "Well, my heart bleeds for those people and I'm all for the boycott, but after all there are other important things in life" — and there it goes.

The eighth rule: *Keep the pressure on,* with different tactics and actions, and utilize all events of the period for your purpose.

The ninth rule: *The threat is usually more terrifying than the thing itself.*

The tenth rule: *The major premise for tactics is the development of operations that will maintain a constant pressure upon the opposition.* It is this unceasing pressure that results in the reactions from the opposition that are essential for the success of the campaign. It should be remembered not only that the action is in the reaction but that action is itself the consequence of reaction and of reaction to the reaction, ad infinitum. The pressure produces the reaction, and constant pressure sustains action.

The eleventh rule is: *If you push a negative hard and deep enough it will break through into its counterside;* this is based on the principle that every positive has its negative. We have already seen the conversion of the negative into the positive, in Mahatma Gandhi's development of the tactic of passive resistance.

One corporation we organized against responded to the continuous application of pressure by burglarizing my home, and then using the keys taken in the burglary to burglarize the offices of the Industrial Areas Foundation where I work. The panic in this corporation was clear from the nature of the burglaries, for nothing was taken in either burglary to make it seem that the thieves were interested in ordinary loot — they took only the records that applied to the corporation. Even the most amateurish burglar would have had more sense than to do what the private detective agency hired by that corporation did. The police departments in California and Chicago agreed that "the corporation might just as well have left its fingerprints all over the place."

In a fight almost anything goes. It almost reaches the point where you stop to apologize if a chance blow lands *above* the belt. When a corporation bungles like the one that burglarized my home and office, my visible public reaction is shock, horror, and moral outrage. In this case, we let it be known that sooner or later it would be confronted with this crime as well as with a whole series of other derelictions, before a United States Senate Subcommittee Investigation. Once sworn in, with congressional immunity, we would make these actions public. This threat, plus the fact that an attempt on my life had been made in Southern California, had the corporation on a spot where it would be publicly suspect in the event of assassination. At one point I found myself in a thirty-room motel in which every other room was occupied by their security men. This became another devil in the closet to haunt this corporation and to keep the pressure on.

The twelfth rule: *The price of a successful attack is a constructive alternative.* You cannot risk being trapped by the enemy in his sudden agreement with your demand and saying "You're right — we don't know what to do about this issue. Now you tell us."

The thirteenth rule: *Pick the target, freeze it, personalize it, and polarize it.*

In conflict tactics there are certain rules that the organizer should always regard as universalities. One is that the opposition must be singled out as the target and "frozen." By this I mean that in a complex, interrelated, urban society, it becomes increasingly difficult to single out who is to blame for any particular evil. There is a constant, and somewhat legitimate, passing of the buck. . . .

It should be borne in mind that the target is always trying to shift responsibility to get out of being the target. There is a constant squirming and moving and strategy — purposeful, and malicious at times, other times just for straight self-survival — on the part of the designated target. The forces for change must keep this in mind and pin that target down securely. If an organization permits responsibility to be diffused and distributed in a number of areas, attack becomes impossible.

I remember specifically that when the Woodlawn Organization started the campaign against public school segregation, both the superintendent of schools and the chairman of the Board of Education vehemently denied any racist segregationist practices in the Chicago Public School System. They took the position that they did not even have any racial-identification data in their files, so they did not know which of their students were black and which were white. As for the fact that we had all-white schools and all-black schools, well, that's just the way it was.

If we had been confronted with a politically sophisticated school superintendent he could have very well replied, "Look, when I came to Chicago the city school system was following, as it is now, a neighborhood school policy. Chicago's neighborhoods are segregated. There are white neighborhoods and black neighborhoods and therefore you have white schools and black schools. Why attack me? Why not attack the segregated neighborhoods and change them?" He would have had a valid point, of sorts; I still shiver when I think of this possibility; but the segregated neighborhoods would have passed the buck to someone else and so it would have gone into a dog-chasing-his-tail pattern — and it would have been a fifteen-year job to try to break down the segregated residential pattern of Chicago. We did not have the power to start that kind of a conflict. One of the criteria in picking your target is the target's vulnerability — where do you have the power to start? Furthermore, any target can always say, "Why do you center on me when there are others to blame as well?" When you "freeze the target," you disregard these arguments and, for the moment, all the others to blame.

Then, as you zero in and freeze your target and carry out your attack, all of the "others" come out of the woodwork very soon. They become visible by their support of the target.

The other important point in the choosing of a target is that it must be a personification, not something general and abstract such as a community's segregated practices or a major corporation or City Hall. It is not possible to develop the necessary hostility against, say, City Hall, which after all is a concrete, physical, inanimate structure, or against a corporation, which has no soul or identity, or a public school administration, which again is an inanimate system.

John L. Lewis, the leader of the radical C.I.O. labor organization in the 1930s, was fully aware of this, and as a consequence the C.I.O. never attacked General Motors, they always attacked its president, Alfred "Icewater-In-His-Veins" Sloan; they never attacked the Republic Steel Corporation but always its president, "Bloodied Hands" Tom Girdler, and so with us when we attacked the then-superintendent of the Chicago public school system, Benjamin Willis. Let nothing get you off your target.

With this focus comes a polarization. As we have indicated before, all issues must be polarized if action is to follow. The classic statement on polarization comes from Christ: "He that is not with me is against me" (Luke 11:23). He allowed no middle ground to the money changers in the Temple. One acts decisively only in the conviction that all the angels are on one side and all the devils on the other. A leader may struggle toward a decision and weigh the merits and demerits of a situation which is 52 per cent positive and 48 per cent negative, but once the decision is reached he must assume that his cause is 100 per cent positive and the opposition 100 per cent negative. He can't toss forever in limbo, and avoid decision. He can't weigh arguments or reflect endlessly — he must decide and act. Otherwise there are Hamlet's words:

> And thus the native hue of resolution
> Is sicklied o'er with the pale cast of thought,
> And enterprises of great pith and moment
> With this regard their currents turn awry,
> And lose the name of action.

Many liberals, during our attack on the then-school superintendent, were pointing out that after all he wasn't a 100 per cent devil, he was a regular churchgoer, he was a good family man, and he was generous in his contributions to charity. Can you imagine in the arena of conflict charging that so-and-so is a racist bastard and then diluting the impact of the attack with qualifying remarks such as "He is a good churchgoing man, generous to charity, and a good husband"? This becomes political idiocy.

PART IV

The Civil War and Reconstruction

Introduction

The Justness of War and Legislating Social Change

In the 1960s and 1970s two issues held this nation's attention like no others: the justification of war and the legislation of social change. Vietnam and civil rights have been *the* issues of the past decades. The war no longer dominates the headlines, of course, but the issues it raised have not lost their importance. We are still concerned about amnesty and pardons for those who claimed that the Vietnam War was unjustified; we still need to consider if the lesson of Vietnam is "Never again." And the civil rights question still demands attention, so long as issues like busing, residential segregation, and welfare continue to trouble us. Even if, by some miracle, America's race problems were to be resolved tomorrow, we would still need to consider the question of whether the passage of laws in other areas of life can change people's behavior significantly.

This nation, like most others, has a long history of involvement in wars. Indeed, we became a nation as a result of one. Since the Revolutionary War, we have fought eight major wars: the War of 1812, the Mexican War, the Civil War, the Spanish-American War, World War I, World War II, the Korean War, and the Vietnam War. This list makes it obvious that during the last sixty years our propensity for this sort of activity has increased. There have been as many wars in the twentieth century as there were in the nineteenth, and we still have almost a quarter of this century before us! There is plenty of time to surpass the old record.

Each time we have gone to war we have told ourselves and the world that our cause was just: that our goals were noble; that we had no other way to achieve them; that we had been forced to choose battle by the evil designs of our enemies. The United States is not alone in making such statements: every nation proclaims that it fights for just ideals, that it is engaged in a defensive war, that it has no choice but to kill its enemies. Faced with the universality of this rhetoric, how do we choose whom to believe? How do we choose when to believe our own leaders, present and future, and how do we judge the merits of the arguments of Hitler, Ho Chi Minh, Stalin, Churchill, Presidents McKinley, Lincoln, or Jefferson Davis? A study of the Civil War should provide some experience in answering such questions.

Before we discuss the idea of a "just" war in the context of the Civil War, we should be aware of some problems in whatever analogies we may be tempted to use. The major problem is that war itself has changed from the mid-nineteenth century to our own age. The justifications for making war are still much the same, but the consequences of choosing war have become vastly more severe. First, there is the reality of the non-discriminatory nature of most modern weapons. Soldiers seldom see the people they kill with today's weapons. Second, bombs do not discriminate between combatants and civilians, no matter how hard pilots and their superiors may try to avoid killing innocent people. Third, the nature of modern warfare is such that the targets of war are not just troops in the field, but the industries and firms that produce supplies for those troops. Because modern technology has produced the possibility, and sometimes the probability, of killing innocent people, the question of the justification of a war today is different from justifying one in which soldiers shot only at other soldiers and where the destruction that took place behind the lines was almost exclusively the destruction of property, not lives. Still, the questions that we must pose of both past and present wars remain: Did the nation really need to go to war? Did it really act during war in as humane a way as possible? Did it gain by war something not possible by any other means? Did the gains in the quality of life outweigh the losses in lives?

The Civil War presents some difficulties in answering these questions. The major difficulty is that the reasons that the North went to war against the South differ from what is probably the major gain of the war. The Civil War began when the South threatened to destroy the Union; a major result of the war was that the Union was preserved, but a more crucial result was that the slaves were freed. Therefore, in deciding if the North was right in going to war, we must assess the extent of the threat to the Union. In evaluating the results of the war, we need to consider not only a secure Union, but the freedom of 4,000,000 slaves, against the losses suffered in that war. The question of a "just" war in the context of the Civil War is thus a complex one. For that reason it is also fascinating.

When the national government freed the slaves at the end of the Civil War, the issue of their freedom was not settled. An unavoidable question was posed: What sort of freedom would they have? Leaving them totally without federal protection was no answer. For 200 years the blacks of the nation had been considered the congenital inferiors of whites, and the end of slavery did not destroy those beliefs. The vast majority of southern whites believed that blacks would not work unless they were slaves. They insisted that unregulated freed slaves would turn to crime or would simply try to live off the state. Further, whites harbored a profound and irrational fear that without the regulations of bondage, intermarriage between the races would take place. These feelings held by a white population that outnumbered blacks by 3 to 1, and which had the experience of ruling slaves, produced an environment that made it impossible, if not criminal, simply to release the slaves from bondage.

The responsibility for securing the freedom of the former slaves thus was taken up by the national government, and immediately raised the issue: To what extent can our laws and their enforcement produce the change needed to give real freedom to the blacks? It was a question that is as familiar in the twentieth century as it was in the nineteenth.

In the modern world the question of legislating social change raises many questions concerning the capacity of laws to produce an egalitarian society. Perhaps the most volatile of recent times has been the issue of busing to achieve racially balanced schools. What courts have asked many people to do is to give up a long-standing tradition in which children attend their neighborhood schools. The issue has immediate impact on the daily lives of individuals. White and black parents are asked (or ordered) to put their children on a bus for a trip that may be over ten miles to a school in a neighborhood that the parents fear, either out of lack of knowledge or from actual knowledge of threatening circumstances. In short, today's issue asks individuals to make changes that they may fear and that they cannot escape.

The United States Supreme Court has said that busing may be used as a tool to achieve balanced schools. The policy has been attempted in some school systems, although resistance to the policy has been loud, and sometimes violent. Can we expect success for busing, or will public opinion force a withdrawal from the concept? Will the law fail to change social patterns? If we believe that busing will fail, does that mean that laws can never change behavior? Such an assumption would be false: since 1954 the pattern of segregation in the South has changed so greatly that there is now less segregation in southern schools than in northern schools.

What conclusions can be drawn about the ability of law to change society? How can we make decisions about future efforts to legislate social change? Confronting the problems of Reconstruction may help generate some new ideas.

The two issues of this section are interrelated. Part of the answer to whether or not the Civil War was justified by its results rests on the actual gains for the freed blacks. We must admit that immediate equal justice under law was not the result of the war. By 1890 the South was a segregated society and the blacks were excluded almost everywhere from economic opportunities as well as from civil and political rights. When social pressures failed in keeping the black "in his place," lynching and other forms of violence were used as persuasion. Not until the mid-twentieth century did the struggle for equality resurface. Not until then were blacks able to collect on the promises made to them in the Civil War era. The moral seems to be that as far as full liberty for the former slaves is concerned, both the war and the legislation of Reconstruction were failures, and 600,000 men died in vain.

On the other hand, would the promise of equality have existed in the twentieth century if slavery had not died a violent death in 1865? If southerners were willing to risk war to save slavery, is it likely that they would have given it up without a war?

The Reconstruction picture is not one of total failure. From about 1867 to 1877, blacks voted in large numbers, held offices ranging from local sheriff to United States senator. As late as the 1890s blacks retained some of these political and civil rights. And gains in education and property ownership, in the creation of a black community, which provided spiritual and social support and growth, laid the foundation for later achievements. Reconstruction was certainly no success story — the fact that a civil rights movement was necessary in our own time is proof of that. Still, interesting questions remain, even though the post-Civil War era did not totally resolve the problem of civil rights. We can and should ask: Was greater success of Reconstruction possible? What would have been the cost of greater success? And apart from the issue of success or failure, there lies the inescapable question: Was it right and necessary to attempt to use national power in this way?

Questions like these haunted the life of William Lloyd Garrison. His personal commitment to ending slavery meant that he could no more escape the challenges of legislating social change than he could avoid wondering whether or not a war that enhanced liberty could ever be just. Struggling with such questions must have been trying for him, because he had to change the very ideas for which he had risked his life: an active pacifist, he would come to accept and support the Civil War; an outspoken idealist, he struggled with the practical realities of using force to carry out his ideals.

Garrison was a man who always fought vehemently for his ideals. He dedicated his life to making his ideals reality. In examining his life, we not only reexamine the issue of agitation, but we direct our attention to the outcome of that agitation: war and reconstruction. And again, we gain the personal, human perspective on past issues that can challenge us to relate our lives to the issues of our own time.

Personalizing the Issues

William Lloyd Garrison:
Agitation and Social Change

According to some political theorists, agitation is often a necessary ingredient for social change. Certainly one of the greatest agitators in American history, William Lloyd Garrison, thought so. Few men have received as much praise or damnation as this short, bald, dynamic little man. Even fewer men would have been as unmoved by the attention they received as this determined idealist. Like most people, Garrison enjoyed praise, but he seldom sought it or showed gratitude when it was given. He was equally oblivious to the hatred and condemnation he

aroused, and although he never courted martyrdom, he always accepted it as a distinct possibility.

One must try to understand Garrison, as difficult as the task may be, because he spent his entire professional career debating the major conflicts of his age. While many other reformers of the day worked endlessly to develop a philosophy of abolitionism, the Great Agitator had only one thought to add to the arguments: "slavery was a crime, a damnable sin." He came to this conclusion early in life and never changed his basic concept. And yet it was this directness, this simplicity, which made him a pervasive force in the abolitionist movement in the 1830s, and an important one after that.

Basically, the answer to the question of his influence can be found in the forces which molded Garrison's mind. Born in 1805 in Newburyport, Massachusetts, to a happily married couple, Abijah and Fanny Garrison, he nonetheless grew up in poverty and loneliness. When Jefferson's Embargo closed the New England ports in 1807, ship's master Abijah Garrison lost the means of his livelihood, turned to drink, and eventually drifted away from his family and died in obscurity.

In the depression which followed the Embargo, Fanny Garrison found it impossible to find enough work to support her three children and keep the family together. Thus the seven-year-old Lloyd was apprenticed to a variety of people; first to a Baptist deacon, Ezekiel Bartlett, who gave him the love and understanding that his father never did, and then in succession, to a shoemaker, cabinetmaker, and printer. The last apprenticeship changed the course of Garrison's life. It lasted seven years, and when completed the young man embarked on a lifelong career as a printer and editor. Although he had almost no formal education, he became a self-educated man during his apprenticeship by reading contemporary and classical writers, particularly the works of Scott, Byron, and Milton.

Despite the fact that he grew up in a foster home, Garrison was very close to his mother, and her Baptist influence was the paramount force on his life. Until her death in 1823, she wrote long letters to her dutiful son advising him of the guidelines for a good Christian life. Her influence, along with that of Deacon Bartlett and the local Baptist minister, almost turned Garrison into a missionary. While he chose instead to become a printer, he was, in his mind, no less the Lord's disciple, as his mother's deeply engrained sense of righteousness controlled his life. Indeed, anyone who has read the *Liberator* cannot fail to note that his most passionate arguments were missionary in tone, urging salvation upon his readers. No one who knew the adult Garrison, even those who were violently opposed to his methods, ever doubted his honesty, integrity, or sincerity. His rigid concept of morality and total dedication created a host of devoted followers and kept men like Wendell Phillips, who were intellectually superior to Garrison, linked to his cause long after other disciples had defected. It also created a host of enemies, some of whom insisted that the New England abolitionist "neighed like a horse" when he discussed ideas contrary to his own, and others who placed a price upon his head.

The second major influence upon the young apprentice was the intellectual climate of his age, which can be summarized briefly as a fanatical belief in the human ability to progress. Moral progress was possible, even to a point of perfection, because this idealistic age promoted the belief that people would always do the "right thing" if someone would only show them "the light." The "light," of course, could be found in the Christian Gospel. This belief created a host of reform movements as idealistic Americans wanted to dedicate their nation to the achievement of the Puritan ideal of the "City Upon a Hill." The reforms touched every aspect of American life, including education, labor, war, dress, health, family, church, crime, and poverty. But the reformers who attacked what they considered evils and demanded change did not hate the society they often castigated; they loved it and wanted only to eradicate its evils. Wendell Phillips spoke for the vast majority of reformers when he stated that there could be no Republic without agitation. Thus the reformers tried to purify their beloved country by attacking all its wrongs.

The intellectual force which created this great optimism was twofold. It was a product of the natural rights philosophy of the Declaration of Independence and the nineteenth-century concept of Christianity. Together they created a militant democracy intolerant of the idea that people could not achieve political and spiritual perfection. These achievements, it was believed, could be accomplished by the incomparable ability to solve all problems as rational Christians. Only a civil war and 600,000 deaths were to shake this faith, and then not completely.

Even more than most of his contemporaries, Garrison was moved by the Christian idealism of his age. Unfortunately, it made him even more intolerant of those who disagreed with him than of his fellow reformers. Later generations would have difficulty understanding why there was so much conflict in an age that idealized the human ability to progress, but this broad faith also meant a specific faith in one's self, and this created conflict as individualistic Americans did not hesitate to challenge each other or their society. Most Americans agreed that the Kingdom of God was possible here on earth, but they also thought that they alone possessed the keys to the Kingdom.

Thus in 1825, when William Lloyd Garrison began his career as a printer, he carried with him the idealism and single-minded dedication of his age. Throughout his career he worked on, owned, or edited many papers, all of which reflected his longing for a moral society in which the Bible settled issues. Whatever cause would purify society became his: nonsmoking, temperance, women's rights, peace, and of course, abolitionism.

The crucial turning point in his career occurred in 1828 when he met the abolitionist Benjamin Lundy, a New Jersey Quaker who was passionately opposed to the "peculiar institution." One of the reasons that there were more antislavery organizations in the South than in the North before 1831 was due, in part, to Lundy's proselytizing. Advocating that "gradual, but total emancipation" was necessary for the Republic to survive, Lundy traveled from town to town, carrying his pack upon his back. Periodically he went to a local print shop and produced an edition of his antislavery paper, *The Genius of Universal Emancipation,* which he mailed to his subscribers. He also organized local antislavery groups.

Like everyone else, Garrison was impressed with Lundy's humble sincerity, and in 1829 he agreed to edit the Baltimore-based *Genius* so Lundy could spend all his time organizing abolitionist crusades. While the *Genius* attacked infidelity, intemperance, and Sabbath-breaking, it was basically devoted to the destruction of chattel slavery in the United States, mainly because it was "the greatest of evils."

At this point, Garrison made one of the few changes in his thinking. Talking, writing, and thinking about the slavery question brought him to the conclusion that both colonization — the establishment of colonies of former slaves in Africa or Latin America — and gradual emancipation were wrong. He concluded that colonization, which was then fashionable in liberal circles, was based on the false assumption that the natural rights philosophy of the Declaration of Independence belonged only to whites and that blacks had to be removed from the country. He also concluded that gradual emancipation was also erroneous because if blacks had the right to freedom, it, like all rights, was not to be compromised. Lundy disagreed with the latter view, but his famous conflict with his colleague came not over these views, but over Garrison's vicious way of stating them. Those who opposed Garrison's views were called "thieves," "blackguards," "moral lepers," "deranged bullies," and "Satanic manstealers." Since there was no doubt in his mind about the validity of his views, he stated them in the strongest language possible. The gentle and more temperate Lundy found this offensive, and a parting of the ways seemed unavoidable.

The argument between the two idealists was temporarily halted by a sea captain named Todd, who sued the abolitionist editor for libel when Garrison called Todd a "murderer . . . fit for the lowest depths of perdition. . . ." The captain had participated in the coastal sea trade in black slaves, and while later generations saw some validity in the charge since the death rate in the coastal trade was 25 percent, the Baltimore jury found Garrison guilty, and he was fined $50 and costs. When the abolitionist would not pay the fine, he was sentenced to jail. He remained there for forty-nine days until a philanthropist, Arthur Tappan of New York, paid the fine for him.

The agitation involved in the libel suit annoyed Lundy, and the two men went their separate ways. Garrison still admired his gentle coworker, but he considered Lundy too timid to be effective. Thus Garrison went back to New England and began a violent series of lectures against the "erroneous" concept of colonization. When they were finished, few important people in the antislavery movement in Boston doubted the falsehood of the colonist's position. Garrison's simple, straightforward arguments that slavery was immoral, barbaric, unchristian, undemocratic, and contrary to the spirit of the Declaration of Independence, seemed very logical to the Boston intellectuals. Although he was later condemned as an extreme radical — which he was — it should be remembered that while Garrison convinced the Bostonians that slavery was an evil because it denied the validity of the Declaration of Independence, John C. Calhoun was trying to convince southerners that there was not one "word of truth" in that famous document, since only a fool could believe that "all men were created equal," as men were born "neither free nor equal."

At this crucial juncture in American history when advocates in one section of the nation wanted to idolize the arguments of the Declaration and opponents in the other wanted to ignore them, Garrison launched his most famous enterprise: *The Liberator*. Whatever he had done before, or was to do after, paled in the minds of his contemporaries when his violently antislavery newspaper first appeared in print in 1831. He meant it when he said that he would be "as harsh as truth, and as uncompromising as justice . . ." and his bold claim that "I WILL BE HEARD . . ." was no idle boast.

What America heard from William Lloyd Garrison was a passionate appeal to end the forced enslavement of black people immediately. There were three ways, he said, that slavery could be ended: by force; by slave revolts; or through an appeal to enlightened opinion. As a pacifist, he rejected the first two possibilities and concentrated on an appeal to public opinion. But his language was so vituperative and his accusations so damning that some abolitionists considered his appeals unsuccessful. Many abolitionists wanted to persuade southerners not to attack their ideas. Garrison, however, thought the main appeal should be made to northerners because southerners were hardly open to argument on this subject.

Soon, despite the fact that he had little following outside of New England, he became the arch villain to southern slave-holders and the epitome of greatness to his loyal followers. His impact in the South was such that he was formally blamed for the Nat Turner insurrection of 1831. It made little difference to southerners that Garrison adopted pacifism as one of his many causes, nor that few abolitionists west of the Hudson accepted either the man or his tactics. What was significant was that Garrison created the impression in small, but important circles — both north and south — that he spoke for millions of northerners.

Despite, or because of, these exaggerations Garrison became the most important voice in the abolitionist crusade in the 1830s. For the next thirty years, like most Americans, he struggled with two of the most important issues of his era: To what extent can one legislate social change? and was there such a thing as a just war? On the first question Garrison concluded that the ultimate authority was God, and that no government that compromised with slaveholders could legislate social change. While most northerners accepted God as the ultimate authority in the abstract, in their immediate world they gave their overt loyalties to their state and federal governments because they had faith in their ability to bring about social change. When Garrison argued that the Constitution was a proslavery document which sanctioned the "peculiar institution," they argued that it was neutral on the slavery question and could be made an antislavery document only by political action. When he argued that slavery was a moral question that could be solved only by the individual's acceptance of the evilness of the institution, they countered that it was a moral question that could be solved by political as well as moral action. Eventually, Garrison's assumptions led him to believe that all governments were false — only people were pure — while his opponents contended that governments reflected people, and thus good people could create good governments that legislated social change.

Some historians have noted that Garrison's contention that people could not legislate social change was suspect since most of the causes he advocated eventually were brought about by social legislation. Others have noted, however, that some of them, like prohibition, were miserable failures. But, for better or worse, his contemporaries eventually concluded that, given proper leadership, people could right all wrongs.

Although Garrison was in the minority on the first question, he came to share the majority opinion on the second question: the justness of war. Like most Americans, he rallied to the call to arms in 1861. Southerners like Lee, who disliked slavery and secession, eventually fought to defend both, while Garrison's loyalty to a Christian God whom he thought hated wars was set aside when he gave his son tacit approval to join the Union army. Previously he had argued that there was a "higher law" than the Constitution that advocated "no union with slaveholders." In arguing this point, he took the radical stand that a person's ultimate allegiance was to God, not institutions, be they secular or religious. But most nineteenth-century Americans openly accepted their institutions as divinely inspired and saw no conflict in their loyalty to both their God and his institutions. The conflict came when they had to decide which divinely inspired institution commanded their utmost loyalty.

Thus beginning in 1840 with the rise of political abolitionism which led to the Liberty, Free Soil, and Republican parties, Garrison became even more isolated. Moral persuasion alone, he argued, could end slavery, and if it could not, then the North should secede from an "iniquitous union" with slaveholders. But beginning in 1850 with the passage of the famous compromise which contained a newer and stiffer Fugitive Slave Law, Garrison saw that social change, even the wrong kind, could be legislated. Many abolitionists came to feel that forceful "resistance to this black bill [the Fugitive Slave Law] was now obedience to God," and northerners who had been indifferent to bondage became antislavery when they realized that the government was trying to make them support slavery.

The changes of the next decade made Garrison realize that after thirty years of being a relatively lonely apostle of freedom for blacks, his ideas on the evils of slavery and no union with slave-holders were about to become generally accepted. While at first *he* could not accept the force which brought these ideas to fruition — political abolitionism — the secession of the South, the Emancipation Proclamation, and the Thirteenth Amendment gave him the long-awaited feeling of "being on the winning side." Success made him temper his ideals and temporarily accept the practical Lincoln as few other abolitionists did. Some abolitionists referred to the Great Emancipator as the "slave hound of Illinois," because he enforced the Fugitive Slave Law early in the war, but Garrison announced that he "had no idea that . . . [he] should live to see hell and death secede." Since they had, however, he was now "with the government . . . to extinguish the flames of hell forever."

Thus the transition from "no union with slaveholders," and a distrust of all governments and institutions, to a support of the Lincoln government, is not as drastic as it first seems. The abolitionist showed his belief in the government's ability to end slavery during the Civil War when his one-time disciple Wendell Phillips wrested control of the Massachusetts Antislavery Society from Garrison, only to be told by his former mentor that its work was done and the organization should be disbanded. Later during Reconstruction, while Phillips and others took up new causes, the sixty-year-old Garrison retired to enjoy the oft-neglected joys of family life.

Like many famous iconoclasts, Garrison enjoyed a stable, wholesome family life. His wife and children noted that he was gentle, kind, and considerate, as warm in person as he was violent in print. His puritanical self-righteousness which convinced him that he was a "soldier of God" also made him accept the family as the most important Christian institution. Whatever professional success one might have, he thought, made no difference if he did not create a Christian family.

And just what professional success did Garrison have? In his own words, the *Liberator* "began without a subscriber (1831) and ended without a farthing (1865)." He was seldom out of debt, and only a huge gift in 1868 from his admirers made it possible for him to stay at home and care for his invalid wife. Yet his life was no failure. In the 1830s he, more than any other American, made people think about the ugliness of black bondage. Prior to his ascendency, most antislavery societies had been in the South. When southern states closed all internal discusion on the slavery question, he became the most outspoken critic of "the cancer in the bosom of the nation," as John Quincy Adams had called slavery. Garrison's violent attacks converted many to the antislavery cause. Although many of his converts later became disciples of other abolitionists, his arguments were the first that many of them accepted. While some abolitionists charged that his intemperate ways did more harm than good to the cause, it must be remembered that the majority of southerners rejected the pleading of the gentle Lundy, and a northern mob killed the mild-mannered Elijah Lovejoy, who advocated gradual emancipation.

Since his death in 1879, Garrison has been called everything from a liability to the antislavery crusade to an irresponsible fanatic. Every one of his actions has been scrutinized and analyzed by some historian to understand what made him such a violent critic of slavery. Yet hindsight, which is always in twenty-twenty vision, makes one wonder not what was wrong with him, but what was wrong with the many Americans who ignored the obvious evils of slavery in a democratic nation for so long.

Issue

The Justness of War

The medieval thinkers rejected religion as a proper cause of a just war, and . . . politics is in the same general class as religion. . . . Is there really any doubt that men can live well under a variety of systems . . . ?

Donald A. Wells, 1969

We do not, as the black race, properly appreciate the old veterans, white or black, as we ought to. . . . Let the younger generation . . . remember that it was through the efforts of these veterans that they and we older ones enjoy our liberty today.

Susie King Taylor, 1902

"There has never been a good war, or a bad peace." To a generation that has seen the horrors of war brought into its own living rooms this statement may ring profoundly true. But ask the slaves of America after the Civil War; ask Hitler's victims after World War II; ask the Americans after the Revolutionary War. These people would probably say, "Yes, war is hell, but there are worse things."

War has revealed people at their most bestial. Women and children, the old and the helpless, have been tortured and killed. Yet for every comment like General Sherman's "War is hell," there can be found a countervailing sentiment. "That faith is true and adorable which leads a soldier to throw away his life in obedience to a blindly accepted duty." The words are those of a soldier and perhaps the greatest Supreme Court Justice, Oliver Wendell Holmes, Jr. Of some young French soldiers it was said, "They were very gentle, they cared nothing for their lives."

To confront the question of the justness of war is to also wrestle with the question, "What would you fight and die for?" Must the answer be "Nothing"? But if the answer is "my country," can we be satisfied? Must we accept the motto, "My country right or wrong," or may we prefer the wish of Albert Camus: "I should like to be able to love both justice and my country"?

The goals of nations that fight, the consequences of war's mass killing, the brutality and heroism of soldiers, the changes or unchanged conditions after the conflict — these are the evidence for assessing the justness of war. The Civil War, the Vietnam War, and others, past and future, require a serious jury.

◆ DOCUMENTS ◆

The Justness of the Rebel Cause

JEFFERSON DAVIS

Jefferson Davis justifies the Confederate cause. Davis spoke to the Confederate Provisional Congress on April 29, 1861, to explain both the general principles which justified secession, and the specific actions of the Lincoln government which required that the shooting start. What are the differences Davis sees between the North and the South? Do these differences justify dividing the Union? Why did the Confederates fire on Fort Sumter? Who started the war in Davis's opinion? Do you agree? What ideals is the South willing to fight, kill, and die for? Does Davis leave anything out of the reasons to fight which should be included?

Strange, indeed, must it appear to the impartial observer, but it is none the less true that all these carefully worded clauses [in the Constitution] proved unavailing to prevent the rise and growth in the Northern States of a political school which has persistently claimed that the government thus formed was not a compact *between* States, but was in effect a national government, set up *above* and *over* the States. An organization created by the States to secure the blessings of liberty and independence against *foreign* aggression, has been gradually perverted into a machine for their control in their *domestic* affairs. The *creature* has been exalted above its *creators;* the *principals* have been made subordinate to the *agent* appointed by themselves. The people of the Southern States, whose almost exclusive occupation was agriculture, early perceived a tendency in the Northern States to render the common government subservient to their own purposes by imposing burdens on commerce as

From James Richardson, ed., *Compilation of the Messages and Papers of the Confederacy* (Nashville: United States Publishing Co., 1905), I, 65–68, 71–73, 75–76, 81–82.

a protection to their manufacturing and shipping interests. Long and angry controversies grew out of these attempts, often successful, to benefit one section of the country at the expense of the other. And the danger of disruption arising from this cause was enhanced by the fact that the Northern population was increasing, by immigration and other causes, in a greater ratio than the population of the South. By degrees, as the Northern States gained preponderance in the National Congress, self-interest taught their people to yield ready assent to any plausible advocacy of their right as a majority to govern the minority without control. They learned to listen with impatience to the suggestion of any constitutional impediment to the exercise of their will, and so utterly have the principles of the Constitution been corrupted in the Northern mind that, in the inaugural address delivered by President Lincoln in March last, he asserts as an axiom, which he plainly deems to be undeniable, that the theory of the Constitution requires that in all cases the majority shall govern; and in another memorable instance the same Chief Magistrate did not hesitate to liken the relations between a State and the United States to those which exist between a county and the State in which it is situated and by which it was created. This is the lamentable and fundamental error on which rests the policy that has culminated in his declaration of war against these Confederate States. In addition to the long-continued and deep-seated resentment felt by the Southern States at the persistent abuse of the powers they had delegated to the Congress, for the purpose of enriching the manufacturing and shipping classes of the North at the expense of the South, there has existed for nearly half a century another subject of discord, involving interests of such transcendent magnitude as at all times to create the apprehension in the minds of many devoted lovers of the Union that its permanence was impossible. . . .

. . . As soon . . . as the Northern States that prohibited African slavery within their limits had reached a number sufficient to give their representation a controlling voice in the Congress, a persistent and organized system of hostile measures against the rights of the owners of slaves in the Southern States was inaugurated and gradually extended. A continuous series of measures was devised and prosecuted for the purpose of rendering insecure the tenure of property in slaves. Fanatical organizations, supplied with money by voluntary subscriptions, were assiduously engaged in exciting amongst the slaves a spirit of discontent and revolt; means were furnished for their escape from their owners, and agents secretly employed to entice them to abscond; the constitutional provision for their rendition to their owners was first evaded, then openly denounced as a violation of conscientious obligation and religious duty; men were taught that it was a merit to elude, disobey, and violently oppose the execution of the laws enacted to secure the performance of the promise contained in the constitutional compact; owners of slaves were mobbed and even murdered in open day solely for applying to a magistrate for the arrest of a fugitive slave; the dogmas of these voluntary organizations soon obtained control of the Legislatures of many of the Northern States, and laws were passed providing for the punishment, by ruinous fines and long-continued imprisonment in jails and penitentiaries, of citizens of the Southern States who should dare to ask aid of the officers of the law for the recovery of their property. Emboldened by success, the theater of agitation and aggression against the clearly expressed constitutional rights of the Southern States was transferred to the Congress; Senators and Representatives were sent to the common councils of the nation, whose chief title to this distinction consisted in the display of a spirit of ultra fanaticism, and whose business was not "to promote the general welfare or insure domestic tranquillity," but to awaken the bitterest hatred against the citizens of sister States by violent denunciation of their institutions; the transaction of public affairs was impeded by repeated efforts to usurp powers not delegated by the Constitution, for the purpose of impairing the security of property in slaves, and reducing those States which held slaves to a condition of inferiority. Finally a great party was organized for the purpose of obtaining the administration of the Government, with the avowed object of using its power for the total exclusion of the slave States from all participation in the benefits of the public domain acquired by all the States in common, whether by conquest or purchase; of surrounding them entirely by States in which slavery should be prohibited; of thus rendering the property in slaves so insecure as to be comparatively worthless, and thereby annihilating in effect property worth thousands of millions of dollars. This party, thus organized, succeeded in the month of November last in the election of its candidate for the Presidency of the United States. . . .

Early in April the attention of the whole country, as well as that of our commissioners, was attracted to extraordinary preparations for an extensive military and naval expedition in New York and other Northern ports. These preparations commenced in secrecy, for an expedition whose destination was concealed only became known when nearly completed, and on the 5th, 6th, and 7th of April transports and vessels of war with troops, munitions, and military supplies sailed from Northern ports bound southward. . . .

Even then, under all the provocation incident to the contemptuous refusal to listen to our commissioners, and the tortuous course of the Government of the United States, I was sincerely anxious to avoid the effusion of blood, and directed a proposal to be made to the commander of Fort Sumter, who had avowed himself to be nearly out of provisions, that we would abstain from directing our fire on Fort Sumter if he would promise not to open fire on our forces unless first attacked. This proposal was refused and the conclusion was reached that the design of the United States was to place the besieging force at Charleston between the simultaneous fire of the fleet and the fort. There remained, therefore, no alternative but to direct that the fort should at once be reduced. This order was executed by General Beauregard with the skill and success which were naturally to be expected from the well-known character of that gallant officer; and although the bombardment lasted but thirty-three hours our flag did not wave over its battered walls until after the appearance of the hostile fleet off Charleston. Fortunately, not a life was lost on our side, and we were gratified in being spared the necessity of a useless effusion of blood, by the prudent caution of the officers who commanded the fleet in abstaining from the evidently futile effort to enter the harbor for the relief of Major Anderson. . . .

. . . Scarcely had the President of the United States received intelligence of the failure of the scheme which he had devised for the reënforcement of Fort Sumter, when he issued the declaration of war against this Confederacy which has prompted me to convoke you. In this extraordinary production that high functionary affects total ignorance of the existence of an independent Government, which, possessing the entire and enthusiastic devotion of its people, is exercising its functions without question over seven sovereign States, over more than 5,000,000 of people, and over a territory whose area exceeds half a million of square miles. He terms sovereign States "combinations too powerful to be suppressed by the ordinary course of judicial proceedings or by the powers vested in the marshals by law." He calls for an army of 75,000 men to act as a *posse comitatus* in aid of the process of the courts of justice in States where no courts exist whose mandates and decrees are not cheerfully obeyed and respected by a willing people. He avows that "the *first* service to be assigned to the forces called out" will be not to execute the process of courts, but to capture forts and strongholds situated within the admitted limits of this Confederacy and garrisoned by its troops; and declares that "this effort" is intended "to maintain the perpetuity of popular government." He concludes by commanding "the persons composing the combinations aforesaid" — to wit, the 5,000,000 of inhabitants of these States — "to retire peaceably to their respective abodes within twenty days." Apparently contradictory as are the terms of this singular document, one point is unmistakably evident. The President of the United States called for an army of 75,000 men, whose *first* service was to be to capture our forts. It was a plain declaration of war which I was not at liberty to disregard because of my knowledge that under the Constitution of the United States the President was usurping a power granted exclusively to the Congress. . . .

. . . A people . . . united and resolved cannot shrink from any sacrifice which they may be called on to make, nor can there be a reasonable doubt of their final success, however long and severe may be the test of their determination to maintain their birthright of freedom and equality as a trust which it is their first duty to transmit undiminished to their posterity. A bounteous Providence cheers us with the promise of abundant crops. The fields of grain which will within a few weeks be ready for the sickle give assurance of the amplest supply of food for man; whilst the corn, cotton, and other staple productions of our soil afford abundant proof that up to this period the season has been propitious. We feel that our cause is just and holy; we protest solemnly in the face of mankind that we desire peace at any sacrifice save that of honor and independence; we seek no conquest, no aggrandizement, no concession of any kind from the States with which we were lately confederated; all we ask is to be let alone; that those who never held power over us shall not now attempt our subjugation by arms. This we will, this we must, resist to the direst extremity. The moment that this pretension is abandoned the sword will drop from our grasp, and we shall be ready to enter into treaties of amity and commerce that cannot but be mutually beneficial. So long as this pretension is maintained, with a firm reliance on that Divine Power which covers with its protection the just cause, we will continue to struggle for our inherent right to freedom, independence, and self-government.

Justice and the Survival of the Union

ABRAHAM LINCOLN

Abraham Lincoln justifies the Union position. On July 4, 1861, Lincoln explained why the Union had to be preserved and what the Confederates had done to begin the fighting. Who was the aggressor at Fort Sumter? Had Lincoln exhausted all remedies short of war? What latitude would Lincoln allow to states' rights? Is it sufficient to provide protection for the southern way of life? What distinguishes the Union cause from the Confederate? What principles is the Union fighting for? Would these principles be destroyed if secession were permitted?

At the beginning of the present Presidential term, four months ago, the functions of the Federal Government were found to be generally suspended within the several States of South Carolina, Georgia, Alabama, Mississippi, Louisiana, and Florida, excepting only those of the Post Office Department.

Within these States, all the Forts, Arsenals, Dock-yards, Customhouses, and the like, including the movable and stationary property in, and about them, had been seized, and were held in open hostility to this Government, excepting only Forts Pickens, Taylor, and Jefferson, on, and near the Florida coast, and Fort Sumter, in Charleston harbor, South Carolina. The Forts thus seized had been put in improved condition; new ones had been built; and armed forces had been organized, and were organizing, all avowedly with the same hostile purpose.

The Forts remaining in the possession of the Federal government, in, and near, these States, were either besieged or menaced by warlike preparations; and especially Fort Sumter was nearly surrounded by well-protected hostile batteries, with guns equal in quality to the best of its own, and outnumbering the latter as perhaps ten to one. A disproportionate share, of the Federal

From Roy P. Basler, ed., *Collected Works of Abraham Lincoln* (New Brunswick, N.J.: Rutgers University Press, 1953), IV, 421–426, 434–435, 438–439.

muskets and rifles, had somehow found their way into these States, and had been seized, to be used against the government. Accumulations of the public revenue, lying within them, had been seized for the same object. The Navy was scattered in distant seas; leaving but a very small part of it within the immediate reach of the government. Officers of the Federal Army and Navy, had resigned in great numbers; and, of those resigning, a large proportion had taken up arms against the government. Simultaneously, and in connection, with all this, the purpose to sever the Federal Union, was openly avowed. In accordance with this purpose, an ordinance had been adopted in each of these States, declaring the States, respectively, to be separated from the National Union. A formula for instituting a combined government of these states had been promulgated; and this illegal organization, in the character of confederate States was already invoking recognition, aid, and intervention, from Foreign Powers.

Finding this condition of things, and believing it to be an imperative duty upon the incoming Executive, to prevent, if possible, the consummation of such attempt to destroy the Federal Union, a choice of means to that end became indispensable. This choice was made; and was declared in the Inaugural address. The policy chosen looked to the exhaustion of all peaceful measures, before a resort to any stronger ones. It sought only to hold the public places and property, not already wrested from the Government, and to collect the revenue; relying for the rest, on time, discussion, and the ballot-box. It promised a continuance of the mails, at government expense, to the very people who were resisting the government; and it gave repeated pledges against any disturbance to any of the people, or any of their rights. Of all that which a president might constitutionally, and justifiably, do in such a case, everything was foreborne, without which, it was believed possible to keep the government on foot. . . .

. . . [T]he assault upon, and reduction of, Fort Sumter, was, in no sense, a matter of self defence on the part of the assailants. They well knew that the garrison in the Fort could, by no possibility, commit aggression upon them. They knew — they were expressly notified — that the giving of bread to the few brave and hungry men of the garrison, was all which would on that occasion be attempted, unless themselves, by resisting so much, should provoke more. They knew that this Government desired to keep the garrison in the Fort, not to assail them, but merely to maintain visible possession, and thus to preserve the Union from actual, and immediate dissolution — trusting, as herein-before stated, to time, discussion, and the ballot-box, for final adjustment; and they assailed, and reduced the Fort, for precisely the reverse object — to drive out the visible authority of the Federal Union, and thus force it to immediate dissolution.

That this was their object, the Executive well understood; and having said to them in the inaugural address, "You can have no conflict without being yourselves the aggressors," he took pains, not only to keep this declaration good, but also to keep the case so free from the power of ingenious sophistry, as that the world should not be able to misunderstand it. By the affair at Fort Sumter, with its surrounding circumstances, that point was reached. Then, and thereby, the assailants of the Government, began the conflict of arms, without a gun in sight, or in expectancy, to return their fire, save only the few in the Fort, sent to that harbor, years before, for their own protection, and still ready to give that protection, in whatever was lawful. In this act, discarding all else, they have forced upon the country, the distinct issue: "Immediate dissolution, or blood."

And this issue embraces more than the fate of these United States. It presents to the whole family of man, the question, whether a constitutional republic, or a democracy — a government of the people, by the same people — can, or cannot, maintain its territorial integrity, against its own domestic foes. It presents the question, whether discontented individuals, too few in numbers to control administration, according to organic law, in any case, can always, upon the pretences made in this case, or on any other pretences, or arbitrarily, without any pretence, break up their Government, and thus practically put an end to free government upon the earth. It forces us to ask: "Is there, in all republics, this inherent, and fatal weakness?" "Must a government, of necessity, be too *strong* for the liberties of its own people, or too *weak* to maintain its own existence?"

So viewing the issue, no choice was left but to call out the war power of the Government; and so to resist force, employed for its destruction, by force, for its preservation. . . .

. . . Much is said about the "sovereignty" of the States; but the word, even, is not in the national Constitution; nor, as is believed, in any of the State constitutions. What is a "sovereignty," in the political sense of the term? Would it be far wrong to define it "A political community, without a political superior"? Tested by this, no one of our States, except Texas, ever was a sovereignty. And even Texas gave up the character on coming into the Union; by which act, she acknowledged the Constitution of the United States, and the laws and treaties of the United States made in pursuance of the Constitution, to be, for her, the supreme law of the land. The States have their *status* IN the Union, and they have no other *legal status*. If they break from this, they can only do so against law, and by revolution. The Union, and not themselves separately, procured their independence, and their liberty. By conquest, or purchase, the Union gave each of them, whatever of independence, and liberty, it has. The Union is older than any of the States; and, in fact, it created them as States. Originally, some dependent colonies made the Union; and, in turn, the Union threw off their old dependence, for them, and made them States, such as they are. Not one of them ever had a State constitution, independent of the Union. Of course, it is not forgotten that all the new States framed their constitutions, before they entered the Union; nevertheless, dependent upon, and preparatory to, coming into the Union.

Unquestionably the States have the powers, and rights, reserved to them in, and by the National Constitution; but among these, surely, are not included all conceivable powers, however mischievous, or destructive; but, at most, such only, as were known in the world, at the time, as governmental powers; and certainly, a power to destroy the government itself, had never been known as a governmental — as a merely administrative power. This relative matter of National power, and State rights, as a principle, is no other than the principle of *generality,* and *locality.* Whatever concerns the whole, should be confided to the whole — to the general government; while, whatever concerns *only* the State, should be left exclusively, to the State. This is all there is of original principle about it. Whether the National Constitution, in defining boundaries between the two, has applied the principle with exact accuracy, is not to be questioned. We are all bound by that defining, without question. . . .

. . . Our adversaries have adopted some Declarations of Independence; in which, unlike the good old one, penned by Jefferson, they omit the words "all men are created equal." Why? They have adopted a temporary national constitution, in the preamble of which, unlike our good old one, signed by Washington, they omit "We, the People," and substitute "We, the deputies of the sovereign and independent States." Why? Why this deliberate pressing out of view, the rights of men, and the authority of the people?

This is essentially a People's contest. On the side of the Union, it is a struggle for maintaining in the world, that form, and substance of government, whose leading object is, to elevate the condition of men — to lift artificial weights from all shoulders — to clear the paths of laudable pursuit for all — to afford all, an unfettered start, and a fair chance, in the race of life. Yielding to partial, and temporary departures, from necessity, this is the leading object of the government for whose existence we contend. . . .

Our popular government has often been called an experiment. Two points in it, our people have already settled — the successful *establishing,* and the successful *administering* of it. One still remains — its successful *maintenance* against a formidable [internal] attempt to overthrow it. It is now for them to demonstrate to the world, that those who can fairly carry an election, can also suppress a rebellion — that ballots are the rightful, and peaceful, successors of bullets; and that when ballots have fairly, and constitutionally, decided, there can be no successful appeal, back to bullets; that there can be no successful appeal, except to ballots themselves, at succeeding elections. Such will be a great lesson of peace; teaching men that what they cannot take by an election, neither can they take it by a war — teaching all, the folly of being the beginners of a war.

War and Victims of Injustice

NEW YORK TIMES

The New York Times *reprints a story describing the brutality of the war. Can any war which includes such activities, however few they may be, be justified? Does the existence of this brutality discredit the activity of soldiers and statesmen who condemned it and fought in more humane ways? Can war ever be fought in humane ways?*

BARBAROUS OUTRAGES PERPETRATED UPON UNION MEN BY THE REBELS

From the Memphis Bulletin

EAST TENNESSEE — From Col. Robert A. Crawford, of Green County, Tennessee, who is a refugee, and was one of the Vice Presidents of the late Convention at Nashville, we learn the following facts in reference to rebel rule in that beautiful "Switzerland of America," East Tennessee. Col. Crawford has a personal knowledge of some of the facts, having left the scene of their enactment quite recently, and vouches for the truth of all of them, as his information was obtained from trustworthy persons, and written down on the spot. Last Summer three young men, brothers named Anderson, left their home in Hawkins County, and attempted to make their way into Kentucky. They were arrested by a squad of Confederate cavalry on Clinch River, about 75 miles from Knoxville, shot, and thrown into the river. Their bodies were found floating in the stream, fifteen miles from their own forsaken homes.

The Scarcity of Salt

In the month of January, 1863, at Laurel, N.C. near the Tennessee border, all the salt was seized for distribution by Confederate Commissioners. Salt was selling at $75 to $100 a sack. The Commissioners declared that the "Tories should have none," and positively refused to give Union men their portion of the quantity to be distributed in that vicinity. This palpable injustice roused the Union men; they assembled together and determined to seize their proportion of the salt by force. They did so, taking at Marshall, N.C. what they deemed to be their just share.

Arrests for Seizing Salt

L. M. Allen was Colonel of the regiment, but had been suspended for six months for crime and drunkenness. Many of the men engaged in the salt seizure left their homes. Those who did not participate in it became the suffer-

---

From the *New York Times*, July 24, 1863, p. 3.

ers. Among those arrested were Joseph Wood about 60 years of age; Dave Shelton, 60; Jus Shelton, 50; Roddy Shelton, 45; Edson King, 60; Halen Moore, 40; Wade Moore, 35; Isaiah Shelton, 15; William Shelton, 12; James Metcalf, 10; Jasper Chunnel, 14; Samuel Shelton, 19, and his brother, aged 17, sons of Lifus Shelton — in all, thirteen men and boys. Nearly all of them declared they were innocent, and had taken no part in appropriating the salt. They begged for a trial, asserting that they could prove their innocence.

The Execution

Colonel Allen, who was with his troops, but not in command, told them they should have a trial, but they would be taken to Tennessee for that purpose. They bid farewell to their wives, daughters, and sisters directing them to procure the witnesses and bring them to the Court in Tennessee, where they supposed their trial would take place. Alas! how little they dreamed what a fate awaited them!

Horrible Barbarities

The poor fellows had proceeded but a few miles, when they were turned from the road into a gorge on the mountain, and halted. Without any warning of what was to be done with them, five of them were ordered to kneel down. Ten paces in front of these five, a file of soldiers were placed with loaded muskets. The terrible reality flashed upon the minds of the doomed patriots. Old man Wood (sixty years of age) cried out, "For God's sake, men, you are not going to shoot us? If you are going to murder us, give us at least time to pray." Colonel Allen was reminded of his promise to give them a trial. They were informed that Allen had no authority; that Keith was in command, and that there was no time for praying. The order was given to fire, the old men and boys put their hands to their faces and rent the air with agonizing cries of despair; the soldiers wavered and hesitated to obey the command. Keith said if they did not fire instantly he would make them change places with the prisoners. The soldiers raised their guns, and the victims shuddered convulsively, the word was given to fire, and the five men fell pierced with rebel bullets. Old men Wood and Shelton were shot in the head, their brains scattered upon the ground, and they died without a struggle. The other three lived only a few minutes.

Murder of a Boy of Twelve Years

Five others were ordered to kneel, among them little Billy Shelton, a mere child, only twelve years old. He implored the men not to shoot him in the face. "You have killed my father and brothers," said he, "You have shot my father in the face; do not shoot me in the face." He covered his face with his hands. The soldiers received the order to fire, and five more fell. Poor little Billy was wounded in both arms. He ran to an officer, clasped him around the legs and besought him to spare his life. "You have killed my old father and my three brothers; you have shot me in both arms — I forgive you all this —

I can get well. Let me go home to my mother and sisters." What a heart of adament the man must have who could disregard such an appeal. The little boy was dragged back to the place of execution, again the terrible word, "fire" was given, and he fell dead, eight balls having entered his body. The remaining three were murdered in the same manner. Those in whom life was not entirely extinct the heartless officers dispatched with their pistols.

The Burial

A hole was then dug, and the 13 bodies were pitched into it. The grave was scarcely large enough; some of the bodies lay above the ground. A wretch named Sergeant N. B. D. Jay a Virginian, but attached to a Tennessee company of the Sixty-fifth North Carolina regiment, jumped upon the bleeding bodies and said to some of the men — "Pat Juba for me, while I dance the damned scoundrels down to and through hell." The grave was covered lightly with earth, and the next day, when the wives and families of the murdered men heard of their fate, searched for and found their grave, the hogs had rooted up one man's body and eaten his head off.

Torturing Defenseless Women

Captain Moonley, in charge of a cavalry force, and Colonel Thomas, in command of a number of Indians, accompanied Keith's men. These proceeded to Tennessee; Keith's men returned to Laurel, and were instructed to say that the cavalry had taken the prisoners with them to be tried, in accordance with the pledge of Colonel Allen. In their progress through the country, many Union men were known to have been killed and scalped by the Indians. Upon the return of Keith and his men to Laurel, they began systematically to torture the women of loyal men, to force them to tell where their fathers and husbands were, and what part each had taken in the salt raid. The women refused to divulge anything. They were then whipped with hickory switches — many of them till the blood, coursed in streams down their persons to the ground; and the men who did this were called soldiers. Mrs. Sarah Shelton, wife of Esau Shelton, who escaped from the town, and Mrs. Mary Shelton, wife of Lifus Shelton, were whipped and hung by the neck till they were almost dead, but would give no information. Martha White an idiotic girl, was beaten, and tied by the neck all day to a tree.

A Woman of Eighty-five Hung

Old Mrs. Unus Riddle, aged eighty-five years, was whipped, hung, and robbed of a considerable amount of money. Many others were treated with the same barbarity. And the men who did this were called soldiers! The daughters of William Shelton, a man of wealth and highly respectable, were requested by some of the officers to sing and play for them. They played and sang a few national airs. Keith learned of it, and ordered that the ladies be placed under arrest and sent to the guard-house, where they remained all night.

Old Mrs. Sallie Moore, 70 years of age, was whipped with hickory rods till the blood ran in streams down her back to the ground; and the perpetrators of this were clothed in the habitments of rebellion, and bore the name of soldiers!

One woman, who had an infant five or six weeks old, was tied in the snow to a tree, her child placed in the doorway in her sight, and she was informed that if she did not tell all she knew about the seizure of the salt, both herself and the child would be allowed to perish. Sergeant N. B. D. Jay, of Captain Reynold's company, and Lieutenant R. M. Deever, assisted their men in the execution of these hellish outrages. Houses were burned and torn down. All kinds of property was destroyed or carried off.

Interference of General Donelson

All the women and children of the Union men who were shot, and of those who escaped, were ordered by General Alfred E. Jackson, headquarters at Jonesburg, to be sent through the lines by way of Knoxville. When the first of them arrived at this place, the officer in charge applied to General Donelson (formerly Speaker of the House of Representatives at Nashville) to know by which route they should be sent from there, whether by Cumberland Gap or Nashville. General Donelson immediately directed them to be released and sent home, saying that such a thing was unknown in civilized countries. They were then sent home and all the refugees met on the road were also turned back.

Killing a Conscript

On the 13th of February, 1863, a squad of soldiers were sent to conscript James McCollum, of Greene County, Tennessee, a very respectable, industrious man, 30 or 35 years of age. They found him feeding his cattle. When he saw some of them he ran to the back of his barn; others were posed behind the barn, and without balking or attempting to arrest him, one of them shot him through the neck, killing him instantly. His three little children who saw it, ran to the house and told their mother; she came out wringing her hands in anguish, and screaming with terror and dismay.

The soldiers were sitting upon the fence. They laughed at her agony, and said they had only killed a "———d Tory." The murdered man was highly esteemed by his neighbors, and was a firm Union man.

In April last, two rebel soldiers, named Wood and Iredell, went to the house of Mrs. Ruth Ann Reah, living on the waters of Lick Creek, Greene County, to conscript her son. The old lady was partially deranged, she commanded the soldiers to leave her house, and raised a stick to strike one of them. He told her if she struck him he would run her through with his bayonet; she gave the blow, and he shot her through the breast.

An Old Man of Sixty Hung

In the same month, Jesse Price, an old man sixty years of age, two sons and two nephews, were arrested in Johnson County, Tennessee, bordering on Virginia, by Colonel Fouke's cavalry, composed of Tennessee and North Carolina men. They were taken to Ash County, North Carolina, to be tried for disloyalty to Jefferson Davis & Company. The old man had been previously arrested, taken to Knoxville, tried and acquitted.

When the five prisoners arrived in Ash County, a groggery-keeper proposed to treat Fouke's men to eight gallons of brandy, if they would hang the old man, his sons and nephews, without a trial. The bargain was struck, and the five unfortunate men were hanged without further ceremony. The brandy was furnished, and some of it drank before the tragedy, the rest afterward.

War, the Midwife of Equal Justice

WILLIAM LLOYD GARRISON

William Lloyd Garrison explains in early 1862 why a pacifist like himself can support the Civil War, and why he wants the Lincoln government to emancipate the slaves. Does Garrison come to grips with the issue of killing in the war? Why is he glad that the South seceded? What benefits will emerge from the war, according to Garrison? Is he willing to support Lincoln even before the president emancipates the slaves?

. . . What have we to rejoice over? . . .

Why, I say, the war! "What! this fratricidal war? What! this civil war? What! this treasonable dismemberment of the Union?" Yes, thank God for it all! — for it indicates the waning power of slavery and the irresistible growth of freedom, and that the day of Northern submission is past. It is better that we should be so virtuous that the vicious cannot live with us, than to be so vile that they can endure and relish our company. No matter what may be said of the Government — how it timidly holds back — how it lacks courage, energy, and faith — how it refuses to strike the blow which alone will settle the rebellion. No matter what may be said of President Lincoln or General McClellan, by way of criticism — and a great deal can be justly said to their condemnation — one cheering fact overrides all these considerations, making them as dust in the balance, and that is, that our free North is utterly unendurable to the slaveholding South; that we have at last so far advanced in our love of liberty and sympathy for the oppressed, as a people, that it is not possible any longer for the "traffickers in slaves and souls of men" to walk in union with us. I call that a very cheering fact. Yes, the Union is divided; but better di-

From Wendell Phillips Garrison and Francis Jackson Garrison, eds., *William Lloyd Garrison: The Story of His Life* (New York: The Century Co., 1889), IV, 43–45.

vision than that we should be under the lash of Southern overseers! Better civil war, if it must come, than for us to crouch in the dust, and allow ourselves to be driven to the wall by a miserable and merciless slave oligarchy! This war has come because of the increasing love of liberty here at the North; and although, as a people, we do not yet come up to the high standard of duty in striking directly at the slave system for its extirpation as the root and source of all our woe — nevertheless, the sentiment of the North is deepening daily in the right direction.

I hold that it is not wise for us to be too microscopic in endeavoring to find disagreeable and annoying things, still less to assume that everything is waxing worse and worse, and that there is little or no hope. No! broaden your views; take a more philosophical grasp of the great question; and see that, criticise and condemn as you may and should in certain directions, the fountains of the great deep are broken up — see that this is fundamentally a struggle between all the elements of freedom on the one hand, and all the elements of despotism on the other, with whatever of alloy in the mixture.

I repeat, the war furnishes ground for high encouragement. "Why," some may exclaim, "we thought you were a peace man!" Yes, verily, I am, and none the less so because of these declarations. Would the cause of peace be the gainer by the substitution of the power of the rebel traitors over the nation for the supremacy of the democratic idea? Would the cause of peace be promoted by the North basely yielding up all her rights and allowing her free institutions to be overthrown? Certainly not. Then, as a peace man, I rejoice that the issue is at last made up, and that the struggle is going on, because I see in it the sign of ultimate redemption. . . .

I do not know that some margin of allowance may not be made even for the Administration. I would rather be over-magnanimous than wanting in justice. Supposing Mr. Lincoln could answer to-night, and we should say to him: "Sir, with the power in your hands, slavery being the cause of the rebellion beyond all controversy, why don't you put the trump of jubilee to your lips, and proclaim universal freedom?" — possibly he might answer: "Gentlemen, I understand this matter quite as well as you do. I do not know that I differ in opinion from you; but will you insure me the support of a united North if I do as you bid me? Are all parties and all sects at the North so convinced and so united on this point that they will stand by the Government? If so, give me the evidence of it, and I will strike the blow. But, gentlemen, looking over the entire North, and seeing in all your towns and cities papers representing a considerable, if not a formidable portion of the people, menacing and bullying the Government in case it dare to liberate the slaves, even as a matter of self-preservation, I do not feel that the hour has yet come that will render it safe for the Government to take that step." I am willing to believe that something of this feeling weighs in the mind of the President and the Cabinet, and that there is some ground for hesitancy, as a mere matter of political expediency. My reply, however, to the President would be: "Sir, the power is in your hands as President of the United States, and Commander-in-

Chief of the army and navy. Do *your* duty; give to the slaves their liberty by proclamation, as far as that can give it; and if the North shall betray you, and prefer the success of the rebellion to the preservation of the Union, let the dread responsibility be hers, but stand with God and Freedom on your side, come what may!" But men high in office are not apt to be led by such lofty moral considerations; and, therefore, we should not judge the present incumbents too harshly. Doubtless, they want to be assured of the Northern heart, feeling, coöperation, approval. Can these be safely relied upon when the decisive blow shall be struck? That is the question, and it is a very serious question. . . .

Nevertheless, I think the Administration is unnecessarily timid and not undeserving of rebuke. I think that this bellowing, bullying, treasonable party at the North has, after all, but very little left, either in point of numbers or power; the fangs of the viper are drawn, though the venomous feeling remains. Still, it has its effect, and produces a damaging, if not paralyzing, impression at Washington.

War and the Irrelevance of Justice
WALT WHITMAN

Walt Whitman offers his understanding of the meaning of the war. What was the full dimension of the killing? Do numbers alone tell the full story? Do you think that Whitman sees any value in the war?

What history, I say, can ever give — for who can know — the mad, determin'd tussle of the armies, in all their separate large and little squads — as this — each steep'd from crown to toe in desperate, mortal purports? Who know the conflict, hand-to-hand — the many conflicts in the dark, those shadowy-tangled, flashing moonbeam'd woods — the writhing groups and squads — the cries, the din, the cracking guns and pistols — the distant cannon — the cheers and calls and threats and awful music of the oaths — the indescribable mix — the officers' orders, persuasions, encouragements — the devils fully rous'd in human hearts — the strong shout, *Charge, men, charge* — the flash of the naked sword, and rolling flame and smoke? And still the broken, clear and clouded heaven — and still again the moonlight pouring silvery soft its radiant patches over all. Who paint the scene, the sudden partial panic of the afternoon, at dusk? Who paint the irrepressible advance of the second division of the Third corps, under Hooker himself, suddenly order'd

From Walt Whitman, *Specimen Days and Collect* (Philadelphia: Rees Welsh and Co., 1882–1883), pp. 35–36, 79–81.

up — those rapid-filing phantoms through the woods? Who show what moves there in the shadows, fluid and firm — to save, (and it did save,) the army's name, perhaps the nation? as there the veterans hold the field. (Brave Berry falls not yet — but death has mark'd him — soon he falls.)

Unnamed Remains the Bravest Soldier

Of scenes like these, I say, who writes — whoe'er can write the story? Of many a score — aye, thousands, north and south, of unwrit heroes, unknown heroisms, incredible, impromptu, first-class desperations — who tells? No history ever — no poem sings, no music sounds, those bravest men of all — those deeds. No formal general's report, nor book in the library, nor column in the paper, embalms the bravest, north or south, east or west. Unnamed, unknown, remain, and still remain, the bravest soldiers. Our manliest — our boys — our hardy darlings; no picture gives them. Likely, the typic one of them (standing, no doubt, for hundreds, thousands,) crawls aside to some bush-clump, or ferny tuft, on receiving his death-shot — there sheltering a little while, soaking roots, grass and soil, with red blood — the battle advances, retreats, flits from the scene, sweeps by — and there, haply with pain and suffering (yet less, far less, than is supposed,) the last lethargy winds like a serpent round him — the eyes glaze in death — none recks — perhaps the burial-squads, in truce, a week afterwards, search not the secluded spot — and there, at last, the Bravest Soldier crumbles in mother earth, unburied and unknown. . . .

The Million Dead, Too, Summ'd Up

The dead in this war — there they lie, strewing the fields and woods and valleys and battle-fields of the south — Virginia, the Peninsula — Malvern hill and Fair Oaks — the banks of the Chickahominy — the terraces of Fredericksburgh — Antietam bridge — the grisly ravines of Manassas — the bloody promenade of the Wilderness — the varieties of the *strayed* dead, (the estimate of the War department is 25,000 national soldiers kill'd in battle and never buried at all, 5,000 drown'd — 15,000 inhumed by strangers, or on the march in haste, in hitherto unfound localities — 2,000 graves cover'd by sand and mud by Mississippi freshets, 3,000 carried away by caving-in of banks, &c.,) — Gettysburgh, the West, Southwest — Vicksburgh — Chattanooga — the trenches of Petersburgh — the numberless battles, camps, hospitals everywhere — the crop reap'd by the mighty reapers, typhoid, dysentery, inflammations — and blackest and loathesomest of all, the dead and living burial-pits, the prison-pens of Andersonville, Salisbury, Belle-Isle, &c., (not Dante's pictured hell and all its woes, its degradations, filthy torments, excell'd those prisons) — the dead, the dead, the dead — *our* dead — or South or North, ours all, (all, all, all, finally dear to me) — or East or West — Atlantic coast or Mississippi valley — somewhere they crawl'd to die, alone, in bushes, low gullies, or on the sides of hills — (there, in secluded spots, their skeletons, bleach'd bones, tufts of hair, buttons, fragments of clothing, are occasionally found yet) — our young men once so handsome and so joyous, taken from us — the son from the mother, the husband from the wife, the dear friend from the dear friend — the clusters of camp graves, in Georgia, the Carolinas, and in Tennessee — the single graves left in the woods or by the road-side, (hundreds, thousands, obliterated) — the corpses floated down the rivers, and caught and lodged, (dozens, scores, floated down the upper Potomac, after the cavalry engagements, the pursuit of Lee, following Gettysburgh) — some lie at the bottom of the sea — the general million, and the special cemeteries in almost all the States — the infinite dead — (the land entire saturated, per-fumed with their impalpable ashes' exhalation in Nature's chemistry distill'd, and shall be so forever, in every future grain of wheat and ear of corn, and every flower that grows, and every breath we draw) — not only Northern dead leavening Southern soil — thousands, aye tens of thousands, of Southerners, crumble to-day in Northern earth.

And everywhere among these countless graves — everywhere in the many soldier Cemeteries of the Nation, (there are now, I believe, over seventy of them) — as at the time in the vast trenches, the depositories of slain, Northern and Southern, after the great battles — not only where the scathing trail passed those years, but radiating since in all the peaceful quarters of the land — we see, and ages yet may see, on monuments and gravestones, singly or in masses, to thousands or tens of thousands, the significant word Unknown.

(In some of the cemeteries nearly *all* the dead are unknown. At Salisbury, N.C., for instance, the known are only 85, while the unknown are 12,027, and 11,700 of these are buried in trenches. A national monument has been put up here, by order of Congress, to mark the spot — but what visible, material monument can ever fittingly commemorate that spot?)

The Real War Will Never Get in the Books

And so good-bye to the war. I know not how it may have been, or may be, to others — to me the main interest I found, (and still, on recollection, find,) in the rank and file of the armies, both sides, and in those specimens amid the hospitals, and even the dead on the field. To me the points illustrating the latent personal character and eligibilities of these States, in the two or three millions of American young and middle-aged men, North and South, embodied in those armies — and especially the one-third or one-fourth of their number, stricken by wounds or disease at some time in the course of the contest — were of more significance even than the political interests involved. (As so much of a race depends on how it faces death, and how it stands personal anguish and sickness. As, in the glints of emotions under emergencies, and the indirect traits and asides in Plutarch, we get far profounder clues to the antique world than all its more formal history.)

Future years will never know the seething hell and the black infernal background of countless minor scenes and interiors, (not the official surface-courteousness of the Generals, not the few great battles) of the Secession war; and it is best they should not — the real war will never get in the books. In the mushy influences of current times, too, the fervid atmosphere and typical events of those years are in danger of being totally forgotten. I have at night watch'd by the side of a sick man in the hospital, one who could not live many hours. I have seen his eyes flash and burn as he raised himself and recurr'd to the cruelties on his surrender'd brother, and mutilations of the corpse afterward. (See, in the preceding pages, the incident at Upperville — the seventeen kill'd as in the description, were left there on the ground. After they dropt dead, no one touch'd them — all were made sure of, however. The carcasses were left for the citizens to bury or not, as they chose.)

Such was the war. It was not a quadrille in a ball-room. Its interior history will not only never be written — its practicality, minutiæ of deeds and passions, will never be even suggested. The actual soldier of 1862–'65, North and South, with all his ways, his incredible dauntlessness, habits, practices, tastes, language, his fierce friendship, his appetite, rankness, his superb strength and animality, lawless gait, and a hundred unnamed lights and shades of camp, I say, will never be written — perhaps must not and should not be.

War and the Ambiguity of Justice
SUSIE KING TAYLOR

In 1902, Susie King Taylor looked back on the war and what the blacks gained from it. What benefits does she find? What problems continue to exist? As a black woman, where would Ms. Taylor be had there been no war? Does she believe she is better off because of the war? Are the benefits of the war a sufficient exchange for the costs?

My dear friends! do we understand the meaning of war? Do we know or think of that war of '61? No, we do not, only those brave soldiers, and those who had occasion to be in it, can realize what it was. I can and shall never forget that terrible war until my eyes close in death. The scenes are just as fresh in my mind to-day as in '61. I see now each scene, — the roll-call, the drum tap, "lights out," the call at night when there was danger from the enemy, the double force of pickets, the cold and rain. How anxious I would be, not knowing what would happen before morning! Many times I would dress, not sure but all would be captured. Other times I would stand at my tent door and try to see what was going on, because night was the time the rebels would try to get into our lines and capture some of the boys. It was mostly at night

From Susie King Taylor, *Reminiscences of My Life in Camp* (Boston, 1902), pp. 50–52, 61–62, 64–66. Published by the author.

that our men went out for their scouts, and often had a hand to hand fight with the rebels, and although our men came out sometimes with a few killed or wounded, none of them ever were captured.

We do not, as the black race, properly appreciate the old veterans, white or black, as we ought to. I know what they went through, especially those black men, for the Confederates had no mercy on them; neither did they show any toward the white Union soldiers. I have seen the terrors of that war. I was the wife of one of those men who did not get a penny for eighteen months for their services, only their rations and clothing. . . .

I look around now and see the comforts that our younger generation enjoy, and think of the blood that was shed to make these comforts possible for them, and see how little some of them appreciate the old soldiers. My heart burns within me, at this want of appreciation. There are only a few of them left now, so let us all, as the ranks close, take a deeper interest in them. Let the younger generation take an interest also, and remember that it was through the efforts of these veterans that they and we older ones enjoy our liberty to-day. . . .

Living here in Boston where the black man is given equal justice, I must say a word on the general treatment of my race, both in the North and South, in this twentieth century. I wonder if our white fellow men realize the true sense or meaning of brotherhood? For two hundred years we had toiled for them; the war of 1861 came and was ended, and we thought our race was forever freed from bondage, and that the two races could live in unity with each other, but when we read almost every day of what is being done to my race by some whites in the South, I sometimes ask, "Was the war in vain? Has it brought freedom, in the full sense of the word, or has it not made our condition more hopeless?"

In this "land of the free" we are burned, tortured, and denied a fair trial, murdered for any imaginary wrong conceived in the brain of the negro-hating white man. There is no redress for us from a government which promised to protect all under its flag. It seems a mystery to me. They say, "One flag, one nation, one country indivisible." Is this true? Can we say this truthfully, when one race is allowed to burn, hang, and inflict the most horrible torture weekly, monthly, on another? No, we cannot sing, "My country, 'tis of thee, Sweet land of Liberty"! It is hollow mockery. The Southland laws are all on the side of the white, and they do just as they like to the negro, whether in the right or not. . . .

One thing I have noticed among my people in the South: they have accumulated a large amount of real estate, far surpassing the colored owners in the North, who seem to let their opportunity slip by them. Nearly all of Brownsville (a suburb of Savannah) is owned by colored people, and so it is in a great many other places throughout the State, and all that is needed is the protection of the law as citizens.

In 1867, soon after the death of my father, who had served on a gunboat during the war, my mother opened a grocery store, where she kept general merchandise always on hand. These she traded for cash or would exchange for crops of cotton, corn, or rice, which she would ship once a month, to F. Lloyd & Co., or Johnson & Jackson, in Savannah. These were colored merchants, doing business on Bay Street in that city. Mother bought her first property, which contained ten acres. She next purchased fifty acres of land. Then she had a chance to get a place with seven hundred acres of land, and she bought this.

In 1870, Colonel Hamilton and Major Devendorft, of Oswego, N.Y., came to the town and bought up a tract of land at a place called Doctortown, and started a mill. Mrs. Devendorft heard of my mother and went to see her, and persuaded her to come to live with her, assuring her she would be as one of the family. Mother went with her, but after a few months she went to Doctortown, where she has been since, and now owns the largest settlement there. All trains going to Florida pass her place, just across the Altamaha River. She is well known by both white and black; the people are fond of her, and will not allow any one to harm her.

Mr. Devendorft sold out his place in 1880 and went back to New York, where later he died.

I read an article, which said the ex-Confederate Daughters had sent a petition to the managers of the local theatres in Tennessee to prohibit the performance of "Uncle Tom's Cabin," claiming it was exaggerated (that is, the treatment of the slaves), and would have a very bad effect on the children who might see the drama. I paused and thought back a few years of the heart-rending scenes I have witnessed; I have seen many times, when I was a mere girl, thirty or forty men, handcuffed, and as many women and children, come every first Tuesday of each month from Mr. Wiley's trade office to the auction blocks, one of them being situated on Drayton Street and Court Lane, the other on Bryant Street, near the Pulaski House. The route was down our principal street, Bull Street, to the court-house, which was only a block from where I resided.

All people in those days got all their water from the city pumps, which stood about a block apart throughout the city. The one we used to get water from was opposite the court-house, on Bull Street. I remember, as if it were yesterday, seeing droves of negroes going to be sold, and I often went to look at them, and I could hear the auctioneer very plainly from my house, auctioning these poor people off.

Do these Confederate Daughters ever send petitions to prohibit the atrocious lynchings and wholesale murdering and torture of the negro? Do you ever hear of them fearing this would have a bad effect on the children? Which of these two, the drama or the present state of affairs, makes a degrading impression upon the minds of our young generation? In my opinion it is not "Uncle Tom's Cabin," but it should be the one that has caused the world to cry "Shame!" It does not seem as if our land is yet civilized. It is like times long past, when rulers and high officers had to flee for their lives, and the negro has been dealt with in the same way since the war by those he lived with and toiled for two hundred years or more. I do not condemn all the Caucasian race because the negro is badly treated by a few of the race. No! for had it not been for the true whites, assisted by God and the prayers of our forefathers, I should not be here to-day.

Personal Heroism and a Just War

OLIVER WENDELL HOLMES, JR.

Oliver Wendell Holmes, Jr., reflects on the lessons of war. What does his idea that there is something admirable in a soldier dying for a cause he doesn't understand mean? What is the "divine" message that war teaches? Do you agree that we need war to teach it? Does Holmes suggest what sorts of things are worth fighting and dying for? Does the possibility that soldiers in the Civil War might have shared these ideas change your evaluation of the meaning and worth of the over 600,000 deaths?

I have heard the question asked whether our war was worth fighting, after all. There are many, poor and rich, who think that love of country is an old wife's tale, to be replaced by interest in a labor union, or, under the name of cosmopolitanism, by a rootless self-seeking search for a place where the most enjoyment may be had at the least cost.

Meantime we have learned the doctrine that evil means pain, and the revolt against pain in all its forms has grown more and more marked. From societies for the prevention of cruelty to animals up to socialism, we express in numberless ways the notion that suffering is a wrong which can be and ought to be prevented, and a whole literature of sympathy has sprung into being which points out in story and in verse how hard it is to be wounded in the battle of life, how terrible, how unjust it is that any one should fail. . . .

. . . I do not know the meaning of the universe. But in the midst of doubt, in the collapse of creeds, there is one thing I do not doubt, that no man who lives in the same world with most of us can doubt, and that is that the faith is true and adorable which leads a soldier to throw away his life in obedience to a blindly accepted duty, in a cause which he little understands, in a plan of campaign of which he has no notion, under tactics of which he does not see the use.

Most men who know battle know the cynic force with which the thoughts of common-sense will assail them in times of stress; but they know that in their

From Oliver Wendell Holmes, Jr., "A Soldier's Faith: An Address Delivered on Memorial Day, May 30, 1895," *Speeches* (Boston: Little, Brown & Co., 1900), pp. 57, 59–60, 62–64.

greatest moments faith has trampled those thoughts under foot. If you have been in line, suppose on Tremont Street Mall, ordered simply to wait and to do nothing, and have watched the enemy bring their guns to bear upon you down a gentle slope like that from Beacon Street, have seen the puff of the firing, have felt the burst of the spherical case-shot as it came toward you, have heard and seen the shrieking fragments go tearing through your company, and have known that the next or the next shot carries your fate; if you have advanced in line and have seen ahead of you the spot which you must pass where the rifle bullets are striking; if you have ridden by night at a walk toward the blue line of fire at the dead angle of Spottsylvania, where for twenty-four hours the soldiers were fighting on the two sides of an earthwork, and in the morning the dead and dying lay piled in a row six deep, and as you rode have heard the bullets splashing in the mud and earth about you; if you have been on the picket-line at night in a black and unknown wood, have heard the spat of the bullets upon the trees, and as you moved have felt your foot slip upon a dead man's body; if you have had a blind fierce gallop against the enemy, with your blood up and a pace that left no time for fear, — if, in short, as some, I hope many, who hear me, have known, you have known the vicissitudes of terror and of triumph in war, you know that there is such a thing as the faith I spoke of. You know your own weakness and are modest; but you know that man has in him that unspeakable somewhat which makes him capable of miracle, able to lift himself by the might of his own soul, un-aided, able to face annihilation for a blind belief. . . .

War, when you are at it, is horrible and dull. It is only when time has passed that you see that its message was divine. I hope it may be long before we are called again to sit at that master's feet. But some teacher of the kind we all need. In this snug, over-safe corner of the world we need it, that we may realize that our comfortable routine is no eternal necessity of things, but merely a little space of calm in the midst of the tempestuous untamed stream-ing of the world, and in order that we may be ready for danger. We need it in this time of individualist negations, with its literature of French and Ameri-can humor, revolting at discipline, loving flesh-pots, and denying that anything is worthy of reverence, — in order that we may remember all that buffoons forget. We need it everywhere and at all times. For high and dangerous action teaches us to believe as right beyond dispute things for which our doubting minds are slow to find words of proof. Out of heroism grows faith in the worth of heroism. The proof comes later, and even may never come. There-fore I rejoice at every dangerous sport which I see pursued. The students at Heidelberg, with their sword-slashed faces, inspire me with sincere respect. I gaze with delight upon our polo-players. If once in a while in our rough riding a neck is broken, I regard it, not as a waste, but as a price well paid for the breeding of a race fit for headship and command.

We do not save our traditions, in this country. The regiments whose battle-flags were not large enough to hold the names of the battles they had fought, vanished with the surrender of Lee, although their memories inherited would have made heroes for a century. It is the more necessary to learn the lesson afresh from perils newly sought, and perhaps it is not vain for us to tell the new generation what we learned in our day, and what we still believe. That the joy of life is living, is to put out all one's powers as far as they will go; that the measure of power is obstacles overcome; to ride boldly at what is in front of you, be it fence or enemy; to pray, not for comfort, but for combat; to keep the soldier's faith against the doubts of civil life, more besetting and harder to overcome than all the misgivings of the battle-field, and to remember that duty is not to be proved in the evil day, but then to be obeyed unquestioning; to love glory more than the temptations of wallowing ease, but to know that one's final judge and only rival is oneself: with all our failures in act and thought, these things we learned from noble enemies in Virginia or Georgia or on the Mississippi, thirty years ago; these things we believe to be true.

> "Life is not lost," said she, "for which is bought
> Endlesse renown."

We learned also, and we still believe, that love of country is not yet an idle name.

> Deare countrey! O how dearely deare
> Ought thy remembraunce, and perpetuall band
> Be to thy foster-child, that from thy hand
> Did commun breath and nouriture receave!
> How brutish is it not to understand
> How much to her we owe, that all us gave;
> That gave unto us all, whatever good we have!

As for us, our days of combat are over. Our swords are rust. Our guns will thunder no more. The vultures that once wheeled over our heads are buried with their prey. Whatever of glory yet remains for us to win must be won in the council or the closet, never again in the field. I do not repine. We have shared the incommunicable experience of war; we have felt, we still feel, the passion of life to its top.

• MODERN ESSAY •

How Much Can a "Just War" Justify?

DONALD A. WELLS

Donald A. Wells supplies criteria by which we can assess whether or not war is just. His essay reflects the intense concern of the nation with the Vietnam War. Does this fact lead him to assess adequately the ideals for which people fight? How would he respond to the question, "Is any peace better than any war?" Judging by the seven conditions for a just war, to what exent was the Civil War just? Can there be a just war in the modern world?

Justification, as is well known, is not an unambiguous term. Even in the context of logical justification the criteria are debatable, but at least in this milieu justification is assumed to be a function of a set of given rules in an agreed-upon system. Within a context of a set of truth claims consistency is a necessary and almost sufficient criterion. In normative discourse, however, justification takes on an honorific and emotion-laden aura. Adequacy here entails notions of "rightness" or "goodness" in addition to putative truth claims. The problem of "The Just War" is, in this latter sense, more than a matter of the occurrence of matters of fact, more than a matter of consistency within a system of given axioms, more than a matter of demonstrating what is permissible legally, and more than an exercise in casuistry.

In a very ordinary sense of the term 'justify' we may merely seek an explanation of why war is waged in the sense of showing the premises that prompted us to the conclusion to wage war. When asked, "Why did you wage this war?" we could reply, "I did it because *x*, *y*, and *z* had occurred," and we might now conclude that the war in question had now been justified. If, on the other hand, we justify war the way an appellant defends himself before the judge, we would then need to show that what we did was consistent with the laws under which we have agreed to operate. But suppose that the justification of war is like the famous "justification of induction" and that its resolution involves us in a metalinguistic search. In fact, the attempts to justify war, or to identify what a just war would be like, share common properties with all these interpretations. In addition, however, there is an implicit contradiction which discussants of war and justice ordinarily recognize. Since the havoc of war is normally classed with immoral actions and evil consequences, what the

From Donald A. Wells, "How Much Can a 'Just War' Justify," *Journal of Philosophy* (December 1969), LXVI, 819–828. Reprinted by permission of *The Journal of Philosophy* and Donald A. Wells.

notion of "the just war" attempts to do is to show that under some circumstances it would be "just" to perform immoral acts and to contribute to evil consequences. Some justifications of war aim to show that actions deemed normally forbidden by moral mandates are now permissible when performed under the aegis of war.

Since the history of ethical speculation has virtually no other instance of the defense of immoral acts under the extenuating circumstance of prudential risk, the "just war" concept needs special attention. It constitutes an anomalous instance in moral discourse, namely, a glaring exception to an otherwise accepted prohibition of acts of human brutality.

Traditionally the doctrine of "the just war" intended to curb excessively inhumane war practices, reduce the likelihood of war, identify who may properly declare war, ensure that the means of war bore a relation of proportion to the ends of war, and generally to promote a conscience on the practice. Incidentally, the concept functioned as a defense of national sovereignty and of the "right" of nations to defend themselves in a basically lawless world. It made national survival feasible, while making international organization unlikely.

Since the notion of "the just war" has been revived after nearly two centuries of silence on the issue, it seems appropriate to look again at the medieval claims to see whether, if they had a defense then, they have any rationale now. The entire discussion for the medievalist rested, of course, on a concession which itself needs reassessment; namely, that war has a place in the moral scheme. The traditional questions about war were prudential, and the discussion centered around such questions as the time, place, and cause for war. Wars were presumed to be neutral means which could be given moral properties under the appropriate conditions. Wars were criticized, if at all, in practice rather than in principle. In this, medieval war discussion shared a common starting point with medieval speculation on capital punishment. It wasn't the fact of killing that was the determinant; rather the reasons given for the acts of killing were decisive.

The Criteria of Saint Thomas

In order for a war to be just, three conditions had to be met: (1) an authoritative sovereign must declare the war; (2) there must be a just cause; and (3) the men who wage the war must have just intentions, so that good actually results from the war. In application of these criteria, the criticisms that did emerge of particular wars were so few as to suggest that princes were basically moral men or that the criteria were too vague to be useful. In addition, the critics were commonly persons not officially in government, so that their protests were a kind of baying at the moon. George Fox, for example, challenged the wars of Cromwell, but then Fox rejected the war method utterly. Franciscus de Victoria, a theological professor at the University of Salamanca in the sixteenth century, chastised his Spanish superiors for the wars against the

Indians[1] — but the remarks of university professors, then as now, were rarely influential in the determination of foreign policy, particularly when such remarks were critical of decisions of state already made.

More recently, Joseph McKenna[2] has revived the "just war" doctrine with an expanded list of seven conditions. They are: (1) the war must be declared by the duly constituted authority; (2) the seriousness of the injury inflicted on the enemy must be proportional to the damage suffered by the virtuous; (3) the injury to the aggressor must be real and immediate; (4) there must be a reasonable chance of winning the war; (5) the use of war must be a last resort; (6) the participants must have right intentions; and (7) the means used must be moral. Our question is: "Can such criteria be made applicable to modern war?" Let us consider this in terms of some general "just war" claims.

A Just War Is One Declared by the Duly Constituted Authority

For a theologian like Saint Augustine or Saint Thomas, who presumed some pervading and ameliorating power from Christian prelates, such a criterion could be considered to be a limitation on careless scoundrels, as well as a limitation on the number of wars that would actually be waged. By the sixteenth century, however, with the proliferation of princes and the fading away of the influence of Christian prelates, a radically new situation had emerged. By this time, the "reasons of state," as Machiavelli elaborated them, permitted every prince to wage war whenever he saw fit. Since by the eighteenth century war had become the sport of kings, it was clear that authorities were not very reliable nor sensitive.

The rise of nationalism made this first criterion undifferentiating. It became increasingly obvious that to grant to any prince the privilege of judging his neighboring prelates was an odd situation. It was this anomaly that led Grotius and Victoria to insist that, although only one side of a war could properly be considered just, in fact persons on both sides could, in good conscience, presume that they had justice on their side. In the absence of any international judge, who could determine the justice of the various national claims? What this criterion did do was to make clear that revolution was not to be allowed. What it could not do was to persuade or compel some prince to forego a war.

If rulers were saints and scholars there might be some reason to suppose that their judgments on war were adequate. Actually, there are no plausible reasons to suppose that secular leaders have intentions that will meet even minimal standards of humaneness. It is not necessary to have in mind Hitler, Tojo, De Gaulle, or Thieu to see that this is so. There is nothing in the nature

---

[1] Franciscus de Victoria, *On the Law of War* (Washington, D.C.: The Carnegie Institute, 1917), sec. 22.

[2] "Ethics and War: A Catholic View," *American Political Science Review* (September 1960): 647–658.

of the process by which leaders are selected to give assurance that Johnson, Trudeau, or Wilson have moral insights that are even as good as the average, let alone sufficiently discerning to be used as the criterion for a just war. These leaders are not presumed by their loyal opposition to be especially gifted in domestic policy. Why imagine that they are so for foreign policy?

Even clerics have a rather poor reputation for moral insight or sound judgment. Witness, for example, the stand of Archbishop Groeber of Freiburg-im-Breisgau, who rejected Christian pacifism for German Catholics on the grounds that Hitler was the duly constituted authority. Pope Pius XII showed no better insight when he rejected the right of conscientious objection for German Catholics at the time of the formation of NATO. This first criterion, therefore, seems to serve no helpful purpose at all. In Vietnam, for example, it would rule out Thieu, since he is warring against his own people, while granting that L.B.J. might be right, and Ho Chi Minh just in killing American troops but not so for killing Vietnamese from the South.

A Just War Uses Means
Proportional to the Ends

Franciscus de Victoria had observed (*op. cit.,* secs. 33, 37) that if to retake a piece of territory would expose a people to "intolerable ills and heavy woes" then it would not be just to retake it. We must be sure, he continued, that the evils we commit in war do not exceed the evils we claim to be averting. But how do we measure the relative ills? This is the problem of a hedonic calculus on which Mill's system foundered. Since Victoria granted princes the right to despoil innocent children if military necessity required it, it ceased to be clear what proportionality meant or whether any limit at all was being proposed.

In a recent paper on this issue Father John A. Connery[3] stated that the morality of the violence depends on the proportionality to the aggression. What is required is some calculus to make this measurement. The latitude with which conscientious persons have interpreted this suggests (what was clear enough to Mill) that we possess neither the quantitative nor the qualitative yardstick for this decision. Pope Pius XII thought the annihilation of vast numbers of persons would be impermissible. John Courtney Murray[4] thought this prohibition was too restrictive. Herbert Hoover thought in 1939 that the aerial bombing of cities should be banned, although he did urge the U.S. to build bombing planes to perform this banned action. Jacques Maritain put bombing from the air in the category of an absolutely proscribed act.[5] In the early period of World War II "saturation bombing" was considered to be too inhumane for American citizens to accept. We then practiced what was euphemistically called "precision bombing." That the terms were empty became

---

[3] "Morality and Nuclear Armament," in William J. Nagle, ed., *Morality and Modern Warfare* (Baltimore: Helicon, 1960), p. 92.
[4] "War and the Bombardment of Cities," *Commonweal* (Sept. 2, 1938).
[5] Nagle, *op. cit.,* p. 107.

obvious when the Air Force announced, at the time of the first test shot of the Atlas missile, that a bomb that lands within fifty miles of its target is considered accurate.

Does the notion of proportionality have any discriminatory meaning? During World War II the English writer, Vera Brittain, attacked both Britain and America in her book *Massacre by Bombing. The Christian Century* urged in editorials that its subscribers should read the book, while taking the position that the bombing of civilians is a necessary part of a just war. The American Bar Association defeated a resolution calling for a condemnation of the bombing of civilians.[6] The *Saturday Evening Post* maintained that anyone who questioned the bombing of civilians was "unstable." [7] MacKinlay Kantor said the book was "soft-hearted." The Reverend Carl McIntyre called the position of the sensitive Mrs. Brittain "un-American and pro-Fascist," and the conservative Boston clergyman, H. J. Ockenga, called the view "un-American" and said it gave aid and comfort to the enemy. Not only do Christian prelates seem a fairly callous lot, but the notion of proportionality has lost sense.

Where should we draw the line? Pope Pius XII decided that Communism was such a cosmic threat that atomic, chemical, and biological bombs could all be justifiably used. But where then is the proportion? The dilemma is not aided by the clerical dictum that "there are greater evils than the physical death and destruction wrought in war" (Nagle, 80). What civilian would be impressed by this amid the rain of bombs? Like "better dead than Red," this is a fiction, enthusiasm for which is directly proportional to the square of the distance from the potential havoc. In any case, there is simply too much horror to be subsumed under the medieval notion of proportionality. Indeed, our State Department's White Paper, which was intended to explain the ends that justified our means in Vietnam, is a monstrously casuistic document. It seems to make no proportional sense to do what we are doing against the Vietnamese if the only reward is American-style elections or freedom from the threat of creeping Communism.

The medieval thinkers rejected religion as a proper cause of a just war, and it is not egregious to point out that politics is in the same general class as religion. After all, is there really any doubt that men can live well under a variety of systems: capitalistic, communistic, monarchic, or democratic? It is equally obvious, I assume, that men may live poorly under any of these systems. Witness the blacks in Georgia, Mississippi, or Washington, D.C. Would any theologian wish to make a case for the bomb on Selma or Chicago? Surely the crimes against men are great there, and if there is any proportion in Hanoi, it would seem to follow that similar acts could be justified in Little Rock.

If there is any reasonable doubt left that the criterion calling for "just means" is simply a verbal genuflection, a brief look at what is currently called

---

[6] *New York Times* (July 15, 1939), p. 3.
[7] *Saturday Evening Post* (Nov. 21, 1942): 128.

"rational nuclear armament" will banish it. A contemporary recommendation by proponents of "rationality" here is to limit bombs to the ½-megaton class. This is fifty times greater than the bomb dropped on Hiroshima. Limitation, proportion, or rationality do not seem to apply to the language of mega-kill. Once a bomb is big enough to kill every person in an area, it is not an expansion of war to use a bomb big enough to kill everyone twice, any more than it can be considered a reduction to reduce from a bomb twice as large as is needed to one the precise size that is needed to decimate the population. And, in addition, to call such a consideration "rational" may be proper to military tacticians, but alien to a concept that aimed at a moral distinction.

War May Be Justly Taken
Only as a Last Resort

In conventional language the notion of "last resort" presupposes a notion of "first resorts." Thus, unless a nation could show that it indeed exhausted first resorts, it would make no sense to claim the right of last resort. Presumably, first resorts would be such alternatives as economic, social, or political boycott, negotiations either through unilateral or multilateral means, or through such an agency as the United Nations, or even the contemplation of some kind of compromise. After these had been exhausted and there appeared to be no further nonviolent alternatives, we would still need to show that the last resort ought, in this case, to be taken. It is always possible that the final resort that can be defended morally is the first resort taken. Too much of the discussion about the "justice" of war as a last resort presumes war to be proper in any case, so that the only genuine questions have to do with timing. With this kind of concession, in the first place, imagine what would happen to discussion of the War Crimes Trials after World War II. The problem facing the German Nazis was simply: "After having exhausted every resort, may we now as a last resort exterminate the Jews?"

The problem facing contemporary theorists of the "just war" is whether modern war is a means that may "justly" be granted as any resort at all. When we begin to speak of "massive retaliation" then perhaps it is time to question war itself. Is there any end at all of sufficient value that the sacrifice of persons on such a scale as is now possible could become "justified"? Something has happened to the medieval notion of last resort when our leaders destroy a city to save it. But the horror of war has never functioned as much of an intellectual deterrent to the justice of war. Thus it is antecedently unlikely that the ability to "overkill" or "mega-kill" makes any rational difference to the medieval concept. If war is a just resort at all, it makes no sense to deny nations its use as a last resort. Once the killing has been sanctioned in the first place, moral discussion, such as the medieval man carried out, takes on the aura of Pentagon calculations.

We find, in this vein, Paul Ramsey, a Protestant advocate of the "just war," endorsing the use of thermonuclear weapons, provided that an important *military target* could not otherwise be eliminated. While Ramsey deplored the death of so many civilians, he assured the survivors that this is not too great a price to pay for civilization. The possibility that surrender would be more moral than war is not even conceded a probability, making it clear that the discussants are speaking only for nations that win wars. The demand for "unconditional surrender" which American statesmen have regularly made, makes it clear that last resorts are the only ones they have in mind. For example, in August, 1958, the U.S. Senate voted 82 to 2 to deny government funds to any person or institution that proposes or actually conducts any study regarding the possible results of the surrender of the U.S. as an alternative to war. The sheer presence of the doctrine of "last resort" makes the compromise contingent on negotiations inadmissible.

What does our "just war" theory say to the American Indians back in the seventeenth century when they were confronted with the white man's power? Was war justified for the Indian as a last resort? It was surely a case of defense, and even white historians grant that the Indians tried many resorts short of war. Since nations with arms are loath to succumb to similar national neighbors, and more especially to do so over concern with whether war is a last resort or whether first resorts still remain, about all the theory tells us is that the "last resort" is bound to be a resort that we actually take.

A Just War Must Be Waged
by Men with Right Intentions

The medieval hub of this argument was the doctrine of the "double effect." A just belligerent intended only as much death as would be proportional to the threat or the offense, and he would intend to kill only combatants. It was presumed that we ought not to kill noncombatants. In the middle ages the weapons made such concern practical. Although the archer might shoot his arrow into the air and not be too clear about where it landed, he was not in doubt about whether he was shooting it at combatant enemies. He might miss a small barn, but he hit the right city. Modern weapons make such sensitivity about the recipients of our missiles inoperable and unfeasible. Not only this, but the number of noncombatants killed in modern war usually far exceeds that of soldiers. Whereas medieval man might pardonably weep for the accidentally slain civilians, modern man intends the death of every civilian slain when he drops his bombs from the air.

In every age, however, the problem of unintended death proved a harassing one, and the pattern of resolution seems to have been to deplete the scope of the class of the noncombatant, until in the present this is a null class. Modern war is total at least in the sense that there are no innocents. We could never have dropped the bombs on Dresden, Nagasaki, Hiroshima, or Tokyo if the class of innocents had had members. But quite apart from whether one could or did intend the death of noncombatants, there would still remain the question whether the end justified the means at all. It was this sheer inapplicability of the doctrine of the "double effect" that prompted John Bennett to reject the notion completely.[8] There is, also, another procedural problem here. The doctrine of the "double effect" is one that does not trouble military or political strategists. Their interest is to win the war, and not to make theological calculations. Indeed, the only concern the military appears to have had over such niceties as intentionality is whether there would be a moral response from the public. We did not, initially, practice saturation bombing in Europe, and we were told later that the military feared a public outcry against it. Once we had practiced it on the Japanese and once military necessity demanded it, Americans lost most of their sensitivity on the problem.

No defense of the intentions of a belligerent could be satisfactorily made unless it could also be shown that the means used were also moral, and this would be so even for the combatants considered to be fair game. Nowhere has the ability of man to tolerate increasing doses of violence and brutality been more evident than in his history of attempts to humanize the weapons. Richard J. Krickus[9] believed that chemical bombs were moral, whereas biological bombs were not, and this because of the difficulty of control in the case of the latter. On the other hand, napalm, anti-personnel shrapnel, and thermonuclear bombs were all "just" in their intended uses. To speak of the just use of the bayonet is difficult enough for mere mortals to grasp, but to use the same approbation for mega-weapons makes the terms "just" and "moral" lose their conventional distinguishing function. Modern man has had long practice in handling these theoretically difficult problems. Since we use gas chambers in the United States for our domestic offenders, it must not have been their method that led to the War Crimes Trials against the Nazis, but simply that they gassed and cremated the wrong persons. Although there may be no way to calculate the relative horror of gas chambers in the two countries or the hedonic ratios of the death of twenty Japanese as compared with the death of twenty Americans, it is precisely this kind of question that the "just war" theorists must answer.

The discussion of "intention" in the thirteenth century, when the weapons were relatively limited in scope so that a king could implement his wish not to harm noncombatants and could practice some kind of proportionality, is something that modern men can no longer carry out. All we can consider is whether to set the projectiles in motion. From that moment on, it makes no sense to speak of proportionality, intentionality, or limitation. But here, men have attempted to think the "unthinkable." What seemed too brutal in one age becomes militarily necessary and, hence, just in the next age. As recently as twenty years ago the arms agencies deleted mention of their chemical-biological research from the public agendas for fear of a public outcry. Now there is no

---

[8] Cf. Paul Ramsey, *War and the Christian Conscience* (Durham, N.C.: Duke University Press, 1961), p. 148.
[9] "On the Morality of Chemical/Biological War," *Journal of Conflict Resolution* (June 1965): 200–210.

need for secrecy, and everyone can witness on television the operations of our nerve gas plant in Newport, Indiana, our disease-bomb research at Fort Detrick, Maryland, and the bubonic plague research of the Hartford Travellers Research Corporation to discover the most efficient means to spread the disease by airplane or on foot. The history of prudential calculation reveals that every weapon sooner or later is added to the list of morally approved ones.

There may be a credible case for claiming that the medieval discussions of the just war added to man's moral insights and implemented his humane concerns. Perhaps without such discussions, the history of war would be even worse than it now is. Such counterfactual conditionals are, however, technically incapable of being assigned weights of probability as to truth or falsity. But what can be determined is that the use of the terms 'just,' 'limited,' 'humane,' 'proportional,' or 'intention' in the context of modern war robs these terms of most of their traditional moral flavor. If it was poor military strategy to assert "thou shalt not kill," it was even worse ethics to claim, "thou mayest napalm thine enemy if thy country is threatened."

One could have hoped that as the scope of weapons increased there would have been an escalation of sensitivity as to their use. But all that happened was that there was an escalation of insensitivity, until today it is hard to imagine what an unjustly fought war would look like that is not already exhibited in the just variety. Conceivably some medieval sword thrusts might have been made justly, and some fortified cities justly sacked. The entire distinction vanishes, however, once we admit weapons that shoot farther than the eye can see. And clearly this distinction has been lost once we use mega-weapons, and even what are called "conventional" weapons like fragmentation bombs and napalm. Since we no longer admit the combatant-noncombatant distinction, what have we left to adjudicate? If the just war ever had moral significance in the past, it is clear today that it justifies too much. In the middle ages the just war was less tragic than the alternatives. Today the just war justifies Armageddon if our hearts be pure, and this is to justify too much.

Issue

Legislating Social Change

We are all created equal, and there it ends. All children are not equal in ability, financial status, or even physical appearance. If such equality is ever achieved, we will have a nation of robots.

Jean Ruffra, 1974

It is precisely because the force of things tends always to destroy equality that the force of legislation should always tend to maintain it.

Charles Sumner quoting Rousseau, 1872

"You can't change hearts with laws." This is perhaps the most enduring piece of folk wisdom in America. Like most folk wisdom, it is true and false. Some heartfelt sentiments defy the law. No legislator, judge, or sheriff can make everyone like oysters or sky diving. Laws which seek to change the social habits of centuries are also likely to fail: the Prohibition amendment is the most obvious example.

Yet further consideration suggests that the question is more complex than these examples indicate. For how do we get our feelings and opinions? They are in large measure the product of our education, our economic circumstances, our chances for work and play, the people we contact. And the law touches on these things every day. Our feelings emerge from the behavior we engage in, and law indisputably shapes behavior.

Yet even if law shapes behavior and behavior molds feelings, there are limits to what laws can do. To be effective, the law must reflect the sentiments of the community. This is especially true in a democracy. The people, not just the police, enforce the laws. Popular sentiment causes people to notify the police, to testify honestly as witnesses, to refuse to break the laws, and to punish those who do. Because it is the law *of* the community and *by* the community, the community has profound reasons to make sure that the law is obeyed.

But what is the community? Can it be said that laws passed and decisions reached in Washington, D.C., or even the state capitol, emerge from the community, express its specific needs and desires? To some extent, the answer is yes. When legislators are elected from a district, the community's will is expressed in laws he or she will help make. The community has participated — but things change. When we do not believe that our community has been heard, when appointed judges, not elected legislators, tell us what to do, when we believe that no one is hearing what we say — at that point, reasons for obeying the law begin to fade.

Community sentiment is not, of course, monolithic. A law may reflect the feelings of one part of the community and not the other: labor, not business; blacks, not whites. Under these conditions a part of the community gives more support to the law than the other parts. All sides, however, have reason to respect the law because it emerged from institutions set up to govern the community to permit response to a changing world.

But if a part of the community feels totally ignored, if it seems that the law endangers its system of social order, and, if this part of the community is powerful, then the law which promotes change faces an uphill fight. Appeals to the ideals of the national community may then have to be supplemented by force to balance the odds.

In the selections which follow, evaluate the sources of community sentiment and of power. Consider what the law was able to do and why. Evaluate the ability of the law to shape behavior, to fulfill the ideals of the national community at the local level. Assess the wisdom and justice of using force to gain equality.

◆ DOCUMENTS ◆

The Limits of Social Change

ANDREW JOHNSON and FREDERICK DOUGLASS

Black leaders discuss with President Andrew Johnson the need for the national government to secure the vote for the freed slaves. What are the experiences of whites and blacks under slavery which Johnson thinks argue against giving the blacks the ballot? Do the leaders of the black delegation answer him adequately on these points? To what extent does the president believe in the majority rights principle? Why do the blacks want the ballot? Does Johnson give adequate consideration to the arguments provided in favor of giving blacks the vote?

From Edward McPherson, ed., "Interview Between President Johnson and a Colored Delegation, February 7, 1866," *The Political History of America During the Period of Reconstruction* (Washington, D.C.: James J. Chapman, 1880), pp. 52–56.

February 7, 1866 — The delegation of colored representatives from different States of the country, now in Washington, to urge the interests of the colored people before the Government, had an interview with the President.

The President shook hands kindly with each member of the delegation.

Address of George T. Downing

Mr. GEORGE T. DOWNING then addressed the President as follows:

We present ourselves to your Excellency, to make known with pleasure the respect which we are glad to cherish for you — a respect which is your due, as our Chief Magistrate. It is our desire for you to know that we come feeling that we are friends meeting a friend. We should, however, have manifested our friendship by not coming to further tax your already much burdened and valuable time; but we have another object in calling. We are in a passage to equality before the law. God hath made it by opening a Red Sea. We would have your assistance through the same. We come to you in the name of the colored people of the United States. We are delegated to come by some who have unjustly worn iron manacles on their bodies — by some whose minds have been manacled by class legislation in States called free. The colored people of the States of Illinois, Wisconsin, Alabama, Mississippi, Florida, South Carolina, North Carolina, Virginia, Maryland, Pennsylvania, New York, New England States, and District of Columbia have specially delegated us to come.

Our coming is a marked circumstance, noting determined hope that we are not satisfied with an amendment prohibiting slavery, but that we wish it enforced with appropriate legislation. This is our desire. We ask for it intelligently, with the knowledge and conviction that the fathers of the Revolution intended freedom for every American; that they should be protected in their rights as citizens, and be equal before the law. We are Americans, native born Americans. We are citizens; we are glad to have it known to the world that you bear no doubtful record on this point. On this fact, and with confidence in the triumph of justice, we base our hope. We see no recognition of color or race in the organic law of the land. It knows no privileged class, and therefore we cherish the hope that we may be fully enfranchised, not only here in this District, but throughout the land. We respectfully submit that rendering anything less than this will be rendering to us less than our just due; that granting anything less than our full rights will be a disregard of our just rights and of due respect for our feelings. If the powers that be do so it will be used as a license, as it were, or an apology, for any community, or for individuals thus disposed, to outrage our rights and feelings. It has been shown in the present war that the Government may justly reach its strong arm into States, and demand from them, from those who owe it allegiance, their assistance and support. May it not reach out a like arm to secure and protect its subjects upon whom it has a claim? . . .

Response of the President

Now, it is always best to talk about things practically and in a common sense way. Yes, I have said, and I repeat here, that if the colored man in the United States could find no other Moses, or any Moses that would be more able and efficient than myself, I would be his Moses to lead him from bondage to freedom; that I would pass him from a land where he had lived in slavery to a land (if it were in our reach) of freedom. Yes, I would be willing to pass with him through the Red sea to the Land of Promise, to the land of liberty; but I am not willing, under either circumstance, to adopt a policy which I believe will only result in the sacrifice of his life and the shedding of his blood. I think I know what I say. I feel what I say; and I feel well assured that if the policy urged by some be persisted in, it will result in great injury to the white as well as to the colored man. There is a great deal of talk about the sword in one hand accomplishing an end, and the ballot accomplishing another at the ballot-box.

These things all do very well, and sometimes have forcible application. We talk about justice; we talk about right; we say that the white man has been in the wrong in keeping the black man in slavery as long as he has. That is all true. Again, we talk about the Declaration of Independence and equality before the law. You understand all that, and know how to appreciate it. But, now, let us look each other in the face; let us go to the great mass of colored men throughout the slave States; let us take the condition in which they are at the present time — and it is bad enough, we all know — and suppose, by some magic touch you could say to every one, "you shall vote to-morrow;" how much would that ameliorate their condition at this time? . . .

The colored man went into this rebellion a slave; by the operation of the rebellion he came out a freedman — equal to a freeman in any other portion of the country. Then there is a great deal done for him on this point. The non-slaveholder who was forced into the rebellion, who was as loyal as those that lived beyond the limits of that State, but was carried into it, lost his property, and in a number of instances the lives of such were sacrificed, and he who has survived has come out of it with nothing gained, but a great deal lost.

Now, upon the principle of justice, should they be placed in a condition different from what they were before? On the one hand, one has gained a great deal; on the other hand, one has lost a great deal, and, in a political point of view, scarcely stands where he did before.

Now, we are talking about where we are going to begin. We have got at the hate that existed between the two races. The query comes up, whether these two races, situated as they were before, without preparation, without time for passion and excitement to be appeased, and without time for the slightest improvement, whether the one should be turned loose upon the other, and be thrown together at the ballot-box with this enmity and hate existing between them. The query comes up right there, whether we don't commence a war of races. I think I understand this thing, and especially is this the case when you force it upon a people without their consent.

You have spoken about government. Where is power derived from? We say it is derived from the people. Let us take it so, and refer to the District of Columbia by way of illustration. Suppose, for instance, here, in this political community, which, to a certain extent, must have government, must have laws, and putting it now upon the broadest basis you can put it — take into consideration the relation which the white has heretofore borne to the colored race — is it proper to force upon this community, without their consent, the elective franchise, without regard to color, making it universal?

Now, where do you begin? Government must have a controlling power — must have a lodgment. For instance, suppose Congress should pass a law authorizing an election to be held at which all over twenty-one years of age, without regard to color, should be allowed to vote, and a majority should decide at such election that the elective franchise should not be universal; what would you do about it? Who would settle it? Do you deny that first great principle of the right of the people to govern themselves? Will you resort to an arbitrary power, and say a majority of the people shall receive a state of things they are opposed to?

Mr. [Frederick] Douglass: That was said before the war.

The President: I am now talking about a principle; not what somebody else said.

Mr. Downing: Apply what you have said, Mr. President, to South Carolina, for instance, where a majority of the inhabitants are colored.

The President: Suppose you go to South Carolina; suppose you go to Ohio. That doesn't change the principle at all. The query to which I have referred still comes up when government is undergoing a fundamental change. Government commenced upon this principle; it has existed upon it; and you propose now to incorporate into it an element that didn't exist before. I say the query comes up in undertaking this thing whether we have a right to make a change in regard to the elective franchise in Ohio, for instance: whether we shall not let the people in that State decide the matter for themselves.

Each community is better prepared to determine the depositary of its political power than anybody else, and it is for the Legislature, for the people of Ohio to say who shall vote, and not for the Congress of the United States. I might go down here to the ballot-box to-morrow and vote directly for universal suffrage; but if a great majority of the people said no, I should consider it would be tyrannical in me to attempt to force such upon them without their will. It is a fundamental tenet in my creed that the will of the people must be obeyed. Is there anything wrong or unfair in that?

Mr. Douglass (smiling): A great deal that is wrong, Mr. President, with all respect.

The President: It is the people of the States that must for themselves determine this thing. I do not want to be engaged in a work that will commence a war of races. I want to begin the work of preparation, and the States, or the people in each community, if a man demeans himself well, and shows evidence that this new state of affairs will operate, will protect him in all his rights, and give him every possible advantage when they become reconciled socially and politically to this state of things. Then will this new order of things work harmoniously; but forced upon the people before they are prepared for it, it will be resisted, and work inharmoniously. I feel a conviction that driving this matter upon the people, upon the community, will result in the injury of both races, and the ruin of one or the other. God knows I have no desire but the good of the whole human race. I would it were so that all you advocate could be done in the twinkling of an eye; but it is not in the nature of things, and I do not assume or pretend to be wiser than Providence, or stronger than the laws of nature.

Let us now seek to discover the laws governing this thing. There is a great law controlling it; let us endeavor to find out what that law is, and conform our actions to it. All the details will then properly adjust themselves and work out well in the end.

God knows that anything I can do I will do. In the mighty process by which the great end is to be reached, anything I can do to elevate the races, to soften and ameliorate their condition I will do, and to be able to do so is the sincere desire of my heart.

I am glad to have met you, and thank you for the compliment you have paid me. . . .

Mr. Douglass: If the President will allow me, I would like to say one or two words in reply. You enfranchise your enemies and disfranchise your friends.

The President: All I have done is simply to indicate what my views are, as I supposed you expected me to, from your address.

Mr. Douglass: My own impression is that the very thing that your excellency would avoid in the southern States can only be avoided by the very measure that we propose, and I would state to my brother delegates that because I perceive the President has taken strong grounds in favor of a given policy, and distrusting my own ability to remove any of those impressions which he has expressed, I thought we had better end the interview with the expression of thanks. (Addressing the President.) But if your excellency will be pleased to hear, I would like to say a word or two in regard to that one matter of the enfranchisement of the blacks as a means of preventing the very thing which your excellency seems to apprehend — that is a conflict of races.

The President: I repeat, I merely wanted to indicate my views in reply to your address, and not to enter into any general controversy, as I could not well do so under the circumstances.

Your statement was a very frank one, and I thought it was due to you to meet it in the same spirit.

Mr. Douglass: Thank you, sir.

The President: I think you will find, so far as the South is concerned, that if you will all inculcate there the idea in connection with the one you urge, that the colored people can live and advance in civilization to better advantage elsewhere than crowded right down there in the South, it would be better for them.

Mr. Douglass: But the masters have the making of the laws, and we cannot get away from the plantation.

The President: What prevents you?

Mr. Douglass: We have not the single right of locomotion through the Southern States now.

The President: Why not; the government furnishes you with every facility.

Mr. Douglass: There are six days in the year that the negro is free in the South now, and his master then decides for him where he shall go, where he shall work, how much he shall work — in fact, he is divested of all political power. He is absolutely in the hands of those men.

The President: If the master now controls him or his action, would he not control him in his vote?

Mr. Douglass: Let the negro once understand that he has an organic right to vote, and he will raise up a party in the Southern States among the poor, who will rally with him. There is this conflict that you speak of between the wealthy slaveholder and the poor man.

The President: You touch right upon the point there. There is this conflict, and hence I suggest emigration. If he cannot get employment in the South, he has it in his power to go where he can get it.

In parting, the PRESIDENT said that they were both desirous of accomplishing the same ends, but proposed to do so by following different roads.

Mr. Douglass, on turning to leave, remarked to his fellow delegates: "The President sends us to the people, and we go to the people."

The President: Yes, sir; I have great faith in the people. I believe they will do what is right.

Reply of the Colored Delegation
to the President

To the Editor of the Chronicle:

Will you do us the favor to insert in your columns the following reply of the colored delegation to the President of the United States?

Geo. T. Downing,
In behalf of the Delegation.

Mr. President:

In consideration of a delicate sense of propriety, as well as your own repeated intimations of indisposition to discuss or to listen to a reply to the views and opinions you were pleased to express to us in your elaborate speech to-day, the undersigned would respectfully take this method of replying thereto. Believing as we do that the views and opinions you expressed in that address are entirely unsound and prejudicial to the highest interests of our race as well as our country at large, we cannot do other than expose the same, and, as far as may be in our power, arrest their dangerous influence. It is not necessary at this time to call attention to more than two or three features of your remarkable address:

1. The first point to which we feel especially bound to take exception is your attempt to found a policy opposed to our enfranchisement, upon the alleged ground of an existing hostility on the part of the former slaves toward the poor white people of the South. We admit the existence of this hostility, and hold that it is entirely reciprocal. But you obviously commit an error by drawing an argument from an incident of a state of slavery, and making it a basis for a policy adapted to a state of freedom. The hostility between the whites and blacks of the South is easily explained. It has its root and sap in the relation of slavery, and was incited on both sides by the cunning of the slave masters. Those masters secured their ascendency over both the poor whites and the blacks by putting enmity between them.

They divided both to conquer each. There was no earthly reason why the blacks should not hate and dread the poor whites when in a state of slavery, for it was from this class that their masters received their slave-catchers, slave-drivers, and overseers. They were the men called in upon all occasions by the masters when any fiendish outrage was to be committed upon the slave. Now, sir, you cannot but perceive that, the cause of this hatred removed, the effect must be removed also. Slavery is abolished. The cause of antagonism is removed, and you must see that it is altogether illogical (and "putting new wine into old bottles," "mending new garments with old cloth") to legislate from slave-holding and slave-driving premises for a people whom you have repeatedly declared your purpose to maintain in freedom.

2. Besides, even if it were true, as you allege, that the hostility of the blacks toward the poor whites must necessarily project itself into a state of freedom, and that this enmity between the two races is even more intense in a state of freedom than in a state of slavery, in the name of Heaven, we reverently ask, how can you, in view of your professed desire to promote the welfare of the black man, deprive him of all means of defence, and clothe him whom you regard as his enemy in the panoply of political power? Can it be that you would recommend a policy which would arm the strong and cast down the defenceless? Can you, by any possibility of reasoning, regard this as just, fair, or wise? Experience proves that those are oftenest abused who can be abused with the greatest impunity. Men are whipped oftenest who are whipped easiest. Peace between races is not to be secured by degrading one race and exalting another, by giving power to one race and withholding it from another; but by maintaining a state of equal justice between all classes. First pure, then peaceable.

3. On the colonization theory you were pleased to broach, very much could be said. It is impossible to suppose, in view of the usefulness of the

black man in time of peace as a laborer in the South, and in time of war as a soldier at the North, and the growing respect for his rights among the people, and his increasing adaptation to a high state of civilization in this his native land, there can ever come a time when he can be removed from this country without a terrible shock to its prosperity and peace. Besides, the worst enemy of the nation could not cast upon its fair name a greater infamy than to suppose that negroes could be tolerated among them in a state of the most degrading slavery and oppression, and must be cast away, driven into exile, for no other cause than having been freed from their chains.

George T. Downing,
John Jones,
William Whipper,
Frederick Douglass,
Lewis H. Douglass,
and others.

The Foundation of Social Change
THIRTEENTH, FOURTEENTH, AND FIFTEENTH AMENDMENTS
TO THE CONSTITUTION

What rights are granted to blacks by these amendments? How far does the enforcement section of the Thirteenth Amendment extend? What is slavery? What is involuntary servitude? Would the Fourteenth Amendment be stronger if it provided a statement guaranteeing national protection for the rights it secures, rather than simply denying the states the right to take away those rights? Does the Fifteenth Amendment actually give the blacks the right to vote?

AMENDMENT XIII

Section I

Neither slavery nor involuntary servitude, except as a punishment for crime whereof the party shall have been duly convicted, shall exist within the United States, or any place subject to their jurisdiction.

Section II

Congress shall have power to enforce this article by appropriate legislation.

AMENDMENT XIV

Section I

All persons born or naturalized in the United States, and subject to the jurisdiction thereof, are citizens of the United States and of the State wherein they reside. No State shall make or enforce any law which shall abridge the privileges or immunities of citizens of the United States; nor shall any State deprive any person of life, liberty or property, without due process of law; nor deny to any person within its jurisdiction the equal protection of the laws.

Section II

Representatives shall be apportioned among the several States according to their respective numbers, counting the whole number of persons in each State, excluding Indians not taxed. But when the right to vote at any election for the choice of Electors for President and Vice-President of the United States, Representatives in Congress, the executive and judicial officers of a State, or the members of the legislature thereof, is denied to any of the male inhabitants of such State, being twenty-one years of age, and citizens of the United States, or in any way abridged except for participation in rebellion or other crime, the basis of representation therein shall be reduced in the proportion which the number of such male citizens shall bear to the whole number of male citizens twenty-one years of age in such State.

Section III

No person shall be a Senator or Representative in Congress, or elector of President and Vice-President, or hold any office, civil or military, under the United States or under any State, who, having previously taken an oath as a member of Congress, or as an officer of the United States, or as a member of any State legislature, or as an executive or judicial officer of any State, to support the Constitution of the United States, shall have engaged in insurrection or rebellion against the same, or given aid or comfort to the enemies thereof. But Congress may, by a vote of two-thirds of each House, remove such disability.

Section IV

The validity of the public debt of the United States, authorized by law, including debts incurred for payment of pensions and bounties for services in suppressing insurrection or rebellion, shall not be questioned. But neither the United States nor any State shall assume or pay any debt or obligation incurred in aid of insurrection or rebellion against the United States, or any claim for the loss or emancipation of any slave; but all such debts, obligations, and claims shall be held illegal and void.

Section V

The Congress shall have power to enforce, by appropriate legislation, the provisions of this article.

AMENDMENT XV

Section I

The right of citizens of the United States to vote shall not be denied or abridged by the United States or by any State on account of race, color, or previous condition of servitude.

Section II

The Congress shall have power to enforce this article by appropriate legislation.

The Demand for Social Change

GENERAL ALFRED TERRY

General Alfred Terry describes race relations in Georgia in August 1869. What are the differing opinions among Georgians about conditions there? Why are the state and local authorities relatively powerless? Why will the use of force improve things? What justifications does Terry provide for giving new power to the national government?

I have delayed making the report thus called for until the present time, in order that I might become acquainted with the condition of affairs in Georgia before expressing any opinion in regard to them. Now I have reluctantly come to the conclusion that the situation here demands the interposition of the national government, in order that life and property may be protected, freedom of speech and political action secured, and the rights and liberties of the freedmen maintained. This opinion is based upon complaints made to me, the reports of officers detailed to investigate alleged outrages, and upon the statements of many persons of respectability and high position from different parts of the State, in whose representations I must repose confidence; some of whom have given me information only under the pledge of secrecy, the state of affairs in their section being such that they feared the extreme of personal violence should it become known that they had been in communication with me.

In many parts of the State there is practically no government. The worst of crimes are committed, and no attempt is made to punish those who commit them. Murders have been and are frequent; the abuse in various ways of the blacks is too common to excite notice. There can be no doubt of the existence of numerous insurrectionary organizations known as "Ku-Klux Klans," who, shielded by their disguise, by the secrecy of their movements, and by the terror which they inspire, perpetrate crime with impunity. There is great reason to believe that in some cases local magistrates are in sympathy with the members of these organizations. In many places they are overawed by

From U.S., Congress, *House Executive Documents,* "Report of the Secretary of War," 41st Cong., 2d sess., 1869–1870, vol. I, pp. 89–91.

them and dare not attempt to punish them. To punish such offenders by civil proceedings would be a difficult task, even were magistrates in all cases disposed and had they the courage to do their duty, for the same influences which govern them equally affect juries and witnesses. A conversation which I have had with a wealthy planter, a gentleman of intelligence and education, and a political opponent of the present national administration, will illustrate this difficulty. While deploring the lamentable condition of affairs in the county in which he lives, he frankly admitted to me that, were the most worthless vagabond in the county to be charged with a crime against the person of a republican or a negro, neither he nor any other person of property within the county would dare to refuse to give bail for the offender, nor would they dare to testify against him, whatever might be their knowledge of his guilt.

That very many of the crimes which have been committed have no political bearing I believe; that some of them were prompted by political animosity, and that most of the numerous outrages upon freedmen result from hostility to the race induced by their enfranchisement, I think cannot be controverted.

The same difficulties which beset the prosecution of criminals are encountered by negroes who seek redress for civil injuries in the local courts. Magistrates dare not do their duty toward them, and instances are not wanting where it has even been beyond the power of a magistrate to protect a negro plaintiff from violence in his own presence while engaged in the trial of his case. I desire it to be understood that in speaking of magistrates I in no degree refer to the judges of the superior courts; they are gentlemen of high character. I have every confidence that they will do their duty fearlessly and impartially, but it is to be observed that even they cannot control grand and petty juries; they cannot compel the former to indict, nor the latter to render unprejudiced verdicts.

The executive of the State would gladly interpose to give to all citizens the protection which is their right, but under the constitution and laws he has power neither to act directly in bringing offenders to justice nor to compel subordinate officers to do their duty. I do not suppose that the great majority of the people of the State, of either race, approve of the commission of these crimes. I believe that not only would they gladly see good order restored, peace and quiet maintained, and the law vindicated, but would lend their aid to secure these ends were they not controlled by their fears. Governed, however, by their apprehensions, and having no confidence that the civil authorities will afford them protection, in many counties they suffer these evils to exist without an effort to abate them, and meekly submit to the rule of the disorderly and criminal minority.

While I have been in command of the department I have endeavored to take no action which could not be justified by the letter of the law, even if Georgia should be held to be restored to its original relations to the general government. I have confined myself to giving support to the civil authorities and moving detachments of troops into some of the disturbed counties, where their presence would exert a good influence, and where they would be ready to act if properly called upon. I think that some good has in this way been accomplished, but the great evil has by no means been reached. As a department commander I can do no more; for whatever may be the status of Georgia, and whatever may be the powers which an officer assigned to command the third district created by the reconstruction acts would possess, it is only an officer so assigned who could exercise them; they are not vested in me by my assignment to the command of this department. Where, therefore, the civil authorities are in sympathy with or are overawed by those who commit crime, it is manifest that I am powerless. In this connection I respectfully call the special attention of the General commanding the army to the reports in regard to the attempt made in Warren County to secure the arrest and punishment of persons charged with crime, which are this day forwarded. It appears to me that the national honor is pledged to the protection of the loyalists and the freedmen of the South. I am well aware that the protection of persons and property is not ordinarily one of the functions of the national government, but when it is remembered that hostility to the supporters of the government is but a manifestation of hostility to the government itself, and that the prevailing prejudice against the blacks results from their emancipation — the act of the government — it would seem that such protection cannot be denied them if it be within the power of the government to give it. I know of no way in which such protection can be given in Georgia except by the exercise of the powers conferred on military commanders by the reconstruction acts.

Law as Social Change
CHARLES SUMNER

Charles Sumner argues for a civil rights bill which will expand the legal protection given by the Constitution and national government to the freed slaves. What ideals does Sumner evoke to support his argument? Why does Sumner believe that public opinion will support his goals? What force does law have in affecting public opinion?

. . . Once Slavery was the animating principle in determining the meaning of the National Constitution: happily, it is so no longer. Another principle is now supreme, breathing into the whole the breath of a new life, and filling it in every part with one pervading, controlling sentiment, — being that great principle of Equality which triumphed at last on the battle-field, and, bearing

From Charles Sumner, "The Supplementary Civil Rights Bill, January 15, 1872," *The Works of Charles Sumner* (Boston: Lee and Shepard, 1883), XIV, 385–387.

the watchword of the Republic, now supplies the rule by which every word of the Constitution and all its parts must be interpreted, as much as if written in its text. . . .

But legislation is not enough. An enlightened public opinion must be invoked. Nor will this be wanting. The country will rally in aid of the law, more especially since it is a measure of justice and humanity. The law is needed now as a help to public opinion. It is needed by the very people whose present conduct makes occasion for it. Prompted by the law, leaning on the law, they will recognize the equal rights of all; nor do I despair of a public opinion which shall stamp the denial of these rights as an outrage not unlike Slavery itself. Custom and patronage will then be sought in obeying the law. People generally are little better than actors, for whom it was once said: —

> Ah, let not Censure term our fate our choice:
> The stage but echoes back the public voice;
> The drama's laws the drama's patrons give;
> For we that live to please must please to live.

In the absence of the law people please too often by inhumanity, but with the law teaching the lesson of duty they will please by humanity. Thus will the law be an instrument of improvement, necessary in precise proportion to existing prejudice. Because people still please by inhumanity, therefore must there be a counteracting force. This precise exigency was foreseen by Rousseau, remarkable as writer and thinker, in a work which startled the world, when he said: —

> It is precisely because the force of things tends always to destroy equality that the force of legislation should always tend to maintain it.

The Ideals and Limitations of Legislation
WILLIAM LLOYD GARRISON

In 1879 William Lloyd Garrison urges support for blacks leaving the South to go to Kansas and demands federal action to protect those who remain. How successful has Reconstruction been, given the emigration described here? What obstacles does Garrison see standing in the way of equal justice? Is Garrison being realistic in calling for a national majority to overcome the white southern majority? What is the force of the ideals he proclaims?

From Wendell Phillips Garrison and Francis Jackson Garrison, eds., *William Lloyd Garrison: The Story of His Life* (New York: The Century Co., 1889), IV, 303–304.

The spectacle of thousands of half-naked, empty-handed, despairing men, women, and children fleeing as for their lives from one part of the country to another, and preferring to risk starvation and death by the way rather than remain where they naturally belong, is one calculated to move pitying Heaven, and to awaken all that is sympathetic and generous in the human breast. Their claims for immediate charitable relief are equally just and imperative; and it is most gratifying to perceive a disposition in various directions to minister to the wants of these poor outcasts. By nothing that they have done, on the score of idleness, dissipation, or disorderly conduct, have they brought this suffering and exposure upon themselves. On the contrary, they have been the only industrious, unoffending, law-abiding, and loyal portion of the population in that quarter, with but few exceptions; and yet their safety is only in flight!

While, therefore, grave, exciting, and relatively important as the present exodus of a few thousands of colored refugees from Mississippi and Louisiana may be, it is only an incident of the hour, demanding succor and aid in various forms until they have time to select their dwelling-places. But what of the four millions of colored people in the entire South? Their exilement is a question not to be seriously entertained for a moment, either as a desirable or possible event. The American Government is but a mockery, and deserves to be overthrown, if they are to be left without protection, as sheep in the midst of wolves. If the nation, having decreed their emancipation, and invested them under the Constitution with all the rights of citizenship, can neither devise nor find a way to vindicate their manhood, then its acts have been farcical, and the local usurpation of a contemptible body of aristocratic factionists is more than a match for the loyalty and strength of the American people; and it is the latter who are as effectually "bulldozed" and ruled by the "shotgun" policy as the colored people themselves. . . .

It is clear, therefore, that the battle of liberty and equal rights is to be fought over again, not in a party sense in the ordinary use of that term, but by the uprising and consolidating of a loyal, freedom-loving North, overwhelming in numbers, resolute in purpose, invincible in action, and supreme in patriotism based upon impartial justice and all-embracing citizenship.

Let the edict go forth, trumpet-tongued, that there shall be a speedy end put to all this bloody misrule; that no disorganizing Southern theory of State rights shall defiantly dominate the Federal Government to the subversion of the Constitution; that the millions of loyal colored citizens at the South, now under ban and virtually disfranchised, shall be put in the safe enjoyment of their rights — shall freely vote and be fairly represented — just where they are located. And let the rallying-cry be heard, from the Atlantic to the Pacific coast, "Liberty and equal rights for each, for all, and forever, wherever the lot of man is cast within our broad domains!"

Law and Social Injustice

PLESSY v. *FERGUSON*

*The United States Supreme Court in 1896 endorses the use of law to enforce
segregation. What limitations does the majority opinion see in the power of
the Fourteenth Amendment? Do you agree that the separation of races in
schools does not imply the inferiority of one of the races? Do you accept the
separation that the majority opinion makes between social, civil, and political
equality? What harmful effects does the dissenting justice, Mr. Harlan, see
resulting from the majority opinion? What relationship does he see between
the power of law and the endurance of prejudice? If law can support the
prejudices of the majority, why may it not also destroy them? Is there a difference between using the power of law to uphold social values and using that
power to undermine those values?*

Justice Brown Delivered the Opinion of the Court

This case turns upon the constitutionality of an act of the General Assembly
of the State of Louisiana, passed in 1890, providing for separate railway
carriages for the white and colored races. . . .

The constitutionality of this act is attacked upon the ground that it conflicts both with the Thirteenth Amendment of the Constitution, abolishing
slavery, and the Fourteenth Amendment, which prohibits certain restrictive
legislation on the part of the States.

1. That it does not conflict with the Thirteenth Amendment, which abolished slavery and involuntary servitude, except as a punishment for crime, is
too clear for argument. . . .

. . . The proper construction of the 14th amendment was first called to
the attention of this court in the *Slaughter-house cases,* 16 Wall. 36, which
involved, however, not a question of race, but one of exclusive privileges. The
case did not call for any expression of opinion as to the exact rights it was
intended to secure to the colored race, but it was said generally that its main
purpose was to establish the citizenship of the negro; to give definitions of
citizenship of the United States and of the States, and to protect from the
hostile legislation of the States the privileges and immunities of citizens of the
United States, as distinguished from those of citizens of the States.

The object of the amendment was undoubtedly to enforce the absolute
equality of the two races before the law, but in the nature of things it could
not have been intended to abolish distinctions based upon color, or to enforce

From *Plessy* v. *Ferguson, United States Reports,* vol. 163, pp. 537 ff (1896).

social, as distinguished from political equality, or a commingling of the two races upon terms unsatisfactory to either. Laws permitting, and even requiring, their separation in places where they are liable to be brought into contact do not necessarily imply the inferiority of either race to the other, and have been generally, if not universally, recognized as within the competency of the state legislatures in the exercise of their police power. The most common instance of this is connected with the establishment of separate schools for white and colored children, which has been held to be a valid exercise of the legislative power even by courts of States where the political rights of the colored race have been longest and most earnestly enforced. . . .

So far, then, as a conflict with the Fourteenth Amendment is concerned, the case reduces itself to the question whether the statute of Louisiana is a reasonable regulation, and with respect to this there must necessarily be a large discretion on the part of the legislature. In determining the question of reasonableness it is at liberty to act with reference to the established usages, customs and traditions of the people, and with a view to the promotion of their comfort, and the preservation of the public peace and good order. Gauged by this standard, we cannot say that a law which authorizes or even requires the separation of the two races in public conveyances is unreasonable, or more obnoxious to the Fourteenth Amendment than the acts of Congress requiring separate schools for colored children in the District of Columbia, the constitutionality of which does not seem to have been questioned, or the corresponding acts of state legislatures.

We consider the underlying fallacy of the plaintiff's argument to consist in the assumption that the enforced separation of the two races stamps the colored race with a badge of inferiority. If this be so, it is not by reason of anything found in the act, but solely because the colored race chooses to put that construction upon it. The argument necessarily assumes that if, as has been more than once the case, and is not unlikely to be so again, the colored race should become the dominant power in the state legislature, and should enact a law in precisely similar terms, it would thereby relegate the white race to an inferior position. We imagine that the white race, at least, would not acquiesce in this assumption. The argument also assumes that social prejudices may be overcome by legislation, and that equal rights cannot be secured to the negro except by an enforced commingling of the two races. We cannot accept this proposition. If the two races are to meet upon terms of social equality, it must be the result of natural affinities, a mutual appreciation of each other's merits and a voluntary consent of individuals. . . . Legislation is powerless to eradicate racial instincts or to abolish distinctions based upon physical differences, and the attempt to do so can only result in accentuating the difficulties of the present situation. If the civil and political rights of both races be equal one cannot be inferior to the other civilly or politically. If one race be inferior to the other socially, the Constitution of the United States cannot put them upon the same plane. . . .

Justice Harlan Dissenting:

In respect of civil rights, common to all citizens, the Constitution of the United States does not, I think, permit any public authority to know the race of those entitled to be protected in the enjoyment of such rights. Every true man has pride of race, and under appropriate circumstances when the rights of others, his equals before the law, are not to be affected, it is his privilege to express such pride and to take such action based upon it as to him seems proper. But I deny that any legislative body or judicial tribunal may have regard to the race of citizens when the civil rights of those citizens are involved. Indeed, such legislation, as that here in question, is inconsistent not only with that equality of rights which pertains to citizenship, National and State, but with the personal liberty enjoyed by every one within the United States. . . .

The white race deems itself to be the dominant race in this country. And so it is, in prestige, in achievements, in education, in wealth and in power. So, I doubt not, it will continue to be for all time, if it remains true to its great heritage and holds fast to the principles of constitutional liberty. But in view of the Constitution, in the eye of the law, there is in this country no superior, dominant, ruling class of citizens. There is no caste here. Our Constitution is color-blind, and neither knows nor tolerates classes among citizens. In respect of civil rights, all citizens are equal before the law. The humblest is the peer of the most powerful. . . .

. . . The present decision, it may well be apprehended, will not only stimulate aggressions, more or less brutal and irritating, upon the admitted rights of colored citizens, but will encourage the belief that it is possible, by means of state enactments, to defeat the beneficent purposes which the people of the United States had in view when they adopted the recent amendments of the Constitution, by one of which the blacks of this country were made citizens of the United States and of the States in which they respectively reside, and whose privileges and immunities, as citizens, the States are forbidden to abridge. Sixty millions of whites are in no danger from the presence here of eight millions of blacks. The destinies of the two races, in this country, are indissolubly linked together, and the interests of both require that the common government of all shall not permit the seeds of race hate to be planted under the sanction of law. What can more certainly arouse race hate, what more certainly create and perpetuate a feeling of distrust between these races, than state enactments, which, in fact, proceed on the ground that colored citizens are so inferior and degraded that they cannot be allowed to sit in public coaches occupied by white citizens? That, as all will admit, is the real meaning of such legislation as was enacted in Louisiana. . . .

If evils will result from the commingling of the two races upon public highways established for the benefit of all, they will be infinitely less than those that will surely come from state legislation regulating the enjoyment of civil rights upon the basis of race. We boast of the freedom enjoyed by our people above all other peoples. But it is difficult to reconcile that boast with a state of the law which, practically, puts the brand of servitude and degradation upon a large class of our fellow citizens, our equals before the law. The thin disguise of "equal" accommodations for passengers in railroad coaches will not mislead any one, nor atone for the wrong this day done. . . .

I am of opinion that the statute of Louisiana is inconsistent with the personal liberty of citizens, white and black, in that State, and hostile to both the spirit and letter of the Constitution of the United States. If laws of like character should be enacted in the several States of the Union, the effect would be in the highest degree mischievous. Slavery, as an institution tolerated by law would, it is true, have disappeared from our own country, but there would remain a power in the States, by sinister legislation, to interfere with the full enjoyment of the blessings of freedom; to regulate civil rights, common to all citizens upon the basis of race; and to place in a condition of legal inferiority a large body of American citizens, now constituting a part of the political community called the People of the United States, for whom, and by whom through representatives, our government is administered. Such a system is inconsistent with the guarantee given by the Constitution to each State of a republican form of government, and may be stricken down by Congressional action, or by the courts in the discharge of their solemn duty to maintain the supreme law of the land, anything in the constitution or laws of any State to the contrary notwithstanding. . . .

The Dimensions of Social Change
W. E. B. DUBOIS

Historian W. E. B. DuBois in 1910 describes the accomplishment of blacks during Reconstruction. What are the successes of the period for blacks? For whites? How did postwar destruction affect the extent of black accomplishment? What actions did blacks take to improve their condition? What failures did they have? How much of the success can be attributed to the use of federal power in the postwar period?

How to train and treat these ex-slaves easily became a central problem of Reconstruction, although by no means the only problem. Three agencies undertook the solution of this problem at first and their influence is apt to be forgotten. Without them the problems of Reconstruction would have been far graver than they were. These agencies were: (a) the negro church, (b) the negro school, and (c) the Freedmen's Bureau. After the war the white

From W. E. B. DuBois, "Reconstruction and Its Benefits," *American Historical Review* (July 1910), XV, 781–782, 787–791, 795–796, 798–799.

churches of the South got rid of their negro members and the negro church organizations of the North invaded the South. The 20,000 members of the African Methodist Episcopal Church in 1856 leaped to 75,000 in 1866 and 200,000 in 1876, while their property increased sevenfold. The negro Baptists with 150,000 members in 1850 had fully a half million in 1870. There were, before the end of Reconstruction, perhaps 10,000 local bodies touching the majority of the freed population, centring almost the whole of their social life, and teaching them organization and autonomy. They were primitive, ill-governed, at times fantastic groups of human beings, and yet it is difficult to exaggerate the influence of this new responsibility — the first social institution fully controlled by black men in America, with traditions that rooted back to Africa and with possibilities which make the 35,000 negro American churches to-day, with their three and one-half million members, the most powerful negro institutions in the world.

With the negro church, but separate from it, arose the school as the first expression of the missionary activity of Northern religious bodies. Seldom in the history of the world has an almost totally illiterate population been given the means of self-education in so short a time. The movement started with the negroes themselves and they continued to form the dynamic force behind it. "This great multitude rose up simultaneously and asked for intelligence." The education of this mass had to begin at the top with the training of teachers, and within a few years a dozen colleges and normal schools started; by 1877, 571,506 negro children were in school. There can be no doubt that these schools were a great conservative steadying force to which the South owes much. . . .

The granting of full negro suffrage meant one of two alternatives to the South: (a) the uplift of the negro for sheer self-preservation; this is what Schurz and the saner North expected; as one Southern superintendent said: "the elevation of this class is a matter of prime importance since a ballot in the hands of a black citizen is quite as potent as in the hands of a white one." Or (b) a determined concentration of Southern effort by actual force to deprive the negro of the ballot or nullify its use. This is what happened, but even in this case so much energy was taken in keeping the negro from voting that the plan for keeping him in virtual slavery and denying him education failed. It took ten years to nullify negro suffrage in part and twenty years to escape the fear of federal intervention. In these twenty years a vast number of negroes had arisen so far as to escape slavery forever. Debt peonage could be fastened on part of the rural South, and was, but even here the negro landholder appeared. Thus despite everything the Fifteenth Amendment and that alone struck the death knell of slavery. . . .

The chief charges against the negro governments are extravagance, theft, and incompetency of officials. There is no serious charge that these governments threatened civilization or the foundations of social order. The charge is that they threatened property, and that they were inefficient. These charges are in part undoubtedly true, but they are often exaggerated. When a man has, in his opinion, been robbed and maltreated he is sensitive about money matters. The South had been terribly impoverished and saddled with new social burdens. In other words, a state with smaller resources was asked not only to do a work of restoration but a larger social work. The property-holders were aghast. They not only demurred, but, predicting ruin and revolution, they appealed to secret societies, to intimidation, force, and murder. They refused to believe that these novices in government and their friends were aught but scamps and fools. Under the circumstances occurring directly after the war, the wisest statesman would have been compelled to resort to increased taxation and would in turn have been execrated as extravagant and even dishonest. When now, in addition to this, the new legislators, white and black, were undoubtedly in a large number of cases extravagant, dishonest, and incompetent, it is easy to see what flaming and incredible stories of Reconstruction governments could gain wide currency and belief. In fact, the extravagance, although great, was not universal, and much of it was due to the extravagant spirit pervading the whole country in a day of inflated currency and speculation. The ignorance was deplorable but a deliberate legacy from the past, and some of the extravagance and much of the effort was to remedy this ignorance. The incompetency was in part real and in part emphasized by the attitude of the whites of the better class. . . .

. . . There might have been less stealing in the South during Reconstruction without negro suffrage but it is certainly highly instructive to remember that the mark of the thief which dragged its slime across nearly every great Northern state and almost up to the presidential chair could not certainly in those cases be charged against the vote of black men. This was the day when a national secretary of war was caught stealing, a vice-president presumably took bribes, a private secretary of the president, a chief clerk of the Treasury, and eighty-six government officials stole millions in the whiskey frauds, while the Credit Mobilier filched fifty millions and bribed the government to an extent never fully revealed; not to mention less distinguished thieves like Tweed.

Is it surprising that in such an atmosphere a new race learning the a-b-c of government should have become the tools of thieves? And when they did was the stealing their fault or was it justly chargeable to their enfranchisement?

Undoubtedly there were many ridiculous things connected with Reconstruction governments: the placing of ignorant field-hands who could neither read nor write in the legislature, the gold spittoons of South Carolina, the enormous public printing bill of Mississippi — all these were extravagant and funny, and yet somehow, to one who sees beneath all that is bizarre, the real human tragedy of the upward striving of down-trodden men, the groping for light among people born in darkness, there is less tendency to laugh and gibe than among shallower minds and easier consciences. All that is funny is not bad. . . .

In the midst of all these difficulties the negro governments in the South accomplished much of positive good. We may recognize three things which negro rule gave to the South:

1. Democratic government.

2. Free public schools.

3. New social legislation.

Two states will illustrate conditions of government in the South before and after negro rule. In South Carolina there was before the war a property qualification for office-holders, and, in part, for voters. The Constitution of 1868, on the other hand, was a modern democratic document starting (in marked contrast to the old constitutions) with a declaration that "We, the People", framed it, and preceded by a broad Declaration of Rights which did away with property qualifications and based representation directly on population instead of property. It especially took up new subjects of social legislation, declaring navigable rivers free public highways, instituting homestead exemptions, establishing boards of county commissioners, providing for a new penal code of laws, establishing universal manhood suffrage "without distinction of race or color", devoting six sections to charitable and penal institutions and six to corporations, providing separate property for married women, etc. Above all, eleven sections of the Tenth Article were devoted to the establishment of a complete public-school system.

So satisfactory was the constitution thus adopted by negro suffrage and by a convention composed of a majority of blacks that the state lived twenty-seven years under it without essential change and when the constitution was revised in 1895, the revision was practically nothing more than an amplification of the Constitution of 1868. No essential advance step of the former document was changed except the suffrage article.

In Mississippi the Constitution of 1868 was, as compared with that before the war, more democratic. It not only forbade distinctions on account of color but abolished all property qualifications for jury service, and property and educational qualifications for suffrage; it required less rigorous qualifications for office; it prohibited the lending of the credit of the state for private corporations — an abuse dating back as far as 1830. It increased the powers of the governor, raised the low state salaries, and increased the number of state officials. New ideas like the public-school system and the immigration bureau were introduced and in general the activity of the state greatly and necessarily enlarged. Finally, that was the only constitution ever submitted to popular approval at the polls. This constitution remained in force twenty-two years. . . .

We are apt to forget that in all human probability the granting of negro manhood suffrage and the passage of the Fifteenth Amendment were decisive in rendering permanent the foundation of the negro common school. Even after the overthrow of the negro governments, if the negroes had been left a servile caste, personally free, but politically powerless, it is not reasonable to think that a system of common schools would have been provided for them by the Southern States. Serfdom and education have ever proven contradictory terms. But when Congress, backed by the nation, determined to make the ne-groes full-fledged voting citizens, the South had a hard dilemma before her: either to keep the negroes under as an ignorant proletariat and stand the chance of being ruled eventually from the slums and jails, or to join in helping to raise these wards of the nation to a position of intelligence and thrift by means of a public-school system. The "carpet-bag" governments hastened the decision of the South, and although there was a period of hesitation and retrogression after the overthrow of negro rule in the early seventies, yet the South saw that to abolish negro schools in addition to nullifying the negro vote would invite Northern interference; and thus eventually every Southern state confirmed the work of the negro legislators and maintained the negro public schools along with the white.

Finally, in legislation covering property, the wider functions of the state, the punishment of crime and the like, it is sufficient to say that the laws on these points established by Reconstruction legislatures were not only different from and even revolutionary to the laws in the older South, but they were so wise and so well suited to the needs of the new South that in spite of a retro-gressive movement following the overthrow of the negro governments the mass of this legislation, with elaboration and development, still stands on the statute books of the South.

◆ MODERN ESSAY ◆

Busing for Social Change

SENATE SUBCOMMITTEE HEARINGS

While Reconstruction was an effort to produce equality in voting and civil rights all over the South, modern efforts for equality focus on smaller places, like school districts, and deal with the education of children. Still the issues remain the same: should it be done? Can it be done? What are the costs of try-ing to the people concerned?

The following testimony before a 1974 Senate committee gives the charac-ter of the modern encounter. What does Ms. Ruffra mean by quality educa-

From U.S., Congress, Senate, Subcommittee on Constitutional Rights of the Committee on the Judiciary, *Busing of Schoolchildren,* 93d Cong., 2d sess., 1974, pp. 129–132, 220–223.

tion? Does her definition include integration? We want to know how far she would carry the argument that the problem of inequality throughout society — not just in the schools — should make us begin integration in other parts of society. What does she see as the harmful results of forced busing? How much attention should be paid to the argument that polarization will be created in a community if the government enforces a law that many in the community don't like? How would Charles Sumner be likely to answer Ms. Ruffra? What role does she see for the law and the Constitution in a society?

What does Morgan see as the consequence of reversing recent change in the movement for equality? Should local communities have to bow before Morgan's alleged majority of the nation? What specific benefits can Morgan point to in order to show the advantages of forced busing? Has law been used here to produce satisfactory social change?

Senator [Sam] Ervin: The next witness is Mrs. Jean Ruffra, who speaks on behalf of herself and the organization known as Save Our Community Schools, Inc., in Louisville, Ky.

Mrs. Ruffra, I would like to welcome you to the committee. The committee has received at least 2,500 telegrams from Kentucky in support of your position and in support of some of these bills.

I am not going to put all of these in the record, but I am going to read only some that were picked out of the sample. One of them is from Mr. and Mrs. Louis E. Douglas. "We fully support S. 1737 that will restrict the Court from busing our grandchildren." One from Mr. and Mrs. Edmond Goldberg: "Busing is bad for everyone." One from L. H. Horton: "I fully support Senate bill 1737 which would restrict the Courts from busing our children."

This is one from Mr. Ronald Douglas which says —

> You have our full support in passing legislation to prohibit forced busing of school children for any reason. Jefferson County, Kentucky is under court orders as of September. Your broad action to correct an unlawful interpretation of the law will endear you to millions of parents who will not surrender their prerogative to the state.

You may proceed.

Testimony of Jean Ruffra, Save Our Community Schools, Inc., Louisville, Ky.

Mrs. Ruffra: Mr. Chairman and Senator Cook, thank you for this opportunity to testify before this committee on behalf of Save Our Community Schools, Inc., representing the citizens of Kentucky.

After hearing the testimony of Congressmen, attorneys, and school board members during these hearings, I feel very humble, but also pleased, to present our views on the busing issues.

Our organization consists of merely parents such as I, who are deeply concerned about our children and our country.

Jefferson County, Ky., is made up of three public school districts. Suits were filed against our school board for merger and desegregation of these three systems. If this is carried out, this system, the metro system, will contain approximately 140,000 students. The district Federal judge ruled that the schools were integrated and no State-imposed segregation exists within the three systems. The sixth circuit court overruled this decision, and an order for total integration and said boundary lines will impose no barriers.

The three school boards are appealing this decision to the Supreme Court. Based on what has happened in other areas, we will very likely have massive busing by this fall.

As a mother of three daughters, I am deeply concerned about the education of my children. Not only am I concerned about my own children, but all children, and as the Senator said, the people in Jefferson County, Ky., are very concerned, by the response of the telegrams. The citizens of Kentucky feel the forced busing issue throughout our country is most serious. As parents, one of the most important concerns of our life is our children. We believe it is our duty to care for our children to the best of our ability, whereas it is the duty of our public school system to provide the best education possible and we also feel it is the duty of our elected officials to protect the constitutional rights of our children.

The majority of people are not opposed to integration, but are opposed to the method forced upon us to achieve integration. The people in Kentucky feel the real issue is quality education for all children. This is not a racial issue and we certainly would hope not a political issue. It is true, some districts are rich in children, but poor with poverty, but because some of our children must suffer from poverty, should we insist the rest suffer along with them?

Every child should be given the opportunity to obtain a quality education regardless of race, color, religion, or national origin. Too much emphasis is placed on where a child attends school. We believe this emphasis should be on the quality of education, not on school location or the ratio of black or white children. The money being spent on forced busing could and should be spent to improve the substandard schools. A quality education is determined by the quality of teachers, administrators, and curriculum.

Forced busing has proven to be more discriminatory to the underprivileged child for whom it was originally intended to benefit. The children being transported many miles from home are deprived from participating in school activities. In many instances, extracurricular school activities are the only available recreation for a child on the poverty level. Forced busing has only changed the children's environment during school hours. When school hours are over, these same children are forced back into an environment more dismal than the one from which they came, because they cannot afford transportation to school sponsored functions. Their neighborhood schools are no longer the center of community activities.

Forced busing has created an economic segregation. In areas where it has been instituted, parents who could afford to, have enrolled their children in private schools to avoid crosstown busing, thereby segregating the underprivileged from the more affluent. The education of every American child, whether he be black or white, is a very personal matter to his parents. We believe the freedom of choice concerning the education of our children should not be available only to the affluent. We believe that parental involvement in the public school system is very important to the school system, the community, the child, and the parent. Our better schools today are the schools in which the parents are actively involved. In areas where forced busing exists, parental involvement is practically nonexistent. This we believe has been the cause of a marked increase in emotional disturbances in children. They no longer have the security resulting from a close knit home, church, community, and school involvement.

Forced busing is not in the best interest of children. The sole purpose of our educational system is to train our youth for the challenges of tomorrow. The use of educational funds for forced busing decreases the funds for educational purposes, thereby downgrading the quality of education rather than enhancing it.

As God in His wisdom has only given us 24 hours in a day to utilize, whereby we find 8 hours for the service of God and a distressed worthy human being, 8 hours for our usual vocation, and 8 hours for refreshment and sleep; forcing any child to spend any part of that 24 hours wastefully and needlessly is an injustice in that that time can never be regained.

We believe that forced busing is depriving 90 percent of the American people of their civil rights and is unconstitutional. In 1954, the Supreme Court ruled in the *Brown* v. *Board of Education,* that separate but equal facilities were unconstitutional. The Court held it was a violation of the 14th amendment for a State to require segregated schools. Our country accepts the legal doctrine that forcible segregation deprives our citizens of equal protection of the laws, but nothing in the *Brown* case requires forcible integration, that is, the mixing of whites and blacks or other races in the public schools to achieve a so-called racial balance. There are no Federal or State laws saying that the public schools must have a racial balance or which require the busing of pupils to achieve a racial balance.

In fact, the Federal Civil Rights Act of 1964 clearly outlaws assigning children to any public school on the basis of color. To assign a child to a school solely by virtue of his race in this most important aspect of his young life is to execute racism, State imposed racism, not essentially different from the pre-*Brown* decision. We believe forced busing is an insult to children; there is the underlying assumption that black children will be upgraded and motivated if they sit beside white children and that society will be improved thereby.

There is nothing in the history of man or government to support this theory. The whole concept is presumptuous and self-defeating. The stated presumption of the busing issue is to achieve equality. We are all created equal, and there it ends. All children are not equal in ability, financial status, or even physical appearance. If such equality is ever achieved, we will have a nation of robots. That all people should remain equal through-out life is not the principle of a democracy. Should we no longer teach our children the meaning of the word "incentive" and teach them to abandon the American dream that by working hard you can improve your status in life? The rights of 90 percent of the American people are being denied when courts order forced busing. Civil rights are those rights belonging to the people, all people. Forced busing is not equal protection of the law, it is equal discrimination under the law.

We live in a violence-prone, permissive type of society in which the rights of the individual are zealously protected. Individual rights are a trademark of today's citizens and the forced implementation of any idea, by its very nature causes polarization. In essence, the courts have said you have the right to decide for yourself whom you worship or whether you worship at all, the right to vote or not to.

Senator Ervin: Do you not believe that the strength and the greatness of America arises out of diversity of people rather than out of making them think the same thoughts and agree on the same propositions?

Mrs. Ruffra: Yes, sir.

Senator Ervin: The Supreme Court of the United States declared, in one case, that parents have a particular right with respect to the question of whether their children should go to school. That was a case involving the issue of whether a State can pass a law requiring children to go to public schools as counterdistinguished from church schools.

Do you not believe that the American parents love their children more than any other human beings on this earth, and for that reason, are more interested in their education than those whose main desire it is to make guinea pigs out of them?

Mrs. Ruffra: Yes, sir, I do.

Senator Ervin: Thank you very much for a most illuminating statement. . . .

Our next witness is Mr. Charles Morgan, Jr., who speaks for the American Civil Liberties Union.

Testimony of Charles Morgan, Jr., American Civil Liberties Union

Mr. Morgan: Senator, our testimony has been previously provided to you; and I trust that it can be included in the record without my reading it.

Senator Ervin: It will be included in the record.

[The prepared statement of Charles Morgan, Jr., follows:]

Prepared Statement of Charles Morgan, Jr.,
Director, Washington Office,
American Civil Liberties Union

Mr. Chairman and members of the Committee, thank you for the opportunity to testify here today. Before moving to my present job here in Washington about 14 months ago, I spent eight years directing the Southern Regional Office of the American Civil Liberties Union, now an organization of 275,000 members. There I was engaged in the trial and appeal of civil liberties and civil rights cases throughout the South.

From 1955 to 1963, I practiced law privately in Birmingham, Alabama. I am a graduate of the public schools of Birmingham, the University of Alabama, and the University of Alabama School of Law.

I appear here today on behalf of the ACLU to express our opposition to the proposals being considered in these hearings.

Mr. Chairman, it was almost two years ago that this Congress was considering a number of proposals similar to those before you today. Chief among them was the so-called "Equal Educational Opportunities Act of 1972," sponsored by the Nixon Administration.

In frequent appearances before many committees, ACLU representatives urged the Congress to reject those proposals. We did so for a wide variety of reasons — all of which I believe have been proven valid by the test of time — but among those many reasons there was always one consistent, underlying theme.

That theme was then, and remains now that all of the proposals now before you will have one effect: namely, they will result in the undermining of the authority, the integrity and the independence of federal courts under the Equality Amendments, and with them, the general public respect for law and order.

I can think of no committee, and Mr. Chairman, I can think of no individual Senator, in whom the American people place more faith when it comes to the Bill of Rights.

Indeed, if I may make a brief personal reference, I would like to say just one word as a Southerner. I think the people of the South believe, perhaps even more strongly than those from anywhere else, in the concept of law and order. I think the South has shown this in the peaceful way in which the overwhelming majority of white Southerners have acknowledged the rule of law, and the decisions of courts, regarding desegregation and the right to equal protection of the laws.

For the Congress now to enact legislation to undermine those principles — legislation which would say, in effect, "never mind those changes so recently made" — would be tragic. It would be a betrayal of those thousands of Americans who, often at great personal risk, placed themselves squarely on the side of the law in the twenty years since 1954.

Yet the four bills under consideration would do just that.

We see one bill, for example, S. 287, which would actually remove *all* public schools cases from the jurisdiction of the federal courts. That is so extreme, I think we need not discuss it here.

Another bill, S. 179, simply says no federal court may require that any pupils be transported to or from school on the basis of their race, color, religion or national origin. Again, we see the goal of undermining the ability of the courts to redress a denial of constitutional rights, even though that denial has been established by a thorough, fair and impartial hearing in a court of law.

Another bill, S. 619, stresses pupil assignment on a neighborhood basis. At first glance, but only at first glance, this concept of the "neighborhood school" sounds innocent enough. It even sounds appealing, conjuring up as it does the images of some of our childhoods — of laughing children skipping through falling leaves, or crossing a grassy field to a nearby school.

The trouble is that many parts of America — by choice — gave up the neighborhood school decades ago. They chose the consolidated school for its better educational facilities, and the bus as the only way to get there.

The other trouble is that in many other parts of America — mainly urban America — neighborhood schools mean segregated schools. They mean segregated schools because of the realities of continuing racial discrimination in jobs and housing, which means segregated neighborhoods.

And the fact is, Mr. Chairman, and we all know this, as a central truth: "white folks ain't going to pay for schools where white children don't go." So when certain schools are all-white, and others are all-black, more tax money, more books and more facilities just somehow always find their way to the white schools than to the black.

Nothing supports the assumption of *Brown* v. *Board of Education,* 347 U.S. 483 (1954) — that slum schools cannot be equalized — more than the reasoning and evidence of pre-*Brown* teacher pay, graduate and law school and undergraduate school decisions including *Sweatt* v. *Painter,* 339 U.S. 629 (1950) [the Texas Law School case] — and more obviously the millions of uneducated black men and women in the North's urban ghettoes, sixty percent of whom were born *and reared* below the Mason and Dixon Line.

Conversely, after desegregation, those same monies and equal school benefits suddenly begin finding their way into all schools on a fair and equal basis. As a black parent from North Carolina put it in a letter to the Washington Post two years ago: "Within one month (after desegregation), the parents of the white children who were being bused managed to get the black school painted, repairs made, new electric typewriters and sewing machines, and the shelves filled with books."

Again recalling my own Southern experience, I know how recently the concept of "neighborhood schools" suddenly wrought such concern. It usually coincided with the time when desegregation was at hand. Neighborhood schools were not always sanctified, in fact, by school systems as recently as the late 1960's where black children were bused as far as 60 or 80 round-trip miles to keep them out of their neighborhood, but white, schools.

One of these bills, S. 619, also cites "serious risks to the health and safety of students" and "risks and harms" supposedly created by busing.

Yet figures from the National Safety Council establish that school busing is actually the safest form of transportation in America — and that includes *walking* to school. ["Your Child and Busing," U.S. Commission on Civil Rights, May 1972, page 13.] Indeed, in some urban centers at peak traffic hours, walking may be the least safe way for children to go to school.

As for "risks and harms," I assume the bill's authors are referring to some alleged psychological damage caused by riding on a bus.

The only truly scientific study on this subject was by one of the nation's most noted child psychologists, Dr. Robert Coles. Dr. Coles rode buses with school children as they traveled to and from newly integrated schools. Based on more than one year's study, he said:

"I never saw children get sick because they were being bused; I never saw children become emotionally disturbed because they were bused; I never saw children's school work suffer because they were bused. Physically, psychologically, educationally, the experience of busing was, in fact, neutral. [Dr. Robert Coles, testimony to the Senate Subcommittee on Education, April 6, 1972.]"

A fourth bill before this committee, S. 1737, refers to "freedom of choice." Like the phrase "neighborhood schools," "freedom of choice" sounded innocuous enough at first hearing.

The problem is, experience has shown that freedom of choice, where tried, was not free. Many ways were found to intimidate and thereby inhibit black children who sought to exercise that freedom, until many of them gave up. Schools remained segregated in fact, if not in name, and the Equality Amendments, along, of course, with black and white children and their chances for a better life through better education, were the victims.

Each of these bills, then, as with all other attempts to draft anti-busing bills, relies on denying our courts the power to enforce the Equality Amendments.

That is reason enough to reject any and all such proposals. But there are other reasons, and I would like to summarize them briefly.

First, these proposals are anachronisms, for the fact is that school desegregation is no longer a major public issue. With the exception of local problem areas whose difficulties should be worked out locally and in accordance with the law, there is simply no public demand for anti-busing legislation. A national law passed to meet an isolated problem might create far more severe problems in a dozen other locales.

Americans are law-abiding people. Two years ago, we quoted many youngsters from many schools, north and south, who said they could get along fine with one another, and their schools could operate peacefully, if adults would just leave them alone and quit stirring up trouble.

We believe the evidence shows that this has happened. Trouble has not been stirred and Americans have again proved law-abiding. They have reached peaceful accords with conscience and the Constitution.

Studies of school desegregation have demonstrated over and over that when citizens of good will made up their minds in advance that they would obey the law and plan their schools accordingly, desegregation took place peacefully.

Where disturbances occurred, they were invariably the result of groups of adults picketing, blockading, shouting obscenities at each other and at little children, even throwing rocks or burning buses. When the adult protests ended, so did disturbances among the youngsters.

The point is, our schools are desegregating peacefully. If there is an isolated case of a badly drawn desegregation plan, the solution is not to upend the law and reverse the gains that have been made (as could be done with the re-opener clause contained in one of the proposed bills, S. 619). The solution to those problems is certainly not new national legislation. The solution for isolated cases is simply the drawing of new and better, if isolated, plans.

Whether politically disastrous or not, two effects of enactment of these proposals will be the stiffening of opposition to desegregation and a simultaneous weakening of the resolve of courts to effect the mandates of the thirteenth, fourteenth and fifteenth amendments.

One effect these proposals definitely will not have is to diminish the desegregation "burden" borne by the white working class. The elimination of busing will not prevent the use of pairing and other desegregation techniques. Buses will continue to transport white and black children to the consolidated schools of the rural south. In southern urban areas those who reside nearest each other — the white and black working class — will be desegregated. Only the white upper middle class children will be sheltered from desegregation and further locked into a Brahmin caste school system which will continue their uneducation in unreal seclusion from the very real world they will soon face.

The other reasons for rejecting these proposed bills go to the myths about desegregation and busing itself. I would like to summarize them briefly.

First, busing is not being ordered by the courts in any wholesale or haphazard way. It is ordered only when it is the only remedy for the redress of constitutional deprivations.

Second, busing is not used to achieve "racial balance," as so many detractors claim. The courts, in fact, have specifically *forbidden* busing for racial balance. The Supreme Court stated in *Swann* v. *Charlotte-Mecklenburg Board of Education* 402 U.S. 1 (1971), that "the use of mathematical ratios was no more than a starting point in the process of shaping a remedy, rather than an inflexible requirement."

Third, busing for desegregation is certainly not "massive," although that word is constantly used by backers of the type of legislation now before this committee.

In fact, of the more than 20 million school children who ride school buses, less than three-percent ride them due to court orders. [Testimony of Elliot Richardson, Secretary of Health, Education, and Welfare, before Senate Subcommittee on Education, March 24, 1972.]

In other words, if all court-ordered busing were halted today, 97% of all youngsters who ride school buses today would still be riding them tomorrow. I think that fact alone should be enough to demonstrate the needlessness of the legislation proposed here today.

Fourth, anti-busing advocates contend that some rides are too long and schedules disruptive. In fact, rides are shorter in many places since desegregation than they were before. And in the few places where schedules are a serious burden on parents, the need is for better planning, and modified desegregation plans, not national legislation.

Fifth, some have implied that court-ordered busing is bankrupting school systems. The fact is that the percentage of education money spent on school transportation is virtually the same (3.6%) as it was 40 years ago (3.5%). ["Your Child and Busing," U.S. Commission on Civil Rights, May 1972.]

In sum, school busing is nothing new. We have been busing school children for about 60 years. Busing only came under attack when used as one device to bring about school desegregation and equal protection of the law.

In view of the Congress's often-stated determination to afford all Americans their full rights under the Constitution, and in view of the fact that all these bills would undermine the ability of our courts to insure those rights, I respectfully urge this committee to reject the proposals being considered today.

I believe this is especially urgent because of the damaging impact these bills would have on our system of law. At a time when this committee is so uniquely charged with the responsibility for protecting civil liberties, rights endangered now more than ever, and a time when this body may soon be called upon to make a decision fundamental to the very future of the rule of law in our society, we respectfully urge that you set aside these proposals of the past and move instead with our children into a future where freedom is the promise of equal education.

1 2 3 4 5 6 7 8 9 0